# Recipes for Home Repair

Quadrangle  NYT  The New York Times Book Co.

ALVIN UBELL AND SAM BITTMAN

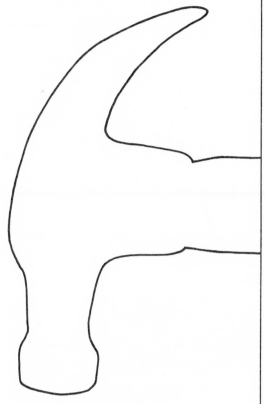

# Recipes for Home Repair

For information address:
Quadrangle/The New York Times Book Co., 10 East 53
Street, New York, N.Y. 10022. Manufactured in the United States
of America. Published simultaneously in Canada by Fitzhenry &
Whiteside, Ltd., Toronto.
Library of Congress Catalog Card Number: 74–77938
International Standard Book Number: 8129–0473–7
Design by Margaret McCutcheon Wagner

**Library of Congress Cataloging in Publication Data**

Ubell, Alvin, 1933-
    Recipes for home repair.

    1. Repairing—Amateurs' manuals. I. Bittman, Sam,
1943-    joint author. II. Title.
TT151.U23 1974    643'.7    74-77938
ISBN 0-8129-0473-7

*For Anna, Lawrence, Charles, and Estelle*
*For Marilyn and the Group*

## ACKNOWLEDGMENTS

We wish to thank the following manufacturers, agencies, and businesses, without whose encouragement and assistance this book would not have been possible.

*American Red Cross*
*American Standard Corporation*
*Accurate Building Inspectors*
*Coyne and Delany Company*
*Davis and Warshow Incorporated*
*Delta Faucet Company*
*General Electric Company*
*Joe & Bill's Hardware*
*Leviton Manufacturing Company, Inc.*
*Minneapolis Honeywell Regulator Company*
*Minnesota Mining and Manufacturing Company*
*New York City Building Department*
*New York City Fire Department*
*Sakrete Incorporated*
*Sears Roebuck and Company*
*The Stanley Works*
*United States Bureau of Standards*
*U.S. Department of Health, Education, and Welfare*
*United States Bureau of Naval Personnel*
*United States Government Printing Office*
*Watta-Crete Company, Inc.*
*Westinghouse*

And special words of deepest thanks and appreciation to Vivian Ubell whose idea started this project; to Bob Ubell for selling it; to our friend, Jeff Weiss, for buying it; to Ed Barber for seeing it through publication; and to all our friends who lent us support and encouragement from first to last.

The authors have done their best to establish the clearest and simplest procedures for the reader. The reader, however, may find that a particular recipe could be improved by shifting steps, or adding a special note, or whatever. The point is, that the authors are interested in any suggestions you might have for the improvement of their book. Write to them in care of Quadrangle/The New York Times Book Co., 10 East 53 Street, New York City 10022.

# CONTENTS

## Part III. Electricity

**Part IV.  Plumbing**

## Part V. Masonry

## Part VI. Charts and Tables

## INTRODUCTION

The faucets leak; the floors squeak; you've got a blackout. You call the plumber, the carpenter, and the electrician, and you're out fifty dollars at the very least.

Perhaps it gives you pleasure to part with money.

Maybe you're heir to the Rockefeller fortune.

For two dollars and a little time you could have fixed everything by yourself. A five-cent washer takes care of the faucet; a can of talcum powder silences the floor; and a twist of the wrist restores light to your home. Approximate time: thirty minutes for each job.

Now that you've taken care of everything, the only remaining problem is to figure out what to do with the forty-eight dollars you've saved.

Interested?

This unique book solves many of the problems of home repair. Simple and easy to understand, it was conceived for men and women who live in apartments or in their own homes—men and women—you—who fall prey to huge annual repair expenditures. You can save enormous amounts of money if you will learn here how simple work can be done independent of the experts.

Above all, this is *not* a book for professional crafts-people. A great many books in recent years started out to be repair guides for the layperson, but they became so tortuously involved and complicated that no one, save perhaps a person in the trade, could follow the directions. In fact, these books contained *no* directions. They assumed that whoever picked up the book already had some understanding of basic skills. A layperson wishing to make a simple repair of a shaky chair was likely to run into a lengthy explanation of carpentry in general. After a sentence or two, he would lay the book down, pick up the phone, and call a carpenter. All of which is perfectly all right if you haven't any time and can afford to pay exorbitant hourly fees to repairpeople.

To be sure, you will run into problems that can be solved only by experts. In those cases, do not hesitate to call in someone who can do the job properly. But most of the work around the house is a single occurrence and so minor that anyone, and we mean anyone, can pull it off with crowning success.

This book further claims uniqueness in its format. There is not a man or woman who, at one time or another, has not used a recipe to prepare a favorite dish. For that reason we present all repair directions as "recipes." A quick glance will tell you what *utensils* and *ingredients* (tools and materials) you'll need, and how much time the job is likely to take. Then follow simple step-by-step procedures, accompanied by clear and precise illustrations.

And we've added one further convenience to help you mark your progress in performing every recipe. To the left of each numbered step, you will notice a small blank box. As you complete a step, put a pencil mark in the box. In that way, your eye will move to the next unmarked box, and you will avoid rereading, and perhaps reperforming, a step you have just completed. It is advisable, however, to read entire Recipe before beginning actual work.

There's nothing to it really, just read and be confident that you can do things of which you never thought yourself capable. The pride and pleasure that come with a job well-done will be yours to enjoy. So will the money you save.

Finally, we wish you all the fun and gratification that comes with locating a problem and finding a successful and speedy solution. We have tested all of our recipes with men and women who had never wielded a hammer or turned a screwdriver, to say nothing of plugging in a soldering iron. The amount of time designated for each repair was not abstractly arrived at; rather, we presented an individual with a task and clocked the procedure. If he or she could do it, so can you. So, go forth and fix!

## KNOWING YOUR OWN HOME

Names are an efficient means of communication; knowing what things are called makes it easier to get to know what those things are. We all get tired of pointing to an object and referring to it as a "whatchamacallit" or "doohickey" or some such abstract phrase. Consider for a moment the brilliant smile that comes to the face of children when they learn for the first time that the great blue expanse above them is called "sky."

Names of things help hook people together in common understanding. And, because this book concerns itself with houses, we'll all feel just a little more at ease if we're speaking the same language.

In Figure A, there is an exhaustive and precise listing of virtually all the architectural terms you'll ever need to know. Study it carefully. Of course, it is not necessary to commit it all to memory; just remember it is here, and, should you come upon a term in the course of reading this book that you do not understand, chances are you'll find the explanation right here.

One other note on the way we have put this book together. We suggest that you pay particular attention to the sections on general information and tools and their uses. A brief amount of time with these instructional recipes will make everything else in the book much easier.

The numbered items below correspond to the "anatomy of the home" in Figure A.

1. *Chimney.* You have known about this ever since Santa Claus days.
2. *Flue Tile Liner.* The flue is the hole in the chimney. The liner, usually of terra cotta, protects the brick from harmful smoke gases.
3. *Chimney Cap.* This top is generally concrete. It protects the brick from weather.
4. *Chimney Flashing.* Sheet metal flashing provides a tight joint between chimney and roof.
5. *Fireplace with Firebrick.* An ordinary brick cannot withstand the heat of direct fire, and so special firebrick is used to line the fireplace.
6. *Ash Dump or Pit.* A trapdoor to let the ashes drop to a pit below, where they may be easily removed.

7. *Ash Cleanout Door.* The door to the ashpit or the bottom of a chimney through which the chimney can be cleaned.
8. *Chimney Breast.* The inside face or front of a fireplace chimney.
9. *Hearth and Hearth Shelf.* The floor of a fireplace that extends into the room for safety purposes.
10. *Ridge.* The top intersection of two opposite adjoining roof surfaces.
11. *Ridge Board.* The board that follows along under the ridge.
12. *Roof Rafters.* The structural members that support the roof.
13. *Collar Beam.* Really not a beam at all. A tie that keeps the roof from sagging.
14. *Insulation.* An insulating material (usually rock wool, or fiber glass) in a blanket form placed between the roof rafters, for the purpose of keeping a house warm in winter, cool in the summer.
15. *Roof Sheathing.* The boards that provide the base for the finished roof.
16. *Roofing.* The wood, asphalt, or asbestos shingles—or tile, slate, or metal—that form the outer protection against the weather. Some roofs have snow guards to keep snow from sliding off.
17. *Cornice.* A decorative element made up of molded members usually placed at or near the top of an exterior or interior wall.
18. *Gutter.* The trough that gathers rainwater from a roof.
19. *Leaders or Downspouts.* The pipe that leads the water down from the gutter.
20. *Storm Sewer Tile.* The underground pipe that receives the water from the leaders and carries it to the sewer, or dry well.
21. *Gable.* The triangular end of a building with a sloping roof.
22. *Barge Board.* The fascia or board at the gable, just under the edge of the roof.
23. *Louvers.* A series of slanted slots arranged to keep out rain, yet allow ventilation.
24. *Corner Post.* The vertical member at the corner of the frame, made up to receive inner and outer covering materials.
25. *Studs.* The vertical wood members of the house, usually 2 by 4s generally spaced every 16 inches.
26. *Sill.* The board that is laid first on the foundation, and on which the frame rests.
27. *Plate.* The board laid across the top ends of the studs to hold them even and rigid.

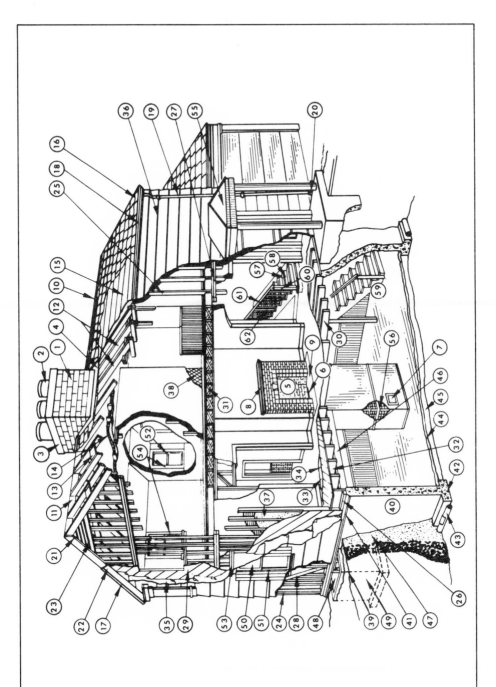

Figure A.
The Home

28. *Corner Bracing.* Diagonal strips to keep the frame square and plumb.
29. *Sheathing.* The first layer of outer wall covering nailed to the studs.
30. *Joist.* The structural members or beams that hold up the floor or ceiling, usually 2 by 10s or 2 by 12s spaced 16 inches apart.
31. *Bridging.* Cross bridging or solid. Members at the middle or third points of joint spans to brace one to the next, to prevent their twisting and to distribute weight evenly.
32. *Subflooring.* The rough boards that are laid over the joist. Usually laid diagonally. Sometimes plywood.
33. *Flooring Paper.* A felt paper laid on the rough floor to stop air infiltration and, to some extent, noise.
34. *Finish Flooring.* Usually hardwood, of tongued and grooved strips.
35. *Building Paper.* Sometimes placed outside the sheathing, not as a vapor barrier, but to prevent water and air from leaking in. Building paper is also used as a tarred felt under shingles or siding to keep out moisture and wind.
36. *Beveled Siding.* Sometimes called clapboards, with a thick butt and a thin upper edge lapped to shed water.
37. *Wall Insulation.* A blanket of wool or reflective foil placed inside the walls.
38. *Metal Lath.* A mesh made from sheet metal onto which plaster is applied.
39. *Finished Grade Line.* The top of the ground at the foundation.
40. *Foundation Wall.* The wall of poured concrete (shown) or concrete blocks that rests on the footing and supports the remainder of the house.
41. *Termite Shield.* A metal baffle to prevent termites from entering the frame (a false sense of security).
42. *Footing.* The concrete pad that carries the entire weight of the house upon the earth.
43. *Footing Drain Tile.* A pipe with open joints to allow underground water to drain in and away before it gets into the basement.
44. *Basement Floor Slab.* The 4- or 5-inch layer of concrete that forms the basement floor.
45. *Gravel Fill.* Placed under the floor slab to allow drainage and to guard against a damp floor.
46. *Girder.* A main beam upon which the floor joists rest. Usually of steel, but also of wood.

47. *Backfill.* Earth, once dug out, that has been replaced and tamped down around the foundation.
48. *Areaway.* An open space to allow light and air to a basement window.
    Also called a light well.
49. *Area Wall.* The wall, of metal or concrete, that forms the open area at basement window.
50. *Window.* The wonderful invention that lets us see through a wall.
51. *Window Frame.* The lining of the window opening.
52. *Window Sash.* The inner frame, usually movable, that holds the glass.
53. *Lintel.* The structural beam over a window or door opening.
54. *Window Casing.* The decorative strips surrounding a window opening on the inside.
55. *Entrance Canopy or Portico.* A roof extending over the entrance door.
56. *Furring.* Falsework or framework necessary to bring the outer surface to where we want it.
57. *Stair Tread.* We put our foot down here.
58. *Stair Riser.* The vertical board connecting one tread to the next.
59. *Stair Stringer.* The sloping board that supports the end of the steps.
60. *Newel.* The post that terminates the railing.
61. *Stair Rail.* The bar used for a hand hold when we use the stairs.
62. *Balusters.* Vertical rods or spindles supporting a rail.

**PART I**

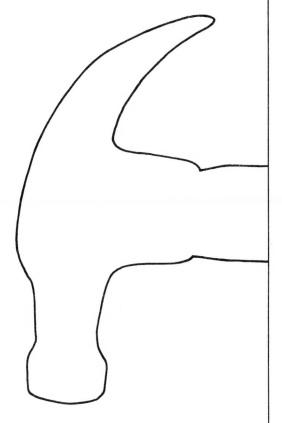

# Tools

# THE USE OF TOOLS

What is a surgeon without a scalpel? an angler without fishing tackle? the engraver without a stylus?

Tools are the extension of the ingenuity of humankind. The implementation of human dreams would have been impossible without them and that painting you just bought and had framed will never be properly hung if you cannot make good use of a hammer, screwdriver, and spirit level.

We have promised a *basic* book on home repair, and there is nothing *more* basic than proper instruction on the use of common tools. Most readers will already have had some experience with most of the tools in the following section. That is a far different thing from using those tools well. Consider the extra and—we hope—helpful hints that follow.

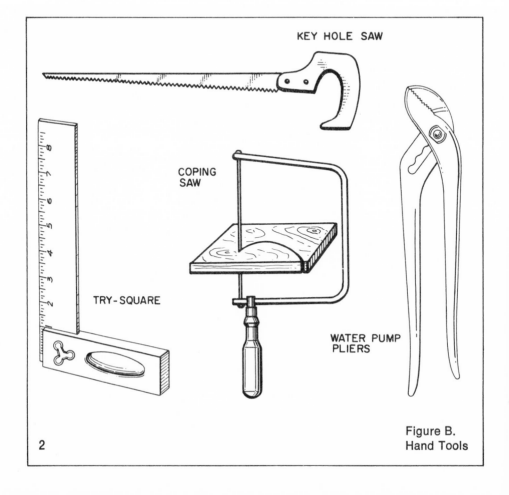

KEY HOLE SAW

COPING SAW

TRY-SQUARE

WATER PUMP PLIERS

Figure B.
Hand Tools

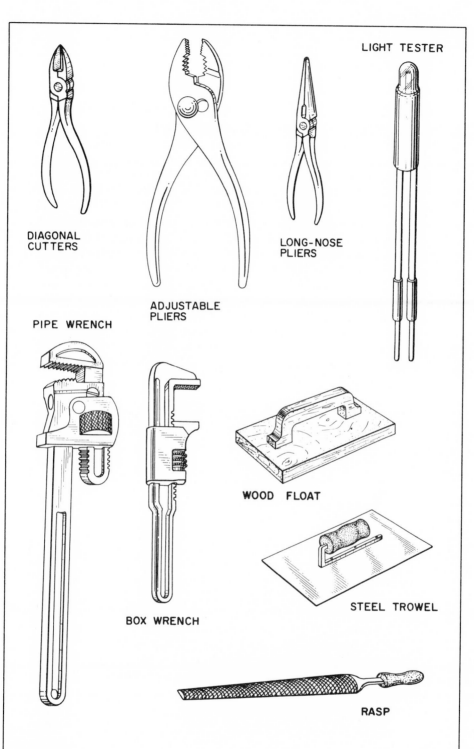

DIAGONAL
CUTTERS

ADJUSTABLE
PLIERS

LONG-NOSE
PLIERS

LIGHT TESTER

PIPE WRENCH

BOX WRENCH

WOOD FLOAT

STEEL TROWEL

RASP

Figure C.
Hand Tools

3

## 1. HOW TO USE A HAMMER

Years ago, Mr. Ubell was apprenticed to a master cabinetmaker where he performed his tasks with great dexterity. The master was displeased with only one thing in his apprentice: he observed how young Mr. Ubell, when working with a hammer, did not hold the tool at the end of its handle, in the proper fashion. Time and time again the master would remind: "Hold the handle!" But the apprentice, otherwise agile and talented for the trade, refused to learn. One day, in a fit of rage at the inability of his apprentice to comprehend that one simple rule, the master grabbed the tool from Mr. Ubell's hands, brought it to a bench, and cut off all but three inches of the handle. "Now," he said, returning it to the flabbergasted youth, "here's your hammer. Use it!"

We relate this incident because many will feel insulted by the title of this recipe. Most people, in truth, can hammer a nail with a degree of efficiency. But before long, they grow weary. This recipe will illustrate a method whereby even the beginner can hammer for an hour and not be overcome with exhaustion.

UTENSILS
*Hammer, 16 ounce with handle vulcanized into head (Fig. 2A)*

INGREDIENTS
*Piece of wood, 2 inches by 3 inches, 12 inches long*
*Assorted nails*
*Piece of wood ¾ inch by ¾ inch, 12 inches long*

### To Hammer in Nail

☐ *1.* Grasp hammer with claw facing upward. Don't choke up on handle (Fig. 1B).
☐ *2.* Hold wrist stiff.
☐ *3.* Arm should be cocked 90 degrees at the elbow.
☐ *4.* Take a few practice swings at the 2-inch by 3-inch piece of wood.
☐ *5.* Gently tap a nail into the wood at 90 degrees (perpendicular).
☐ *6.* Raise hammer as described above and strike confidently, but without great force, at the head of the nail.
☐ *7.* Repeat, adding force and velocity with each swing, until nail has been completely driven into wood.

### To Remove Nail

☐ 1. Using the edge of one claw of the hammer, pry the head of the nail from the wood until it can be slid into claw slot.

☐ 2. Place the ¾-inch by ¾-inch piece of wood beneath the head of the hammer for additional leverage (Fig. 1C).

☐ 3. Jerk the nail out.

*Note:* Repeat this recipe several times until you become proficient in both driving the nail into the wood and removing it.

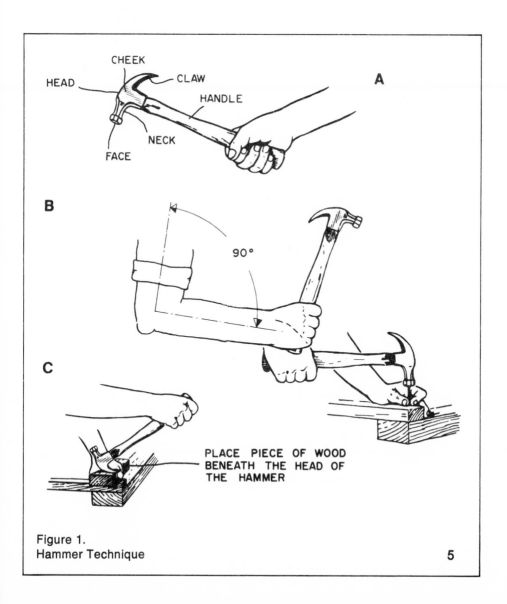

Figure 1.
Hammer Technique

## 2. HOW TO USE A SCREWDRIVER

A strong society is held together by the frequent and consistent presence of a good screw. A well-fitted screw implies togetherness; a loose screw suggests imperfection and decay. In this recipe we offer you the means to hold the world together.

Just one note: Screwing is done in two directions, clockwise and counterclockwise. These terms simply mean: in the direction of the movement of the hands of a clock, or the reverse of that movement (Fig. 2A).

To be able to screw efficiently, however, one must have the right equipment in addition to direction.

UTENSILS
*Set of screwdrivers:*
  *1 offset screwdriver, Phillips one end, flat blade other end*
  *1 2-inch-long flat blade with ⅛-inch tip*
  *1 4-inch-long flat blade with ⅛-inch tip*
  *1 6-inch-long flat blade with 5/16-inch tip*
  *1 8-inch-long flat blade with ⅜-inch tip*
  *1 4-inch Phillips head with #2 point*
  *1 6-inch Phillips head with #3 point*
  *1 stubby Phillips head with #2 point*
  *1 stubby flat blade with ¼-inch tip*
*Awl or nail*
*Hammer*
*Drill and set of bits*

INGREDIENTS
*Set of assorted screws*
*Bar of soap*
*Block of wood*

### Procedure for Installation of Screw

☐  *1.* Select screw from assortment and screwdriver to match.
☐  *2.* Gently tap nail or awl into wood block with hammer (Fig. 2B).
☐  *3.* Remove nail or awl.

☐ *4.* Drill shank hole and pilot hole (Fig. 2C).
☐ *5.* Rub threads of screw with soap.
☐ *6.* Insert screw into nail hole, twisting lightly into place in clockwise direction.
☐ *7.* Lay the handle of the screwdriver into your palm as though it were an extension of your hand (Fig. 2C).
☐ *8.* Keeping screwdriver in line with screw, twist screw into wood in clockwise direction.

### Procedure for Removal of Screw

☐ *1.* Find a screw already embedded in wood.
☐ *2.* Select a screwdriver whose point matches slot in screwhead.
☐ *3.* Keeping screwdriver on even line with screw, remove the screw by turning in a counterclockwise direction.

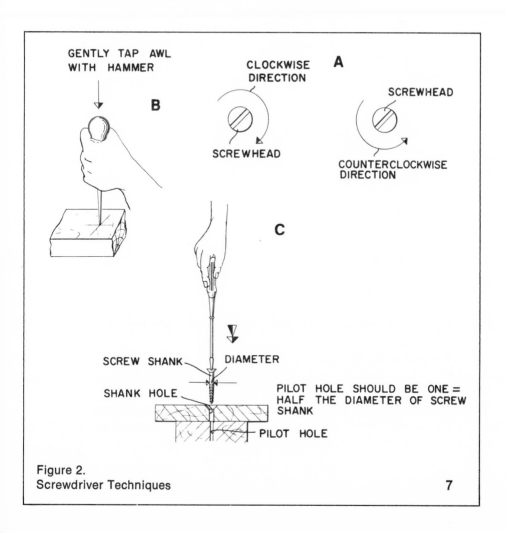

Figure 2.
Screwdriver Techniques

7

## 3. HOW TO USE A CROSSCUT SAW

So you think you know how to handle a saw, eh? Far be it from us to say no; but we know of many experienced, handy people who claim that, without instruction, it took them years before they got the knack. But, we know the knack, and we can teach it to you in the next few minutes.

The crosscut saw is devised to cut perpendicular or across the grain of a piece of wood. There are two types: the handsaw (Fig. 3A) and the backsaw (Fig. 3B), which has a piece of steel vulcanized to the top of the blade. The handsaw is used primarily for basic cutting, while the backsaw is for more intricate cutting on smaller pieces of wood and moldings. However, both saws are operated identically: if you learn how to use one, you learn how to use the other.

Because they are precision tools, both saws should be kept clean and sharp at all times and stored in a cool, dry place.

UTENSILS

*Handsaw, 11 points per inch*
*Backsaw, 14 points per inch*

INGREDIENTS

*Plank of wood*
*Paraffin wax*

☐  *1.* Grip handle of saw in your dominant hand and hold securely as shown in Figure 3C.
☐  *2.* Place piece of wood on a low bench. If you are right-handed, the wood should extend over the right side of the bench. If you are left-handed, wood should extend over left side of bench.
☐  *3.* Rest opposite knee (left, if right-handed; right if left-handed) on the plank as shown in Figure 3D.
☐  *4.* Now grasp edge of board with inactive hand as shown, and lean the saw against the thumb of that hand.
☐  *5.* Having placed the heel of the saw against your thumb, draw the saw upward toward you. Keep your wrist stiff as you pull, and allow your elbow to bend to its maximum. In this position, your shoulder should also be kept loose, so the arm, from the shoulder to the elbow, can swing like a pendulum.
☐  *6.* Now that there is a groove in the wood, slide your inactive hand a few inches away from the cut, but maintain its grasp.
☐  *7.* With the toe of the saw in the groove, slide the saw forward

gently, still holding the wrist rigidly. A loose wrist will make for a crooked cut.

*Note:* Hardly any pressure should be exerted on the saw, and especially not on the back stroke. The weight of the saw itself, plus the pendulumlike motion of your arm, will do all the work. If saw binds, rub paraffin wax on both sides of saw teeth.

☐ 8. Now saw through the wood, gaining momentum as you go. Try to master the pendulum swing, as this takes the pain out of sawing. If your line is crooked, you haven't got it yet.

☐ 9. Keep sawing until you are just about across the wood. Reach your inactive hand over to the end of the plank, which is about to fall, and continue sawing very slowly, so that when you cut through, the wood will not splinter.

☐ 10. Repeat these steps with both handsaw and backsaw until you have become proficient.

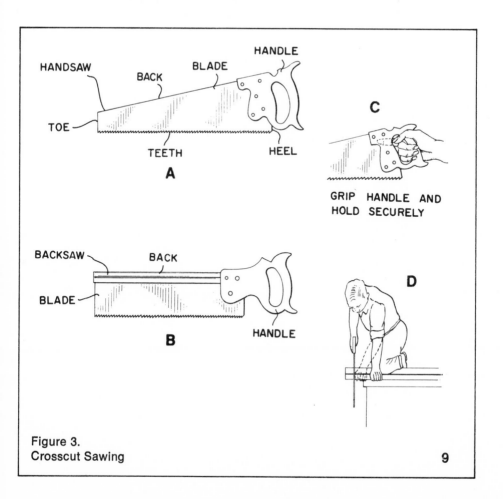

Figure 3.
Crosscut Sawing

9

## 4. HOW TO USE A HACKSAW

Though the hacksaw is specifically designed to cut through metal, it is often used to saw wood and plastic. And because of the unique frame design, the blade may be inserted both parallel and perpendicular to the frame, as shown in Figure 4. The technique for using a hacksaw is identical to that of a crosscut saw.

UTENSILS
*Hacksaw frame*
*Hacksaw blade, 12 inches,*
  *with 24 teeth per inch*
*Table vise*
*Hacksaw blade, 12 inches,*
  *with 32 teeth per inch*
*C-clamp*

INGREDIENTS
*Piece of pipe or heavy iron*
*Can of machine oil*
*Piece of sheet metal*
*Block of wood*

☐  *1.* Adjust hacksaw frame so end post and handle post are slightly more than 12 inches apart. This is done by putting pressure on the end post until frame releases from notch and can be moved.
☐  *2.* Set forward and rear blade holders so pins are perpendicular to the frame (Fig. 4A).
☐  *3.* Place the 24-teeth-per-inch blade onto the forward and rear pins so teeth are facing away from handle (Fig. 4B).
☐  *4.* Turn wing nut so that blade is secure in frame. To operate effectively, blade must be under tension at all times.
☐  *5.* Insert pipe securely into vise, one end protruding a few inches.
☐  *6.* Grasping the hacksaw handle firmly in one hand, lay the blade on the pipe ½ inch from the vise. The closer to the vise you cut, the fewer the vibrations and the more accurate the cut.
☐  *7.* Take long, easy strokes over the pipe until a groove is formed.
☐  *8.* Continue the strokes, exerting additional, but not excessive pressure.
☐  *9.* If the cutting becomes difficult, apply a few drops of lubricating oil to the blade.
☐ *10.* Relieve pressure before cutting through the pipe. Also watch your toes when the pipe end falls to the floor.
☐ *11.* Remove pipe from vise.

☐ 12. Remove blade from frame and replace with 32-teeth-per-inch blade.
☐ 13. Lay sheet metal onto piece of wood and clamp together with C-clamp. Insert both securely into vise, making sure that sheet metal is flush with the upper edge of the wood.
☐ 14. With the sheet metal facing you, lay the hacksaw blade on the wood and make several long, easy strokes as described above. You will notice that, as you cut the wood, you also cut through the sheet metal. Incidentally, this is the only safe method we know.
☐ 15. Do not twist blade and exert too much pressure, as this will break the blade.

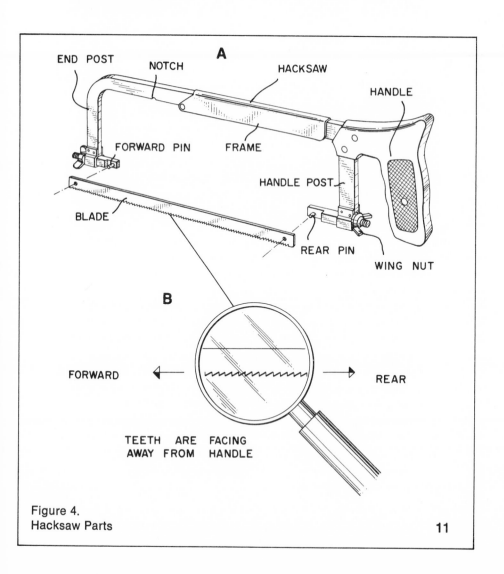

Figure 4.
Hacksaw Parts

11

## 5. HOW TO USE A HAND DRILL

The hand drill is used for the rapid drilling of small holes in wood and metal. Holes in wood should be started with an awl, to center the hole. Holes in metal should be started with a center punch. Note: When drilling through metal, be sure to relieve pressure just before breaking through to avoid breaking the bit. Bits for wood and metal come in a variety of sizes.

UTENSILS
*Hand drill*
*Assortment of wood and*
   *metal bits*
*Small table vise with protector*
   *block*
*Awl*
*Center punch for metal drills*
*Hammer*

INGREDIENTS
*Several pieces of wood of*
   *varying thickness*

☐ *1.* Open chuck (Fig. 5A) slightly larger than diameter of bit.
☐ *2.* Insert bit and tighten chuck by pushing clockwise on the crank with one hand while holding chuck tight with thumb and forefinger of the other hand (Fig. 5B).
☐ *3.* To remove bit, hold the chuck with thumb and forefinger of one hand and turn crank counterclockwise with the other hand (Fig. 5E).
☐ *4.* With a hammer and awl, punch small hole in wood (Fig. 5C). Use center punch for metal (Fig. 5D).
☐ *5.* Clamp wood or metal into the table vise so that hole punched with awl or center punch is visible.
☐ *6.* To prepare for horizontal drilling, grasp drill handle in one hand and crank handle in the other hand.
☐ *7.* Place bit against hole firmly and turn crank steadily in a clockwise direction. Do not wobble the drill, as this will create an oversized hole and could possibly break the bit.
☐ *8.* It is sometimes desirable to hold the drill by the side handle and press your body against the frame handle (Fig. 5F).
☐ *9.* Repeat this process several times until you can drill steadily.

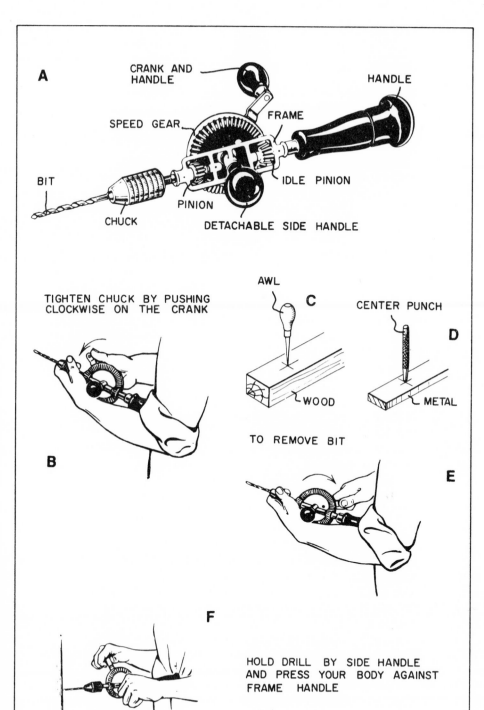

A

CRANK AND HANDLE

HANDLE

SPEED GEAR

FRAME

BIT

IDLE PINION

PINION

CHUCK

DETACHABLE SIDE HANDLE

TIGHTEN CHUCK BY PUSHING CLOCKWISE ON THE CRANK

AWL C

CENTER PUNCH D

WOOD

METAL

B

TO REMOVE BIT

E

F

HOLD DRILL BY SIDE HANDLE AND PRESS YOUR BODY AGAINST FRAME HANDLE

Figure 5.
Hand Drill and Its Use

13

## 6. HOW TO USE AN ELECTRIC DRILL

The electric drill, with its many attachments, is one of the most versatile tools you can have around the house. In addition to its drilling functions, which are many, the electric drill can be used as a light sanding device and as a buffer. Best of all, the electric drill requires no special skill and is extremely easy to handle. One word of caution, however: It is essential that your wall outlet be grounded if it is not of the three-pronged variety. See Recipe 63 on Installing a 3-Pronged Grounded Adapter.

UTENSILS
*Hammer*
*Awl*
*Table vise or C-clamp*
*Electric drill, grounded with*
  *three-pronged plug*
*Variety of bits*
*Center punch*

INGREDIENTS
*Several blocks of wood*
*Several strips of metal*
*Can of machine oil*

☐ *1.* With hammer and awl, punch a small hole in a block of wood (Fig. 6A).
☐ *2.* Insert block of wood in vise so hole is exposed.
☐ *3.* Loosen chuck with chuck key as shown in Figure 6B.
☐ *4.* Insert drill bit.
☐ *5.* Tighten chuck with key.
☐ *6.* Cradle the barrel of the drill in the palm of one hand.
☐ *7.* Grasp the handle and the trigger with the other hand.
☐ *8.* Squeeze trigger to start drill.
☐ *9.* Now place spinning drill bit against punched hole with a degree of force (Fig. 6C). Do not push too hard, as this will cause wobbling, and wobbling will result in an oversized hole and possibly break the bit.
☐ *10.* Relieve pressure on drill just before breaking through the wood.
☐ *11.* Repeat process on several other blocks of wood until you have gained confidence and some measure of proficiency.
☐ *12.* With hammer and center punch, punch a dimple in the surface of the metal and insert metal into vise.
☐ *13.* Repeat steps 8–11. If drilling through steel, add a few drops of machine oil to the hole. This will prevent the buildup of heat friction. (Brass requires no lubrication.)

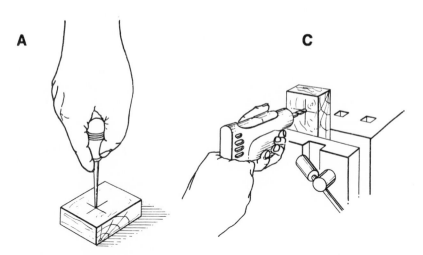

A

PUNCH A SMALL HOLE IN
A BLOCK OF WOOD

C

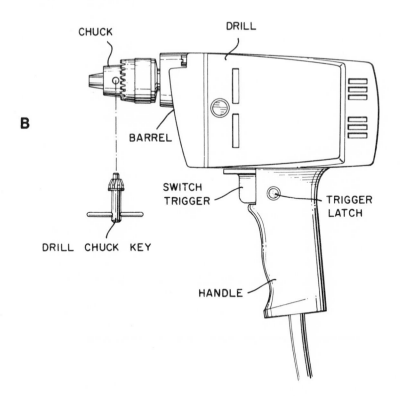

B

CHUCK

DRILL

BARREL

DRILL CHUCK KEY

SWITCH
TRIGGER

TRIGGER
LATCH

HANDLE

Figure 6.
Electric Drill Techniques

15

## 7. HOW TO USE FILES

Your tool kit should always include a variety of files and handles to match. They are used for smoothing, cutting, or removing small amounts of metal and wood. They come in a variety of shapes and sizes, and each one is designed to perform a specific type of work. The practice recipe below is designed for all types of files, and you would do well to become acquainted with as many types as possible to see what each can do. Caution: Never use a file without a tight-fitting handle. It can result in serious injury.

UTENSILS
*Table vise*
*File(s) and handle(s)*
*Chalk*
*File brush*

INGREDIENTS
*Several blocks of wood*
*2 2-inch dowels or old*
*    broom handle*
*Several pieces of metal pipe*

- ☐  *1.* Insert block of wood in vise.
- ☐  *2.* Grasp the handle of the file in one hand (Fig. 7A).
- ☐  *3.* Grasp the point of the file in the other hand.
- ☐  *4.* Place the middle of the face of the file on the wood.
- ☐  *5.* The first stroke should be started with light pressure near the point of the file.
- ☐  *6.* Push file across wood and increase pressure as you go, so that each file tooth will do its share of the job.
- ☐  *7.* When the file is pushed all the way across the surface of the wood, raise file and start all over. Never use pressure on return stroke. Make sure your strokes are slow and steady. Too much speed will cause your file to "rock," and that will round off the edges of your wood.
- ☐  *8.* As you file, the teeth of the file will clog up with some of the wood shavings and prevent efficient filing. This is known as "pinning." Rubbing chalk between the teeth of the file can help to prevent this condition. But, better clean the file frequently with a brush, as shown in Figure 7B. Brush with a pulling motion parallel to the rows of teeth, diagonally across the file, not up-and-down the length of the file.
- ☐  *9.* Clean the file after fifteen strokes and alter your angle of filing at the same time.
- ☐  *10.* Now repeat entire process with dowels or broom handle, so that you get practice in filing a rounded surface.
- ☐  *11.* Repeat entire practice procedure on metal.

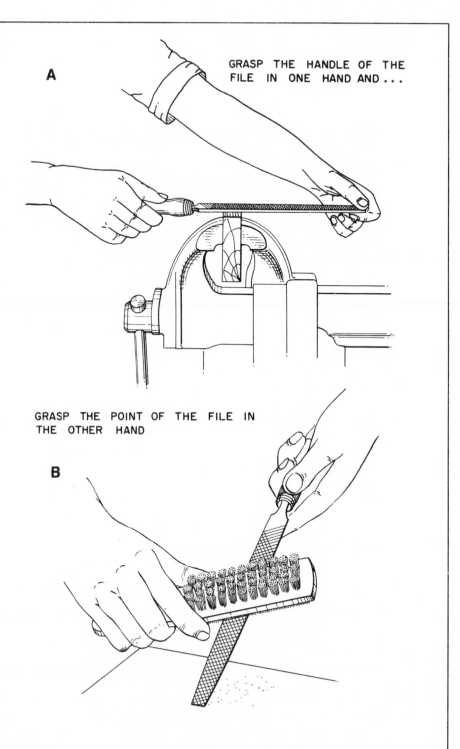

A

GRASP THE HANDLE OF THE
FILE IN ONE HAND AND...

GRASP THE POINT OF THE FILE IN
THE OTHER HAND

B

Figure 7.
The File

## 8. HOW TO USE A WOOD CHISEL

Contrary to popular belief, the wood chisel is not a tool used for heavy work. It is a sharp, delicate instrument; and in the hands of an expert woodworker, it is not unlike a scalpel in the hands of a surgeon. It is used to cut and shave wood and must be kept sharp at all times so precision work can be done with it. Never, never use a wood chisel as a prying tool, as this will ruin the bevel edge forever. Never use the wood chisel on metal either. Only occasionally does the wood chisel require the assistance of a wooden mallet for the purpose of embedding the cutting edge deeply into a piece of wood. For the purpose of the practice recipes below, it is essential you work on a bench or table surface and utilize a small vise or C-clamp to hold the wood securely.

UTENSILS
*Combination square vise
   or C-clamp
Sharp pencil
Crosscut saw or hacksaw
¾-inch general purpose chisel
   with wooden or plastic
   handle
Wooden mallet*

INGREDIENTS
*Piece of lumber, 2 inches by
   3 inches, 12 inches long*

### To Cut a ½-Inch-Deep Dado (Groove)

☐  1. Working from one end of lumber, measure off 3 inches with square and mark with pencil (Fig. 8A).
☐  2. Now measure off 5 inches from the same end (Fig. 8A). Mark as above.
☐  3. Turn wood clockwise on its side and extend lines drawn on face (Fig. 8B).
☐  4. Turn wood counterclockwise to the other side and extend lines as above.
☐  5. Mark off ½ inch from top edge on both sides of the face (Fig. 8B). These are the depth lines of the dado to be chiseled out.
☐  6. Now turn wood so original face is up and mark off ¼-inch lines from one edge to the other (Fig. 8C).
☐  7. Place wood in vise and clamp securely.
☐  8. Starting from either the extreme left-hand side or the right, saw down along face lines to depth lines drawn on sides.

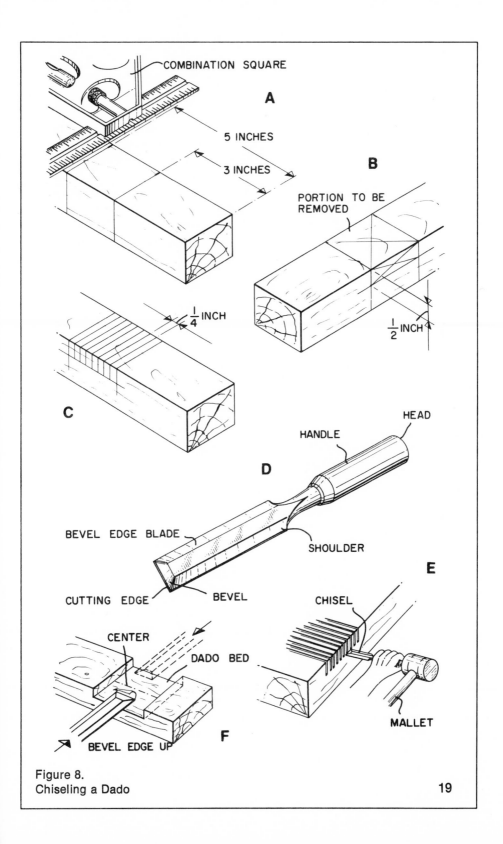

COMBINATION SQUARE

**A**

5 INCHES

3 INCHES

**B**

PORTION TO BE REMOVED

$\frac{1}{2}$ INCH

$\frac{1}{4}$ INCH

**C**

HEAD

HANDLE

**D**

BEVEL EDGE BLADE

SHOULDER

CUTTING EDGE

BEVEL

**E**

CHISEL

CENTER

DADO BED

BEVEL EDGE UP

**F**

MALLET

Figure 8.
Chiseling a Dado

19

Just make sure that the saw lines on the outer two markings are *inside,* not outside, the lines.

☐ 9. With chisel (Fig. 8D) in one hand and mallet in the other, tap away at the narrow rows of wood until they are all removed (Fig. 8E).

☐ 10. Now grasp the handle of the chisel and the shoulder of the blade in one hand.

☐ 11. With bevel edge up, place chisel flat on the dado bed at the left side of the dado and shave toward the center until smooth (Fig. 8F).

☐ 12. Repeat process from right side to center until the dado is smooth.

## 9. HOW TO USE A COLD CHISEL

A cold chisel (Fig. 9A) is a tool you will use primarily in masonry projects, principally for chipping away at old mortar, concrete, cement, and plaster. Occasionally, however, it may be used on metal for making holes or cutting edges.

Before beginning work with a cold chisel, you should first have some proficiency in the use of a hammer; for without it, your swing will be hesitant—and he who hesitates is lost. You must have no fear when you wield a hammer. If you are uncertain, please reread Recipe 1 on How to Use a Hammer.

UTENSILS

*Cold chisel*
*Ball peen hammer*
*Pair of goggles to
    protect eyes*

INGREDIENTS

*Piece of broken concrete*

☐ 1. Put on protective goggles.

☐ 2. Grasp chisel in hand firmly, but loose enough so you do not absorb the shock when the hammer strikes the chisel head.

☐ 3. Hold chisel at an angle to the concrete so that the lower bevel of the chisel is parallel (Fig. 9B).

☐ *4.* Grasp the hammer near the end of the handle and tap head of chisel gently until you establish a confident rhythm.

☐ *5.* Now raise the hammer above the shoulder and strike the head of the chisel with some force. Do this slowly until your rhythm is established. The amount of force used is determined by the nature of the material on which you are working. The heavier the material, the more forceful the striking should be.

*Note:* To prevent injury, the head of the chisel and the head of the hammer should be kept free of oil or dirt at all times. In addition, watch for "burring" on the chisel head after extensive use (Fig. 9C). When this condition arises, have the head of the chisel reground until smooth (Fig. 9D). This will avoid cuts on the hands and will prevent metal chips from flying about. Use goggles at all times.

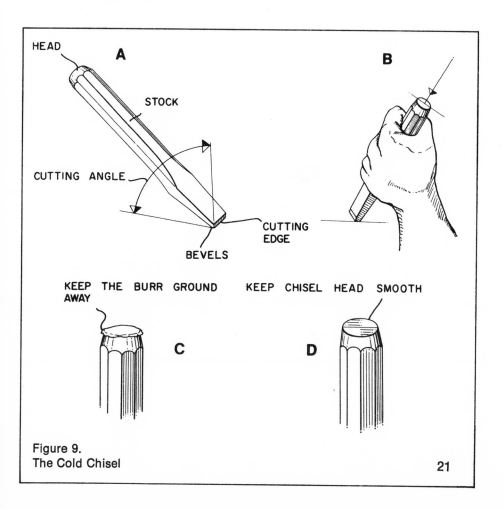

Figure 9.
The Cold Chisel

21

## 10. HOW TO USE A JACK PLANE

Because the plane is made of many parts, we suggest, for openers, that you check closely with the illustrations (Fig. 10) as we describe this tool.

A plane is primarily a shaving instrument, and its blade must be kept sharp and clean at all times to insure precision work. You will notice that it has two handles, one at the front of the tool, and one at the rear. Never, never use the plane with one hand! It is dangerous.

Knowing how to adjust the plane blade for varying cutting depths is essential, and it is easy to learn. Simply turn the adjusting nut clockwise until the blade protrudes to your specifications. The more the blade protrudes, the deeper the cut it will make, so be careful! You must also be certain that the blade is extending evenly from the mouth of the plane. The adjustment is made by moving the lateral adjusting lever to the right or left as needed. If the blade itself is loose, remove the cam lever cap and tighten lever cap screw with screwdriver, turning in a clockwise direction.

UTENSILS
INGREDIENTS
*Table vise*
*Block(s) of wood*
*Jack plane*

☐ 1. Insert piece of wood in vise and clamp tightly.
☐ 2. Grasp the rear handle of the plane in one hand, with the index finger pointing forward as shown in Figure 10A. Grasp the front handle with the thumb and forefinger of the other hand, or you may lay the palm of that hand firmly over the handle.
☐ 3. Position yourself firmly at the back of the wood in the vise.
☐ 4. Lay the toe of the blade on the wood and slide the plane forward, exerting pressure on both the toe and heel. If the blade is protruding too far, readjust depth by turning adjusting nut in a counterclockwise direction (Fig. 10B).
☐ 5. Once you have reached the end of the wood, remove pressure from the toe and return plane to starting position.
☐ 6. Repeat stroke, making sure that you are planing the edge of the wood, not its corners.
☐ 7. If the wood begins to chip apart, remove it from the vise and turn it around. You have been planing against the grain (Fig. 10C).

□ 8. Repeat planing strokes several times until you can make one long, clean shaving, which should be paper thin (Fig. 10D). Then pat yourself on the back.
□ 9. Planing the end grain of the wood is a little trickier. First, turn wood over so end-grain is up, and tighten vise securely.
□ 10. Grasp the plane as before, but do not attempt a single-length cut. Plane halfway on the edge, and then turn the piece of wood around in the vise, and plane in from that end to the center.
□ 11. Repeat these steps on several pieces of wood until you are really in control of the tool.

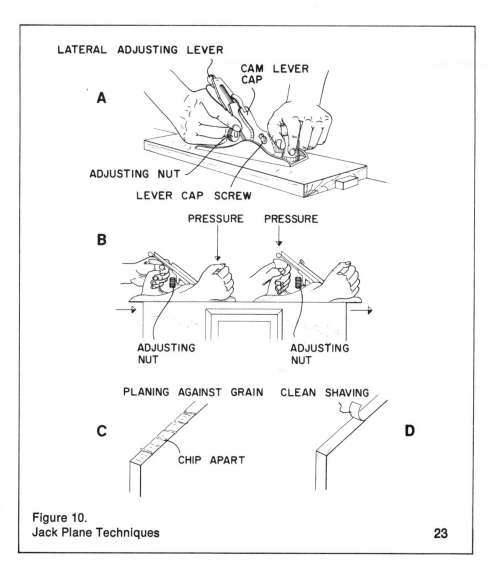

Figure 10.
Jack Plane Techniques

23

## 11. HOW TO USE A SPIRIT LEVEL

A spirit level is a precision instrument and will not perform its delicate work if abused. Don't use it to bang in nails. Use a hammer.

The level is used to create perfectly horizontal and/or vertical planes. Some men will even establish a perfect 45-degree angle to the perpendicular; but that is rarely used by the layman.

The following practice recipe will show you how to test the accuracy of a level and, at the same time, instruct you in most of its uses. It is advisable that you perform these tests at the hardware store, before you purchase.

The ideal level for home use is approximately 18 inches long with double spirit level tubes at every opening on the face.

| UTENSILS | INGREDIENTS |
|---|---|
| *Spirit level* | *Several pieces of thin cardboard*<br>*Roll of masking tape* |

☐  *1.* Set level on tabletop. Any table will do.
☐  *2.* Check the spirit tubes, and you'll notice that two lines have been drawn on each one (Fig. 11A).
☐  *3.* If the bubble is to the right of the two lines, then place a piece of cardboard beneath the left end. If bubble is to the left of the lines, place cardboard beneath right end.
☐  *4.* Keep adding or removing cardboard until bubble is centered between the two lines (Fig. 11B).
☐  *5.* Once the bubble is centered, turn the level over on the other side and rest it on the cardboard pieces already in place (Fig. 11C). The bubble should still be in center.
☐  *6.* Now turn level around and replace over cardboard. Bubble should still be centered. If the bubble has shifted in any of the changed positions, that means that the level is defective and must not be purchased.
☐  *7.* Now lay the narrow edge of the level against the wall. If the bubble leans toward the wall, cardboard must be placed beneath the bottom end of the level and taped in place.
If the bubble leans away from the wall, cardboard must be taped at the top end of the level. Adjust until bubble is centered.

□ 8. Now turn level over and test again. Bubble should be centered.
□ 9. Now turn level around and test once again. Bubble should still be centered.
□ 10. If bubble is not in between the lines when the level is shifted around, this indicates that the vertical calibration of the tool is not in working order.

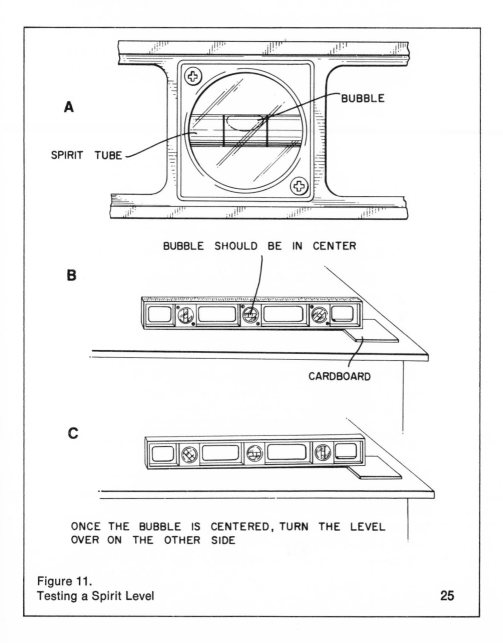

A

BUBBLE

SPIRIT TUBE

BUBBLE SHOULD BE IN CENTER

B

CARDBOARD

C

ONCE THE BUBBLE IS CENTERED, TURN THE LEVEL OVER ON THE OTHER SIDE

Figure 11.
Testing a Spirit Level

25

## 12. HOW TO USE A SOLDERING IRON

In more trying times than these, there was a hue and cry for a "chicken in every pot." Today, for the do-it-yourselfer, the slogan ought to be "A soldering iron for every home." This reasonably priced tool is virtually indispensable for modern people. With it, wonders can be performed: toys, electrical appliances, plugs, and even jewelry can be repaired in the home. The following recipes will teach you all you need to know about this device.

Most metals, with the exception of aluminum, white metal, and porous cast iron can be soldered. Those most easily soldered are tin, all sheet metals (except aluminum), brass, and copper. All soldering should be done on a surface where damage would be of little concern—preferably wood.

UTENSILS
*25- or 30-watt soldering iron
   with medium-small tip*
*Fine emery cloth*
*Small, fine file*

INGREDIENTS
*Soldering paste or flux
   (nonacid)*
*Cotton cloth or pad*
*2 small tin can lids*
*Piece of electrical wire*

### Preheating Soldering Iron

☐  *1.* When soldering iron (Fig. 12A) is new, tip should be cleaned with emery cloth.
☐  *2.* If iron is old, tip should be filed and reshaped.
☐  *3.* Plug into outlet and heat tip until it turns bright orange or red.
☐  *4.* Dip heated tip into soldering flux, and avoid inhaling fumes.
☐  *5.* Touch a short length of solder coil to heated tip (Fig. 12B). The melted solder will run freely, creating a shiny, silvery surface on the tip.
☐  *6.* Remove solder coil and wipe tip clean of excess with cloth or pad.

### Soldering Tin Lids

☐  *1.* Preheat soldering iron.
☐  *2.* With emery cloth, clean off small edge of each tin lid.
☐  *3.* Wipe soldering paste on cleaned surface of one lid.
☐  *4.* Press heated tip onto fluxed area.
☐  *5.* Touch end of solder coil to the point at which the heated

tip and tin lid meet. The solder will flow freely over the surface.

☐ 6. Remove soldering iron and solder coil.

☐ 7. Repeat process with other tin lid.

☐ 8. Turn one lid over and place on the other, so both soldered surfaces are in contact (Fig. 12C).

☐ 9. Press heated soldering tip onto overlapped surface until solder beneath melts and overflows from edges.

☐ 10. Remove soldering iron and allow lids to cool. Once cool, the lids will be solidly welded together.

## Soldering Electrical Wire

☐ 1. Strip back a piece of electrical wire so stranded ends are exposed.

☐ 2. Twist ends together tightly in clockwise direction.

☐ 3. Dip twisted ends into soldering paste.

☐ 4. Touch heated soldering iron tip and solder coil to twisted ends (Fig. 12D). Avoid inhaling fumes. The flowing solder will seal wire strands.

☐ 5. Let cool.

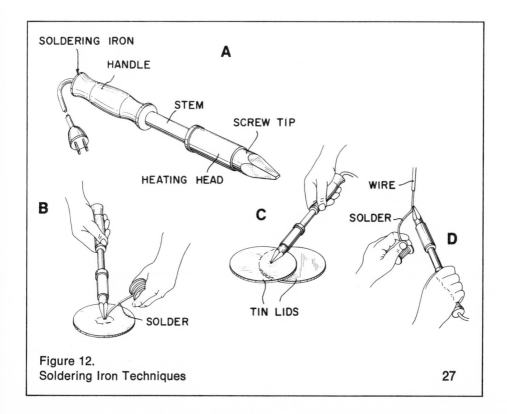

Figure 12.
Soldering Iron Techniques

27

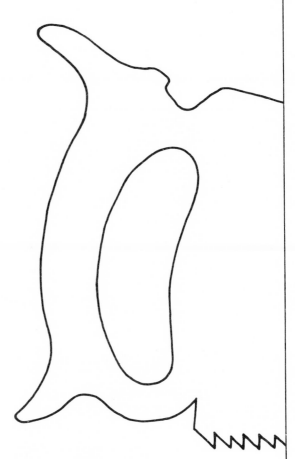

# PART II

# Carpentry

Working with wood is not only a craft that can bring you hours of pleasure, it is an art, or it *can* be. While we are not offering a course in the art of woodworking, we do offer a beginning to a hobby that can transcend the commonplace chores of simple repairs of wooden objects.

Tools, as we said, are essential to complete woodworking tasks. What follows is a more than adequate list. You need not purchase them all at one time, though that is not a bad idea.

*1 claw hammer*
*1 tack hammer*
*1 ball peen hammer*
*1 set of screwdrivers (see Recipe 2 on How to Use a Screwdriver)*
*Wood files (smooth, medium, rough) and handles to match*
*1 crosscut handsaw*
*1 coping saw*
*1 small jack plane*

*Assortment of wood screws*
*Assortment of woodworking nails*
*Assortment of tacks*
*Small hand drill and assortment of bits*
*Assortment of open-coat sandpaper*
*Plastic wood*
*White polyvinyl glue*

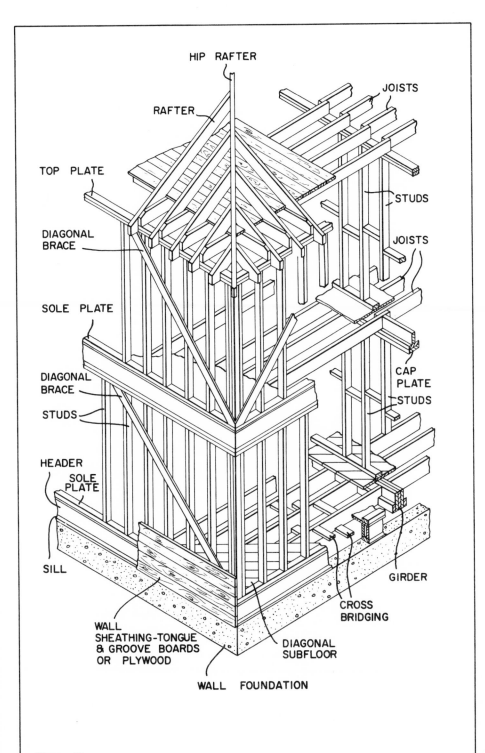

HIP RAFTER

RAFTER

JOISTS

TOP PLATE

STUDS

DIAGONAL BRACE

JOISTS

SOLE PLATE

CAP PLATE

DIAGONAL BRACE

STUDS

STUDS

HEADER

SOLE PLATE

SILL

GIRDER

CROSS BRIDGING

WALL SHEATHING-TONGUE & GROOVE BOARDS OR PLYWOOD

DIAGONAL SUBFLOOR

WALL FOUNDATION

Figure D.
Platform Framing for a Typical Two Story House

31

## 13. SHAKY CHAIR

To sit on a chair and wind up on the floor is not only a painful humiliation, it is also a chance for a serious injury. So, if your chairs have been wobbling lately, pick yourself up and get your seat together.

UTENSILS
*Pencil*
*Rasp*
*Hammer*
*Wooden block, ¾ inch wide*
  *and 2 to 3 inches long*
*Heavy rope or twine*
*3 to 4 sticks, ½ inch by ½*
  *inch, 6 to 8 inches long*

INGREDIENTS
*White polyvinyl glue*

APPROXIMATE TIME: 90 TO 120 MINUTES

□ 1. Disassemble all loose sections of chair, and mark each for easy reassembly.
□ 2. With rasp, scrape away old glue from around dowel ends (Fig. 13A).
□ 3. Scrape away all old glue inside dowel holes (Fig. 13A).
□ 4. Apply glue to cleaned dowel ends and reassemble chair.
□ 5. With hammer and wooden block, tap at all intersecting sections to secure dowels firmly in holes.
□ 6. Wrap rope several times around legs and tie ends in square knot.
□ 7. Insert ½-inch sticks between rope strands at several locations (Fig. 13B), and twist around, creating the effect of a turnbuckle or tourniquet (Fig. 13C). This will tighten all joints.
□ 8. Tap all sections again with hammer and wooden block.
□ 9. Set chair on level surface to make sure all legs are resting evenly on the floor.
□ 10. If one leg is higher than the others, tap that corner of the chair with hammer and block until that leg is even with others.
□ 11. Let dry overnight.
□ 12. Remove rope.

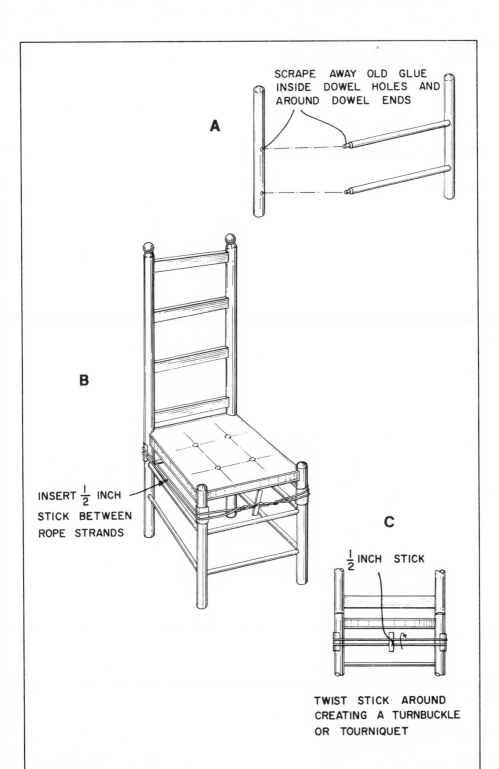

SCRAPE AWAY OLD GLUE INSIDE DOWEL HOLES AND AROUND DOWEL ENDS

**A**

**B**

INSERT $\frac{1}{2}$ INCH STICK BETWEEN ROPE STRANDS

**C**

$\frac{1}{2}$ INCH STICK

TWIST STICK AROUND CREATING A TURNBUCKLE OR TOURNIQUET

Figure 13.
Tightening a Chair Leg

## 14. LOOSE TABLE LEGS

A wobbly table and civilized dining do not go together, especially when one's soup goes sloshing out of the plate and into the lap. You think that's funny? Does the tablecloth think it's funny? Follow this recipe, and you'll never have to worry about a wet lap again.

UTENSILS
*Small adjustable wrench*

INGREDIENTS
*Toothpicks*
*White polyvinyl glue*

APPROXIMATE TIME: 15 MINUTES

☐ *1.* Locate the loose leg or legs causing the wobble.
☐ *2.* At that point, look under the table and find a diagonal metal bracket in which there is a bolt known as a stair-rail bolt (Fig. 14A).
☐ *3.* Lift that corner of the table with one hand, if the table is light, and tighten bolt with adjustable wrench in a counter-clockwise direction (Fig. 14A). If the table is heavy, you will need assistance. You might even want to turn the table upside down to gain easy access to the bolt.
☐ *4.* Tighten all loose bolts.
☐ *5.* If bolt accidentally slips out of leg, as it sometimes will, perform the following steps (Fig. 14C). Insert three or four small pieces of toothpicks into bolt hole. Squeeze in liberal amount of white polyvinyl glue. Let dry. Reinsert bolt and tighten securely.

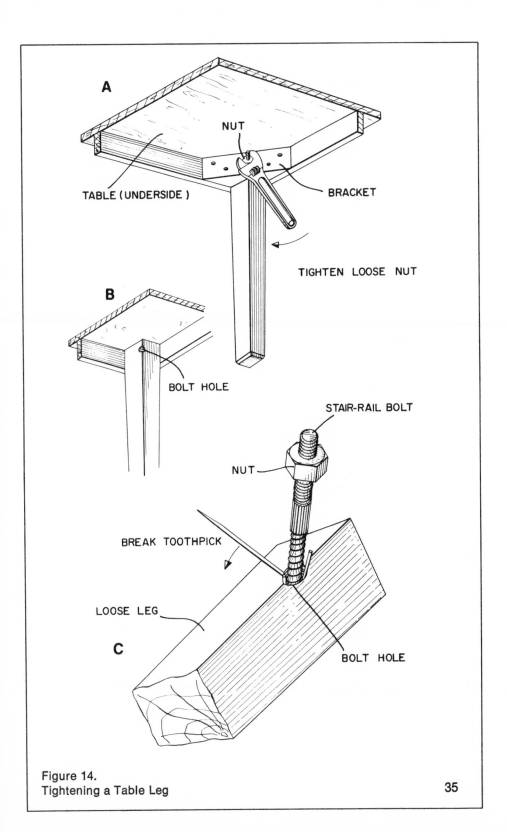

A

NUT

TABLE (UNDERSIDE)

BRACKET

TIGHTEN LOOSE NUT

B

BOLT HOLE

STAIR-RAIL BOLT

NUT

BREAK TOOTHPICK

LOOSE LEG

C

BOLT HOLE

Figure 14.
Tightening a Table Leg

## 15. REPAIRING BROKEN FURNITURE LEGS

A thin chair or sofa or table leg breaking is not a frequent occurrence; but when it happens, it is far more expedient to fix it yourself than to call someone in for help. The only possible difficulty you'll encounter is having to turn over the piece of furniture so you won't be forced to work lying down. Don't tackle really heavy furniture by yourself.

UTENSILS
*Rasp*
*Diagonal cutters*
*4-penny (or larger) nails,*
    *depending on the diameter*
    *of the leg*
*Electric or hand drill*
*Small fine file*

INGREDIENTS
*Masking tape*
*Paraffin wax*
*Casein or white polyvinyl glue*
*Roll of waxed paper*
*4 to 5 feet of strong twine*

APPROXIMATE TIME: 30 MINUTES

- ☐ 1. Turn over piece of furniture so legs are pointing up (Fig. 15A).
- ☐ 2. If leg has been broken before, clean away old glue with rasp.
- ☐ 3. Tape broken pieces of leg together in original position with masking tape (Fig. 15B).
- ☐ 4. With diagonal cutters, cut off the head of a 4-penny nail.
- ☐ 5. Insert nail in drill for use as bit.
- ☐ 6. Drill two holes through leg at right angle to break (Fig. 15B).
- ☐ 7. Insert a 4-penny nail into each drilled hole so nails are protruding at both ends of hole (Fig. 15C).
- ☐ 8. Remove masking tape from leg.
- ☐ 9. Rub paraffin wax on finished sections of leg, but avoid waxing broken joint, as wax will prevent glue from sticking.
- ☐ 10. Apply glue into the broken joint, making sure both sides of the break are glued.
- ☐ 11. Squeeze sections firmly together until glue oozes out of joint.
- ☐ 12. Wrap joint with waxed paper and hold in place with several tight turns of twine.
- ☐ 13. Permit to dry overnight.
- ☐ 14. Remove twine and waxed paper.
- ☐ 15. Cut off protruding nails as close to the leg as possible with diagonal cutters.
- ☐ 16. File nail end until flush with surface of leg.
- ☐ 17. Turn furniture piece right side up.

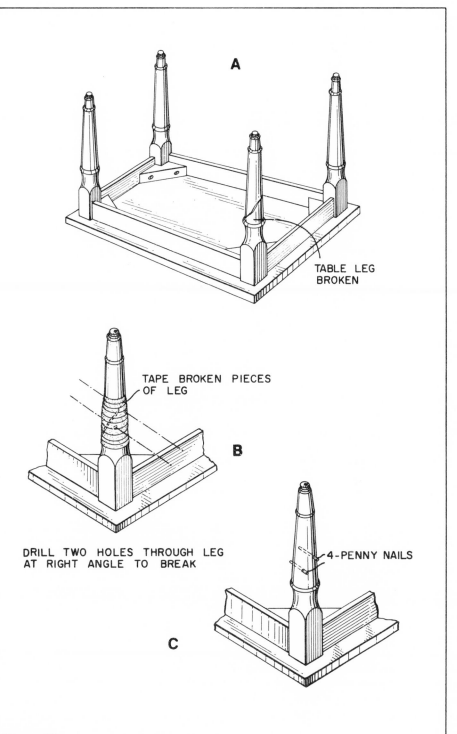

A

TABLE LEG
BROKEN

TAPE BROKEN PIECES
OF LEG

B

DRILL TWO HOLES THROUGH LEG
AT RIGHT ANGLE TO BREAK

4-PENNY NAILS

C

Figure 15.
Procedures for Broken Table Leg

## 16. REPAIRING LOOSE AND BROKEN BALUSTERS

This is one recipe we cannot make light of. A wobbly balustrade (Fig. 16A) is dangerous, especially if there is someone in your home who relies on its strength to walk up and down stairs. Take a half hour, if you have this problem, and stop worrying about someone breaking his neck.

UTENSILS
*Electric or hand drill with*
  *⅛-inch bit*
*Hammer*
*Nail set with small point*
*Diagonal cutter*
*C-clamp*
*Damp sponge*

INGREDIENTS
*White polyvinyl glue*
*1-pound box of 2-inch finishing*
  *nails*
*Roll of ¾-inch masking tape*

APPROXIMATE TIME: 30 TO 45 MINUTES

☐   *1.* At a 45-degree angle, drill 2 inches into wood where baluster and tread intersect (Fig. 16B).
☐   *2.* Repeat on all loose balusters. See step 6 if applicable.
☐   *3.* Squeeze glue into drilled holes until glue overflows from cracks.
☐   *4.* Repeat at all points, wiping away excess glue with damp sponge.
☐   *5.* Let dry overnight.
☐   *6.* If balusters are split or broken where drilling is to take place, follow these directions before performing steps 3, 4, and 5.
☐     a. Remove bit from drill.
☐     b. With diagonal cutter, cut off head of finishing nail.
☐     c. Insert nail into drill as a bit.
☐     d. Drill through broken section.
☐     e. Squeeze glue into drilled hole.
☐     f. Drive in uncut finishing nail through glue and set with nail set.
☐     g. If the splintered baluster had shed pieces of wood, it would be advisable to replace these pieces as well as possible and tape them into place before beginning step 1.
☐     h. Proceed with steps 3, 4, 5.

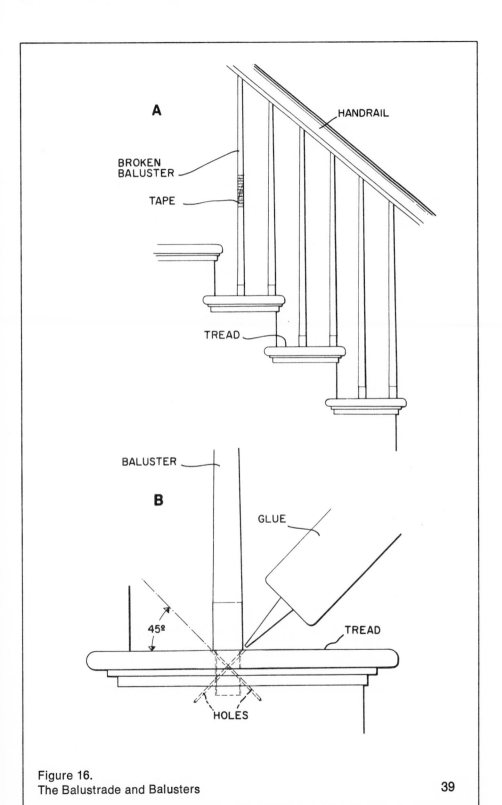

**A**

HANDRAIL

BROKEN
BALUSTER

TAPE

TREAD

**B**

BALUSTER

GLUE

45º

TREAD

HOLES

Figure 16.
The Balustrade and Balusters

## 17. DRAWERS STICK

This problem is even more annoying than the drawer that is just off kilter, because if your life depends on getting some underwear out of that drawer, well . . .

Here's a practical and speedy solution to the problem.

UTENSILS
*Extension cord with light bulb socket and a 75-watt bulb*

INGREDIENTS
*Sheet of coarse grade, ½-grit sandpaper (see Abrasives chart)*
*Paraffin wax or silicone spray*

APPROXIMATE TIME: 15 TO 30 MINUTES

☐  1. If drawer is stuck really fast and cannot be removed from cabinet, try your best to open it at least a few inches.
☐  2. Place extension cord and bulb into the drawer (Fig. 17A).
☐  3. Plug extension cord into wall.
☐  4. Allow lighted bulb to remain in drawer for 15 minutes until heat from bulb shrinks wood. This will allow you to remove drawer easily.
☐  5. Place drawer on tabletop and sandpaper sides of the drawer as well as the tops and bottoms of drawer runners as shown in Figure 17B.
☐  6. Rub paraffin or apply silicone spray on tops and bottoms of drawer runners and sides of drawer.
☐  7. Replace drawer into cabinet. If still tight, it will be necessary to sandpaper that side of the drawer that is still binding.

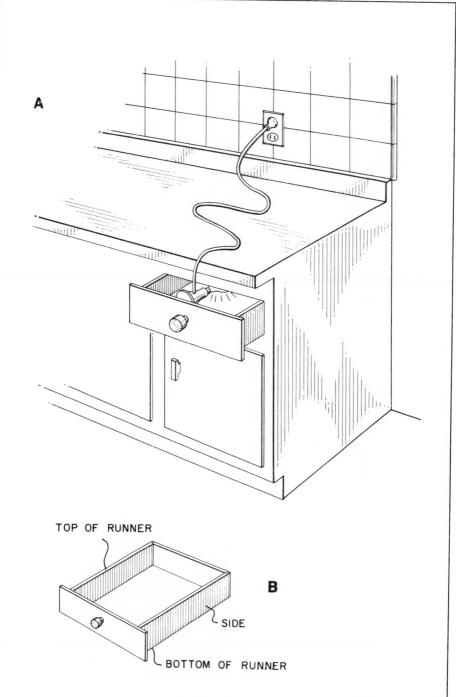

A

TOP OF RUNNER

B

SIDE

BOTTOM OF RUNNER

Figure 17.
Repairing a Sticking Drawer

## 18. DRAWER REPAIR

You're looking for something in your dresser drawer. You try to pull the drawer open, and only the right side moves. Or maybe it's the left side that gives an inch or two. Or maybe nothing gives. If you can get the drawer out (see Recipe 17), then we'll show you how to refit it if the joints are loose. Loose joints are the major reason for this malady.

UTENSILS
*Pencil*
*Wood chisel*
*Hammer*

INGREDIENTS
*Polyvinyl glue*
*24 2-penny finishing nails*
*Paraffin wax*

APPROXIMATE TIME: 60 MINUTES

☐ *1.* Place drawer on tabletop with front of drawer facing you (open section up).
☐ *2.* Mark on the inside of drawer, where it will not be seen *front, rear, left, right,* as shown in Figure 18A.
☐ *3.* Gently tap with hammer all glue joints in the direction in which they disassemble until all sections are apart.
☐ *4.* Clean away all old glue with chisel. The cleaner the joints, the more secure the fitting when you reassemble.
☐ *5.* Notice that there is a groove running along the bottom of all sections with the possible exception of the rear. Do not place glue in this groove! (Fig. 18B).
☐ *6.* Apply glue to all joints except the bottom groove.
☐ *7.* Reassemble the left, right, and front sections as shown in Figure 18B.
☐ *8.* Starting from the rear, slip bottom section into groove (Fig. 18B).
☐ *9.* Now you may replace rear section into glue joints.
☐ *10.* Placing drawer on table so left side is on the table and right side is up, drive several nails through right side of drawer into front and rear sections, as shown in Figure 18C.
☐ *11.* Turning drawer over so right side is on the table and left side is up, repeat nailing procedure.
☐ *12.* If drawer does not have a grooved rear section, turn drawer upside down, and make sure that the bottom section slides all the way into the groove and is flush with front section. Drive several nails through bottom into rear. All nailed sections should be snug.

□ *13.* With ruler, measure diagonal distance from right front to left rear, and from left front to right rear.
□ *14.* They should be identical measurements. If not, a little gentle squeezing on the long sides will finally get the measurements within 1/16 inch.
□ *15.* Allow joints to dry as drawer sits on a flat surface.
□ *16.* Rub sides of drawer and bottom with paraffin wax and then replace in cabinet.

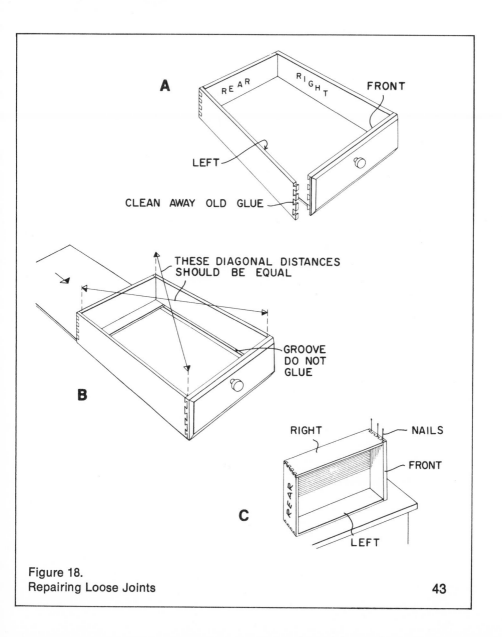

Figure 18.
Repairing Loose Joints

43

## 19. SQUEAKY FLOORS

Creaking floors in your home need not indicate either a defect in the structure or ghosts lurking about the premises. If your floors squeak, don't be alarmed: merely follow this simple recipe.

UTENSILS                          INGREDIENTS
*Flat thin chisel*                *Talcum powder*
*Hammer*
*Broom*
*Vacuum cleaner*

APPROXIMATE TIME: 30 MINUTES

☐ *1.* Locate the source of the squeak.
☐ *2.* Open tight floorboards slightly: insert chisel in cracks, tap with hammer, and move chisel lightly from side to side (Fig. 19A).
☐ *3.* Sprinkle talcum powder into the cracks (Fig. 19B). A few taps on the floor with the hammer will shake the powder into the joints.
☐ *4.* Sweep powder over squeaky area with broom.
☐ *5.* Vacuum all excess powder, but be careful not to remove too much from the cracks.
☐ *6.* If squeak persists, repeat the process.

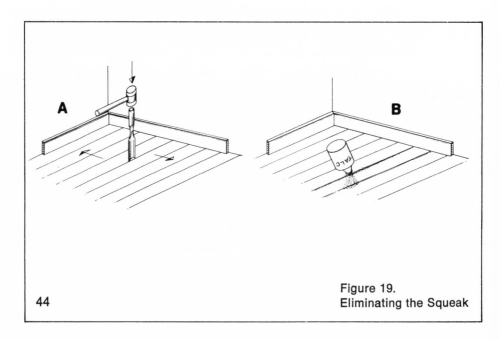

44

Figure 19.
Eliminating the Squeak

## 20. A BROKEN WINDOWPANE

If the youngster next door accidentally hurls a football through your bedroom window, and the day happens to be Friday, chances are you'll have a chilly weekend. That is, if you rely on a glazier to do the job. Here is a simple recipe that will restore warmth to your home and keep money in your pockets.

UTENSILS
*Pair of heavy gloves*
*Electric iron or small*
  *propane torch*
*Putty knife*
*Pliers*
*Scissors*
*Small paintbrush*

INGREDIENTS
*Large piece of cardboard*
  *or shirt board*
*1 piece single-thickness glass*
*Box of cornstarch*
*Can of putty or glazing*
  *compound*
*Can of boiled linseed oil*
*Box of glazier's points*

APPROXIMATE TIME: 90 MINUTES

☐  1. Wearing gloves to avoid being cut, remove all broken glass from window frame.
☐  2. Heat old putty on window frame with electric iron or propane torch, and remove with putty knife and pliers.
☐  3. With pliers, or with edge of putty knife, remove glazier's points (small triangular metal wedges) from window frame.
☐  4. Cut a piece of cardboard to fit window frame, reducing measurement uniformly by ⅛ inch.
☐  5. Take cardboard template to glazier or hardware store and have a piece of glass cut to exact size.
☐  6. Sprinkle cornstarch on your hands and on the work surface you'll be using. This will prevent putty from sticking.
☐  7. Remove all the putty from the can and roll into a rope.
☐  8. Brush a light coat of linseed oil onto frame where glass and putty will be inserted.
☐  9. Cut putty rope into 6-inch lengths and squeeze into corner of window frame (Fig. 20A).
☐ 10. Press glass securely into frame (Fig. 20B).
☐ 11. Remove all but 1/16 inch of putty squeezed out by pressure of glass.
☐ 12. Now wedge glazier's points into frame with blade of putty knife (Fig. 20C, 20D). Space the points approximately 8 inches apart.

☐ *13.* Cut remainder of putty rope into 6-inch lengths and repeat step 9.
☐ *14.* Remove all excess putty with putty knife and smooth.

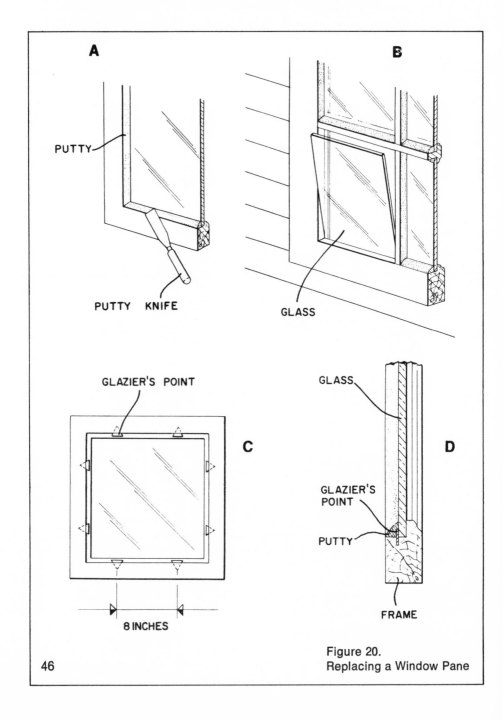

Figure 20.
Replacing a Window Pane

## 21. SASH CORD REPLACEMENT

This is perhaps the most difficult task the home repairperson will ever face. But don't take this as a reason to be discouraged! Follow the procedure closely, rely heavily on the detailed sketches, and you'll do just fine!

UTENSILS
Claw hammer
Old wood chisel
Pliers
Medium flat blade screwdriver
10-foot length of twine
    or fishing cord
½-ounce fishing weight
Diagonal cutters
Wooden stick, 2 feet long

INGREDIENTS
Length of sash chain or cord
    2 feet longer than height
    of window
Sash chain hooks
Sash chain spine coils
Can of silicone spray lubricant
    or paraffin wax

APPROXIMATE TIME: BOTTOM SASH—60 MINUTES;
TOP SASH—90 MINUTES

☐ 1. Remove window stop bead from side of window frame that has the broken sash cord (Fig. 21A). If there are two broken cords, it will be necessary to remove stops from both sides. Pry gently with claw hammer. Do not break.

☐ 2. Raise bottom sash and remove weather stripping (metal strips grooved into edge of sash frame), if any, by prying up with chisel. Do not damage weather stripping.

☐ 3. Remove protruding nails by pulling them *through* with claw hammer or pliers.

☐ 4. Now remove sash from frame.

☐ 5. On each side of frame, there are wood panels called *pockets* (Fig. 21B). Remove screws holding each in place and remove panel, revealing sash weight.

☐ 6. If the sash cord on the upper sash is also broken, this step and steps 7 and 8 are necessary. All succeeding steps apply to all. If that upper sash cord is broken, it is necessary to remove the upper sash by gently dislodging parting strip as shown in Figure 21C. Lower window and remove weather stripping, if any, as in step 2.

☐ 7. Raise window and prop up with stick.

☐ 8. At bottom of upper sash track, next to parting strip, there is a pocket that must be removed.

□ 9. Tie twine to fishing weight, and push over top of pulley, as shown in Figure 21B.

□ 10. Carefully lower weight until it is visible in pocket below.

□ 11. Tie the end of twine to one end of cord or chain. See Figure 22B.

□ 12. Now pull fish weight until chain or cord is visible in pocket.

□ 13. Slip end of chain or cord through hole in weight and attach a hook, as shown in Figure 21D, to secure chain to weight, or, if using sash cord, tie a knot as shown in Figure 21B.

□ 14. Now pull chain so that weight is pulled up inside frame until it stops.

□ 15. Place window on sill, as shown in Figure 21A, and cut chain with diagonal cutters 2 inches beyond hole in side of sash. If using cord, cut 3 inches beyond hole.

□ 16. Take sash chain spring coil and attach as shown in Figure 21E. Tie a knot to attach, if using cord.

□ 17. Push coil into hole inside of sash, and repeat on other sashes as necessary.

□ 18. Place sash into position and ride window up and down to insure that cord and/or chain is of proper length.

□ 19. Replace pockets.

□ 20. Replace weather stripping and all moldings.

□ 21. Spray tracks with silicone spray or rub with paraffin. This will guarantee a smooth operation.

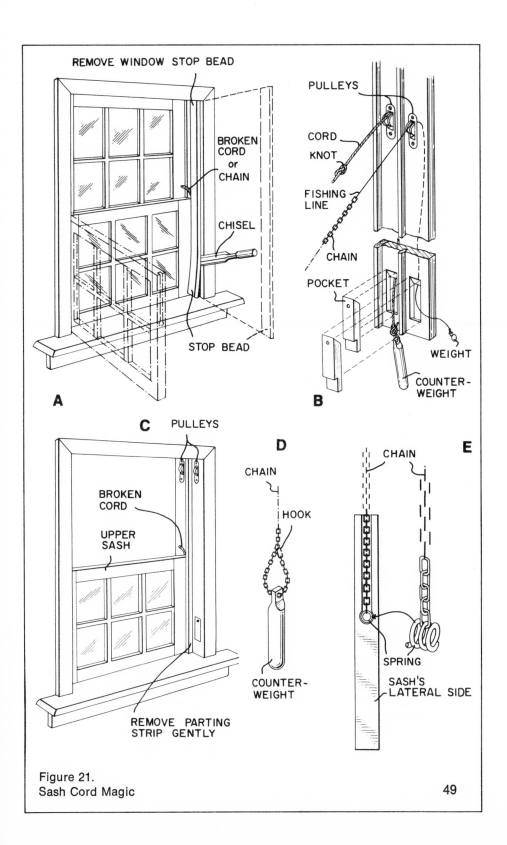

REMOVE WINDOW STOP BEAD

BROKEN CORD or CHAIN

CHISEL

STOP BEAD

**A**

PULLEYS

CORD

KNOT

FISHING LINE

CHAIN

POCKET

WEIGHT

COUNTER-WEIGHT

**B**

**C** PULLEYS

BROKEN CORD

UPPER SASH

REMOVE PARTING STRIP GENTLY

**D**

CHAIN

HOOK

COUNTER-WEIGHT

**E**

CHAIN

SPRING

SASH'S LATERAL SIDE

Figure 21.
Sash Cord Magic

49

## 22. STICKING WINDOWS

There are house painters and there are "Shmearers." House painters are people who take their time, select the proper paint, prepare the area well, and do their work efficiently and neatly. The "shmearer," on the other hand, stalks into the place, pries open a few cans of paint, and slops it onto walls, windows, floors, stoves, refrigerators, silverware, and furniture. It is this "shmearer" who is responsible for windows that won't open because of caked paint. Here's how to undo his handiwork.

UTENSILS
*Claw hammer*
*Pliers*
*2-inch flat chisel*
*3-inch putty knife*
*Hatchet*
*6-inch piece of 2 by 4*

INGREDIENTS
*Paraffin wax or wax candles*
  *or silicone spray or soap*

APPROXIMATE TIME: 15 TO 60 MINUTES

- ☐ *1.* First check to see if stuck windows have been nailed shut.
- ☐ *2.* If this is the case, remove nails with hammer or pliers.
- ☐ *3.* If not, you must now check for caked paint between sash and frame.
- ☐ *4.* If that's the problem, place chisel between sash and frame and gently chip away accumulated paint.
- ☐ *5.* If you have easy access to outside frame, check there for caked paint and chip away as in step 4.
- ☐ *6.* Now—from the outside—try to pry at bottom of sash with chisel and hammer. Don't overdo.
- ☐ *7.* Place hatchet under sash and hammer into joint as shown in Figure 22B.
- ☐ *8.* Repeat prying.
- ☐ *9.* Repeat tapping, placing 2 by 4 block on frame and gently striking with hammer. The block will prevent damage to window.
- ☐ *10.* You should now be able to open window.
- ☐ *11.* Once window is open, rub tracks with wax, silicone, or soap.
- ☐ *12.* Repeat process with upper sash and other windows as necessary.
- ☐ *13.* If it is impossible to work outside, lay putty knife between sash and stop and tap gently into frame (Fig. 22A).

☐ *14.* Continue all around sash, and repeat steps 9 and 10. You may now try to open window carefully.

☐ *15.* Repeat steps 11 and 12.

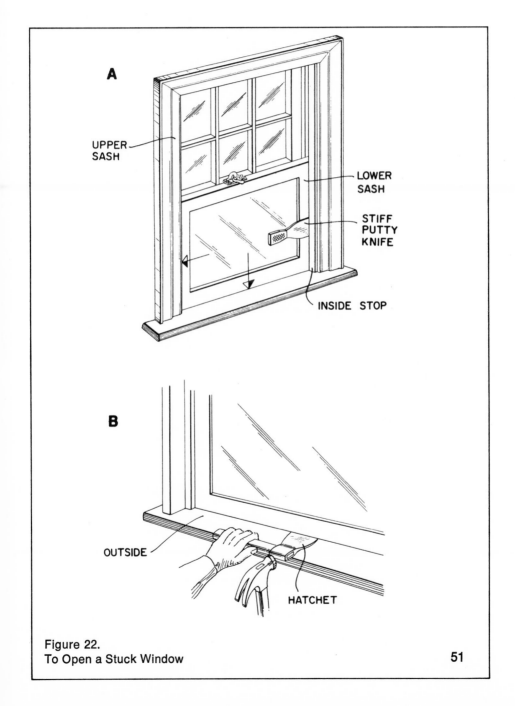

Figure 22.
To Open a Stuck Window

## 23. RATTLING WINDOWS

You never know your windows rattle until the wind blows. Unfortunately, the wind blows just about every day. If you want the rat-tat-tat, forget this recipe. If you want to get rid of it, read on.

UTENSILS

*Ruler*
*Pencil*
*Shears*
*Small hammer*

INGREDIENTS

*Pad of paper*
*Linoleum*
*Carpet tacks*
*Paraffin wax or silicone spray*

APPROXIMATE TIME: 30 TO 45 MINUTES

☐ *1.* If your lower sash is rattling, raise sash as high as possible, and measure the distance from the bottom of sash to windowsill. Add 6 inches (Fig. 23A).

☐ *2.* Note measurement on paper.

☐ *3.* Now measure thickness of sash and subtract ⅛ inch (Fig. 23A).

☐ *4.* Note this dimension on paper.

☐ *5.* Cut strips of linoleum to the measurements taken. Two strips for each sash should be more than adequate.

☐ *6.* If the upper sash is rattling, lower the window and measure the distance from the top of sash to top of window frame opening, and add 6 inches.

☐ *7.* Note measurement on paper.

☐ *8.* Measure thickness of sash and note measurement.

☐ *9.* Cut strips as directed in step 5.

☐ *10.* Starting at the right side of window, slip 6 inches of linoleum strip between window frame and top of sash as shown in Figure 23B, making sure bottom of strip is in contact with the sill.

☐ *11.* If window has metal weather stripping, it will be necessary to slip linoleum underneath.

☐ *12.* Nail linoleum into position with carpet tacks and hammer.

☐ *13.* Repeat on other side and upper sash if necessary.

☐ *14.* Rub linoleum with paraffin wax or silicone spray.

☐ *15.* Run window up and down.

☐ *16.* If window continues to rattle, repeat steps 10, 12, and 13 as necessary, adding linoleum strips as necessary.

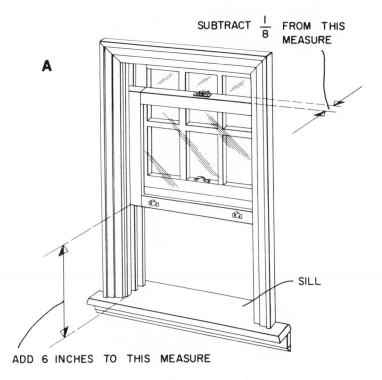

SUBTRACT $\frac{1}{8}$ FROM THIS MEASURE

**A**

SILL

ADD 6 INCHES TO THIS MEASURE

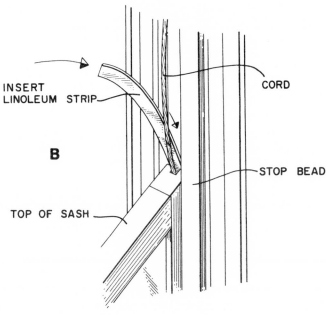

INSERT LINOLEUM STRIP

CORD

**B**

STOP BEAD

TOP OF SASH

Figure 23.
To Stop the Rattle

53

## 24. CENTER LATCH FOR DOUBLE-HUNG WINDOW

The center latch is far and away the most commonly used window locking device; and the reason it's been around so long is because it is so reliable. A good window latch, particularly in urban areas, is vital for a homeowner's or apartment dweller's peace of mind.

UTENSILS
*Ruler*
*Hammer*
*Center punch or awl*
*Cake of soft soap*
*Medium flat blade screwdriver*

INGREDIENTS
*Center-latch sash lock*
*Petroleum jelly*

APPROXIMATE TIME: 15 TO 20 MINUTES

☐  1. Close window tightly.
☐  2. Mark off center of joined sash frame as shown in Figure 24A.
☐  3. Take turning latch section of lock and place on the center mark of the upper frame of the lower sash, as shown in Figure 24B.
☐  4. With hammer and awl, punch two holes through screw holes on the latch section of sash lock (Fig. 24B).
☐  5. Rub screw threads over soap bar.
☐  6. Drive screws in clockwise until secure.
☐  7. Now place hook section of lock on center mark of lower frame of upper sash (Fig. 24C). Make sure it is lined up evenly with latch section.
☐  8. Punch holes as before.
☐  9. Soap screws and drive securely into place, turning clockwise.
☐ 10. Lubricate latch with petroleum jelly.

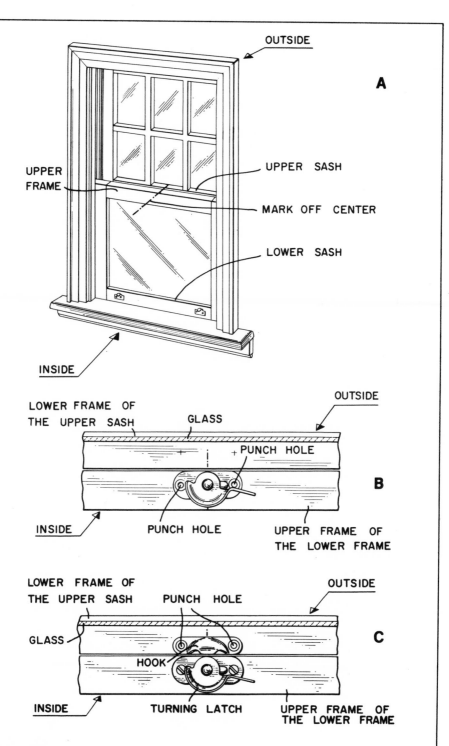

Figure 24.
To Lock a Window

55

## 25. NAIL LATCHES FOR DOUBLE-HUNG WINDOWS

The nail latch may be used in conjunction with any other latch on your window for additional protection. We like it a great deal because it has good safety value and a homey quality. And you'll like it because it just takes a few minutes to install.

UTENSILS
*Electric or hand drill*
*3/16-inch diameter high-*
    *speed bit*

INGREDIENTS
*4-inch common nails (count*
    *on 4 per double sash)*

APPROXIMATE TIME: 10 MINUTES PER SASH

☐  *1.* Close window securely.
☐  *2.* Drill holes into both sides of sash as shown in Figure 25A. If done correctly, the holes will extend through the sash into window frame.
☐  *3.* Insert a nail into each hole. Window is now securely locked.
☐  *4.* Nails may be removed to open windows.
☐  *5.* An alternate method is illustrated in Figure 25B.

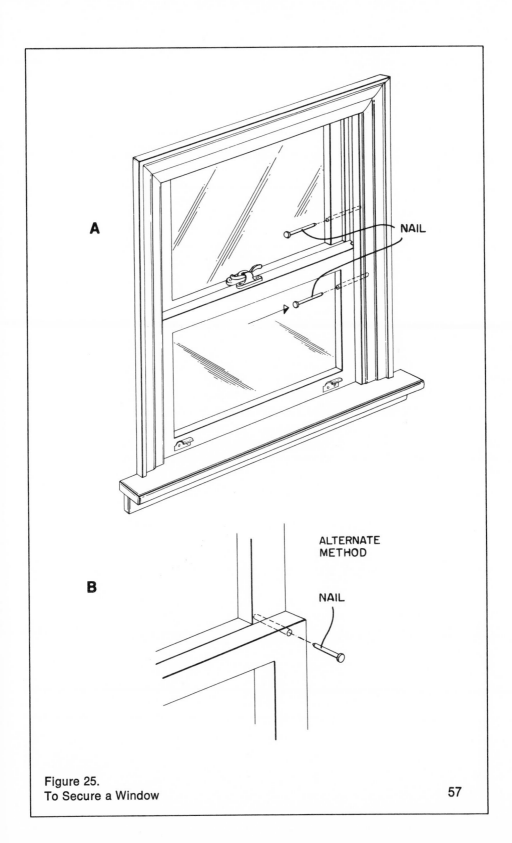

**A**

NAIL

**B**

ALTERNATE
METHOD

NAIL

Figure 25.
To Secure a Window

## 26. DOOR STICKS

We know you'd prefer not to, but let's talk about doors that won't open when you want them to. You stand there tugging and tugging, and nothing gives. Do you remember the last time the kid was locked in the bathroom behind such a door? Or you were, while a party was going on in your own home, and you had to yell for help?

Doors stick for a variety of reasons. Here's a universal solution.

UTENSILS
*Hammer*
*Medium flat blade screwdriver*
*Jack plane (sharp blade)*

INGREDIENTS
*Pencil*
*Masking tape*

APPROXIMATE TIME: 60 MINUTES

☐ *1.* Discover where door is sticking, and mark area(s) with erasable pencil (Fig. 26A).
☐ *2.* Starting at bottom, remove pins from door hinges as shown in Figure 26B.
☐ *3.* Label each pin with masking tape so it can be identified and returned later to its original position.
☐ *4.* Now shake door slightly, and it will come away from frame.
☐ *5.* Set door on floor, hinge-side down.
☐ *6.* Examine outer edges of door to see which areas have been rubbed or chafed.
☐ *7.* Measure and mark 1/16 to 1/18 inch parallel to chafed surface.
☐ *8.* Plane down to mark.
☐ *9.* If top or bottom of door has been chafed, take special care not to plane over edges, as this will cause splintering. Using marks as directed in steps 7 and 8, plane chafed areas from the edge toward the center, as shown in Figure 26C.
☐ *10.* Bevel all edges and corner with plane as shown in Figure 26D.
☐ *11.* Rehang door and replace hinge pins in original positions.
☐ *12.* Procedure may be repeated to achieve perfect fit.
☐ *13.* A ⅛-inch space at sides and top is optimum. A ¼- to ⅛-inch space at bottom is standard.

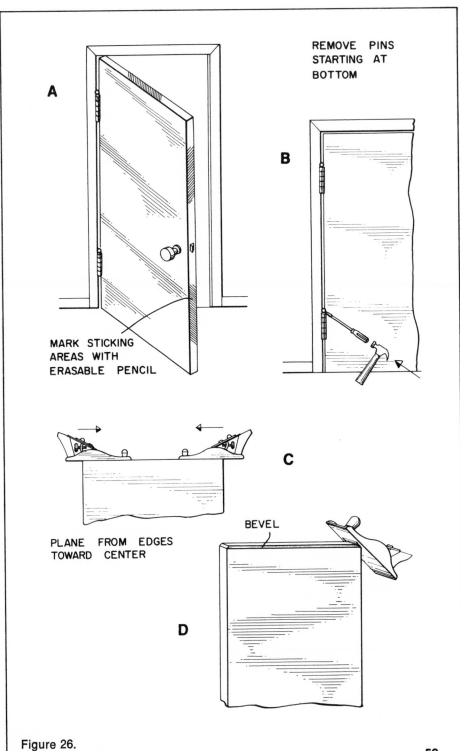

A

**REMOVE PINS STARTING AT BOTTOM**

B

**MARK STICKING AREAS WITH ERASABLE PENCIL**

C

**PLANE FROM EDGES TOWARD CENTER**

**BEVEL**

D

Figure 26.
Repairing a Sticking Door

59

## 27. RATTLING DOORS: ADJUSTING THE DOORSTOP

The usual cause for a rattling door is an improper fit of the doorstop on the doorjamb. What's worse, it sounds a lot like a burglar letting himself into your home during the night. There are three procedures for correcting this nerve-racking malady. This is the first.

UTENSILS
*Hammer*
*Flat chisel*
*Pocketknife*
*Pliers*
*Nail set*

INGREDIENTS
*24 1-inch finishing nails*
*Putty or plastic wood*

APPROXIMATE TIME: 30 TO 45 MINUTES

☐ 1. You will notice there is a space between the doorstop and the door. That's why you have a rattle. Very carefully remove doorstop on latch side of door. Do not crack this delicate molding. Pry it up gently with hammer and chisel (Fig. 27A), and then remove with claw end of hammer.

☐ 2. If you are having a rough time prying the stop from its position, it will be necessary to carve away accumulated paint with pocketknife before continuing (Fig. 27B).

☐ 3. Once the doorstop has been removed, pull out protruding nails with pliers (Fig. 27C). Make no attempt to hammer them through.

☐ 4. Replace doorstop in its old location, or try to. You'll notice that it will be offset slightly from its former position (Fig. 27D). This is good, for it has now been moved closer to the door.

☐ 5. Drive in three nails: one at the top, one at the bottom, and one in the middle (Fig. 27E).

☐ 6. Close door and test the fit.

☐ 7. If the fit is flush, drive in several additional nails to secure doorstop to frame. If the fit is not good, remove the three nails and move stop closer to door. Now repeat steps 5, 6, and 7.

☐ 8. Set finishing nails below the surface of molding (stop) and fill with putty (Fig. 27E).

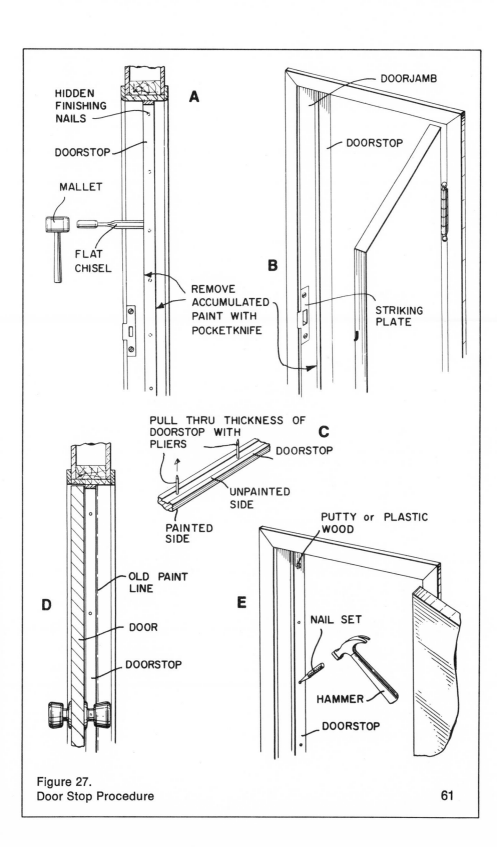

**A**

HIDDEN FINISHING NAILS

DOORSTOP

MALLET

FLAT CHISEL

REMOVE ACCUMULATED PAINT WITH POCKETKNIFE

**B**

DOORJAMB

DOORSTOP

STRIKING PLATE

**C**

PULL THRU THICKNESS OF DOORSTOP WITH PLIERS

DOORSTOP

UNPAINTED SIDE

PAINTED SIDE

**D**

OLD PAINT LINE

DOOR

DOORSTOP

**E**

PUTTY or PLASTIC WOOD

NAIL SET

HAMMER

DOORSTOP

Figure 27.
Door Stop Procedure

61

# 28. RATTLING DOORS: MOVING THE LATCH STRIKE

Now if you're still hearing thieves in the night, or other creaking phenomena coming from the direction of that troublesome door, the cause might well be in the poor way the latch and the door are working together. Take a look. If this is your problem, follow this procedure.

UTENSILS
*Ruler*
*Pencil*
*Medium flat blade screwdriver*
*Medium Phillips screwdriver*
*Flat chisel*
*Hammer*
*Awl*

INGREDIENTS
*White polyvinyl glue*
*Toothpicks*
*Pad of paper*

APPROXIMATE TIME: 30 TO 45 MINUTES

- [ ] *1.* Close door and stand on stop side.
- [ ] *2.* Press hard on stop side of door, and you'll notice a space between doorstop and door.
- [ ] *3.* Measure that space with ruler and mark measurement down on paper (Fig. 28A).
- [ ] *4.* Open door and remove strike from jamb, as shown in Figure 28B, turning screws counterclockwise.
- [ ] *5.* Using previously noted measurement, mark off line from strike bed as shown in Figure 28C.
- [ ] *6.* Carefully chisel away that section of wood where strike is to be reset. This will create a deeper bed for strike in the jamb. See Figure 28C.
- [ ] *7.* Fill old screw holes with toothpicks and glue, making sure surface is even (Fig. 28D).
- [ ] *8.* Reset strike in new bed (Fig. 28D).
- [ ] *9.* Punch holes with awl through holes in strike plate.
- [ ] *10.* Insert screws and screw in clockwise direction with screwdriver.
- [ ] *11.* It will (should) not rattle.

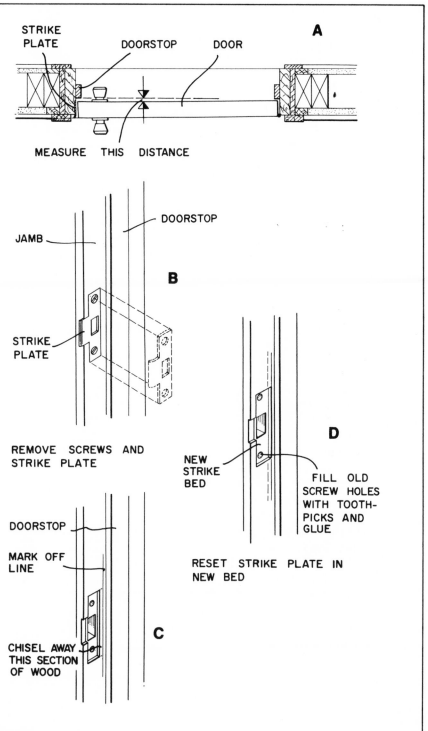

STRIKE PLATE

DOORSTOP   DOOR   **A**

MEASURE   THIS   DISTANCE

DOORSTOP

JAMB

**B**

STRIKE PLATE

REMOVE  SCREWS  AND STRIKE PLATE

NEW STRIKE BED

**D**

FILL OLD SCREW HOLES WITH TOOTH-PICKS AND GLUE

RESET  STRIKE  PLATE  IN NEW BED

DOORSTOP

MARK OFF LINE

CHISEL AWAY THIS SECTION OF WOOD

**C**

Figure 28.
Latch Strike Procedure

63

## 29. RATTLING DOORS: RUBBER TACK

Now we hate to sound like a broken record, but if the #$@& door is still rattling, this is absolutely guaranteed to do the trick.

UTENSILS
*Hammer*

INGREDIENTS
*Rubber tack button (available at hardware store)*

APPROXIMATE TIME: 5 MINUTES

☐ *1.* With hammer, nail rubber tack into the very highest corner at the top of the latch side of the door facing stop. See Figure 29A.

☐ 2. Once nailed into place, the rubber tack button creates a springlike action as it comes in contact with the door, thus eliminating the rattling (Fig. 29B).

*Note:* We have no further advice if your door continues to rattle. Maybe you should move.

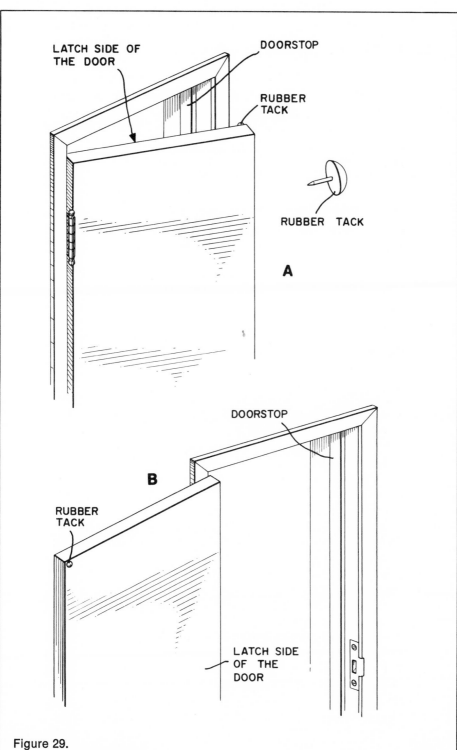

LATCH SIDE OF THE DOOR

DOORSTOP

RUBBER TACK

RUBBER TACK

A

DOORSTOP

B

RUBBER TACK

LATCH SIDE OF THE DOOR

Figure 29.
Rubber Tack Procedure

65

## 30. LOOSE DOOR HINGES

Rotted and chipping wood in the door frame and doorjamb are the most common reasons hinges come loose. At best, the symptoms are annoying; at worst, they are extremely dangerous and could result in the door actually falling away from the frame and causing injury to some innocent bystander. If you have a door with this malady, get going on the cure.

UTENSILS
*Scissors*
*Pencil*
*Hammer*
*Screwdriver*

INGREDIENTS
*Masking tape*
*Toothpicks*
*White polyvinyl glue*
*Bar of soap*
*Extra screws, if necessary*

APPROXIMATE TIME: 30 TO 45 MINUTES

- [ ] *1.* Cut small tabs of masking tape and place on leaves of each hinge (Fig. 30A).
- [ ] *2.* Place one piece of tape adjacent to hinge on wood frame and the door.
- [ ] *3.* Starting at the top, mark the hinge leaves as follows: door side 1, 2, 3; jamb side A, B, C.
- [ ] *4.* If there are three hinges, remove the pin in center hinge first by tapping out of position with hammer and screwdriver.
- [ ] *5.* Tape the pin and mark it, so you can return it to original location.
- [ ] *6.* Repeat process on bottom hinge pin.
- [ ] *7.* Now swing door and remove top pin and mark as before.
- [ ] *8.* Jiggle door, and it will come away. Rest it against wall.
- [ ] *9.* Unscrew hinges from frame and jamb.
- [ ] *10.* Dip toothpicks into polyvinyl glue.
- [ ] *11.* Insert toothpicks into all screw holes by tapping into place with hammer (Fig. 30B). Insert as many toothpicks as necessary for tight fit.
- [ ] *12.* Break off protruding toothpicks so they are flush with surface (Fig. 30B).
- [ ] *13.* Rub all screws into a bar of soap so threads are filled.
- [ ] *14.* Replace any missing screws with wood screws to match old ones.
- [ ] *15.* Replace hinge leaves where they belong and rescrew into

position on door frame and jamb. Make sure screws are tight and secure.

- [ ] *16.* Replace door into hinge slots.
- [ ] *17.* Reinsert hinge pins in original hinges, starting at top.

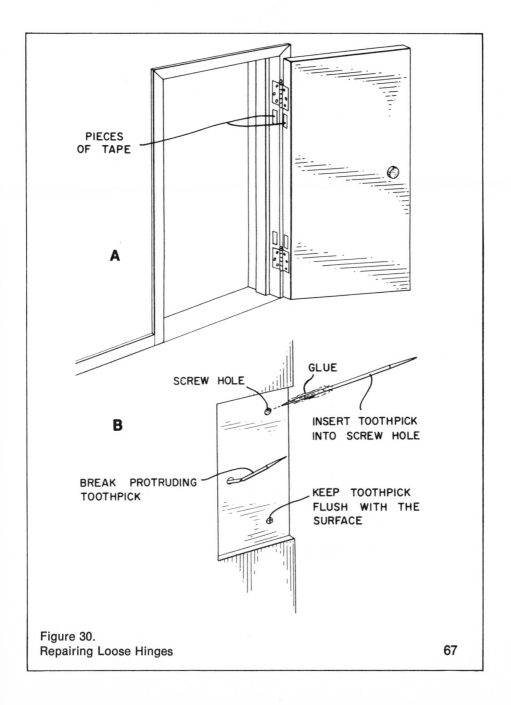

PIECES OF TAPE

**A**

GLUE

SCREW HOLE

**B**

INSERT TOOTHPICK INTO SCREW HOLE

BREAK PROTRUDING TOOTHPICK

KEEP TOOTHPICK FLUSH WITH THE SURFACE

Figure 30.
Repairing Loose Hinges

## 31. INSTALLING A WALL BUMPER

If you're the sort of person who doesn't like holes in his walls, this is the recipe for you. Free-swinging doors, particularly heavy doors with weighty knobs, have a tendency to damage the walls they open against. Here is a surefire way to prevent such a problem.

UTENSILS
*Pencil*
*Awl*
*Hammer*
*Screwdriver*
*Hand or electric drill*
*Wood, carbide, plaster, or*
  *masonry bit, 3/16 inch*

INGREDIENTS
*Knob wall stop*
*Epoxy glue set*
*3/16-inch fiber anchor for*
  *masonry wall (see chart*
  *on screws)*

APPROXIMATE TIME: 15 TO 30 MINUTES

□ *1.* Mark the spot where knob hits wall (Fig. 31A).
□ *2.* Place bumper of the knob wall stop over mark.
□ *3.* Using the awl, punch holes into wall through bumper screw holes (Fig. 31B).
□ *4.* If wall is plasterboard:
□   a. Drive screws into wall, but don't tighten all the way.
□   b. Now remove bumper and screws.
□   c. Mix glue as directed.
□   d. Apply glue to back of bumper.
□   e. Install bumper and screws on wall and tighten securely (Figs. 31C and 31D).
□ *5.* If wall is concrete or brick:
□   a. Drill screw holes with carbide bit.
□   b. Insert fiber anchor into the holes.
□   c. Proceed now as in step 4, a through e.

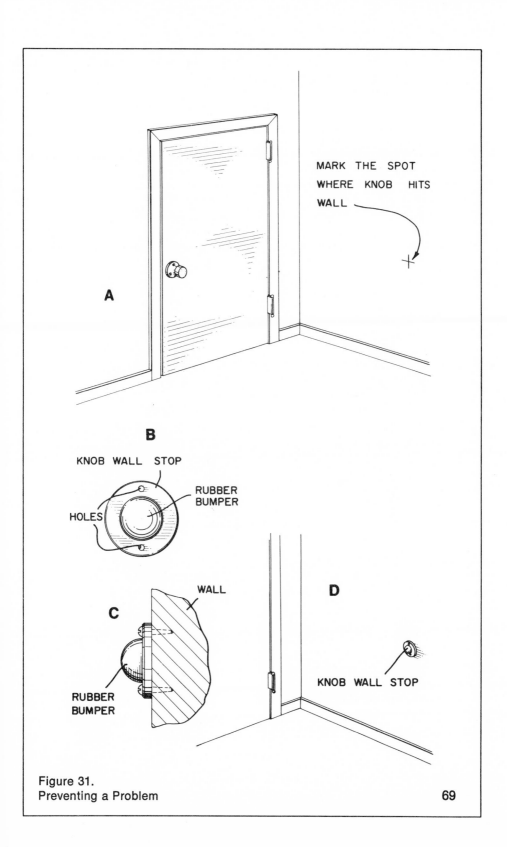

MARK THE SPOT
WHERE KNOB HITS
WALL

A

B

KNOB WALL STOP

RUBBER
BUMPER

HOLES

WALL

C

RUBBER
BUMPER

D

KNOB WALL STOP

Figure 31.
Preventing a Problem

69

## 32. SOLID-TYPE WALL BUMPER

If you don't care for the wall bumper in Recipe 31, we herein offer you another variety. It's just as easy to install, and performs its task to the same end: to protect your walls.

UTENSILS
*Ruler*
*Pencil*
*Hammer*
*Awl*
*Electric or hand drill*
*Carbide bit to fit fiber anchor*
*Pliers*

INGREDIENTS
*Solid-type wall bumper*
*Epoxy glue set*
*Fiber anchors and screws to fit*
*    bumper (see chart on screws)*

APPROXIMATE TIME: 15 TO 30 MINUTES

☐  *1.* On the wall, measure in 1½ inches from the latch-side edge of the door, 3 to 4 inches from the floor (Figs. 32A and 32B). Mark the spot with pencil.
☐  *2.* At that spot, punch in a small hole with the awl.
☐  *3.* Insert bumper screw into position. If secure, remove.
☐  *4.* Mix epoxy glue.
☐  *5.* Apply glue to flange of screw and reinsert snugly into hole (Fig. 32C).
☐  *6.* If wall is masonry:
☐      a. Drill hole with carbide bit and insert fiber anchor.
☐      b. Apply glue to back of bumper.
☐      c. Using pliers, screw bumper securely into position on the wall.

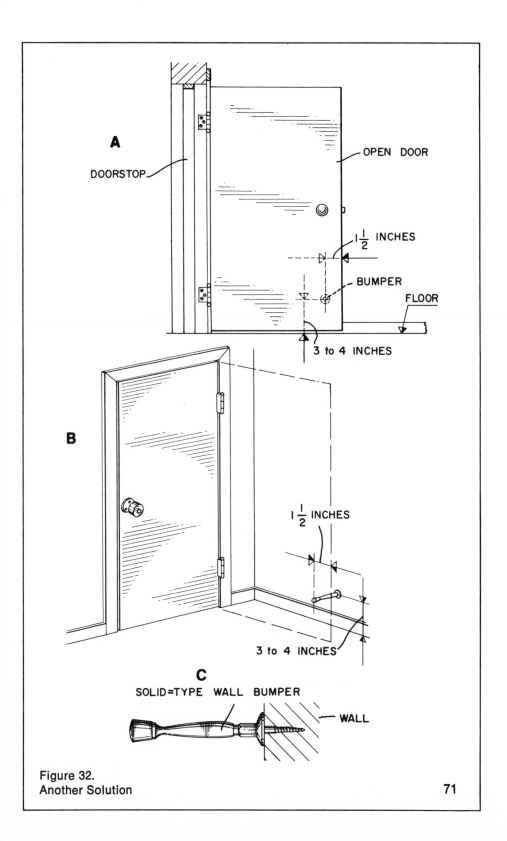

**A**

DOORSTOP

OPEN DOOR

$1\frac{1}{2}$ INCHES

BUMPER

FLOOR

3 to 4 INCHES

**B**

$1\frac{1}{2}$ INCHES

3 to 4 INCHES

**C**

SOLID=TYPE WALL BUMPER

WALL

Figure 32.
Another Solution

71

## 33. INSTALLING A FLOOR BUMPER

Here is still another door stopper to choose from! This one looks quite snazzy, though it functions for precisely the same purpose as those we've already mentioned. Once again, dear reader, the choice is yours.

UTENSILS
*Pencil*
*Ruler*
*Hammer*
*Awl*
*Screwdriver*
*Hand or electric drill*
*Carbide bit to fit lead shield*
   *(for concrete floors only)*

INGREDIENTS
*Floor bumper (Fig. 33A)*
*Fiber anchor to fit bumper*
   *screw*

APPROXIMATE TIME: 15 TO 30 MINUTES

☐　*1.* Swing door to where you would like it stopped.
☐　*2.* With pencil, mark that spot on the floor on hinge side and edge of door. See Figure 33B.
☐　*3.* Measure 2 inches from the edge of door toward hinge on the hinge side of door.
☐　*4.* From that spot, measure 1 inch away from door in door's swing path, as shown in Figure 33B.
☐　*5.* Punch hole into floor at this spot with awl.
☐　*6.* Screw door stopper to floor with wood screws (Fig. 33C).
☐　*7.* If floor is concrete:
☐　　　a. Drill hole and insert fiber anchor.
☐　　　b. Screw bumper into floor. Rubber tip should face door.

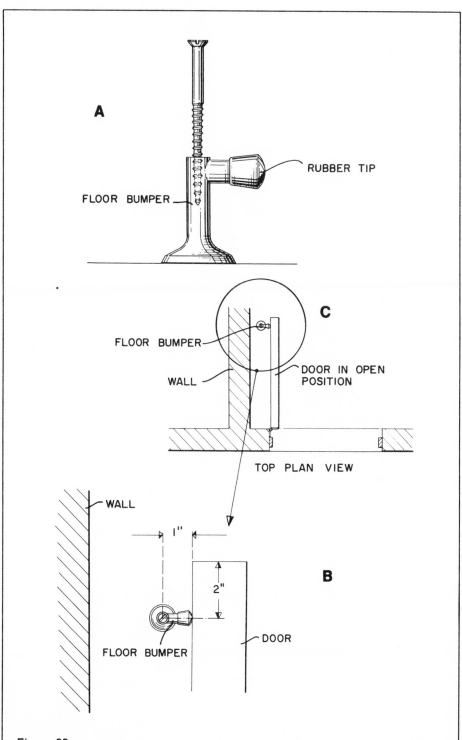

A

RUBBER TIP

FLOOR BUMPER

C

FLOOR BUMPER

WALL

DOOR IN OPEN
POSITION

TOP PLAN VIEW

WALL

1"

2"

B

FLOOR BUMPER

DOOR

Figure 33.
Floor Bumper Procedure

## 34. HINGE-TYPE STOPPER

Here's something a little different and perhaps simplest of all to install. As in the previous three recipes, the purpose of the device is to prevent damage to the wall. This is the last possibility, so make up your mind.

UTENSILS
*Hammer*
*Screwdriver*

INGREDIENTS
*Hinge-type stopper*

APPROXIMATE TIME: 5 TO 10 MINUTES

☐  *1.* With hammer and screwdriver gently tap out pin from either top or bottom door hinge (Fig. 34A).
☐  *2.* Now insert hinge pin through the hole of hinge stopper (Fig. 34B).
☐  *3.* Insert entire assembly into door hinge (Fig. 34C).
☐  *4.* Adjust stopper screw for desired swing.

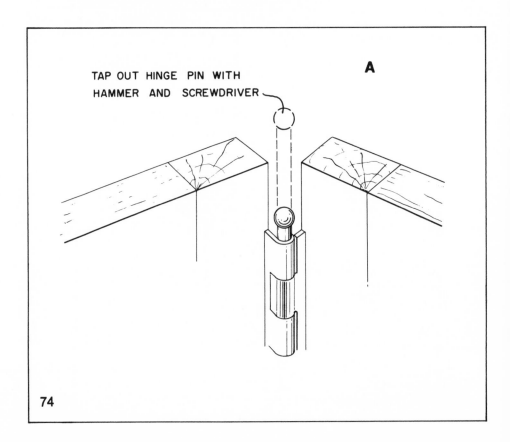

TAP OUT HINGE PIN WITH
HAMMER AND SCREWDRIVER

**A**

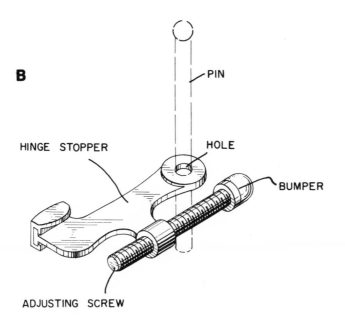

**B**

HINGE STOPPER

PIN

HOLE

BUMPER

ADJUSTING SCREW

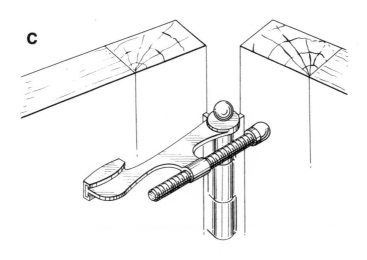

**C**

Figure 34.
Installing a Hinge-Type Stopper

## 35. SAGGING CLOTHING ROD

For some reason, a sagging coat rod reminds us of a poor soul upon whose back rests the weight of the world. He somehow manages the weight, but develops a chronic case of stooped shoulders. To straighten him up, do the following:

UTENSILS
*Screwdriver*
*Hammer*

INGREDIENTS
*Piece of pipe, the length and
    diameter of original rod
    (either black or galvanized)*
*Paint thinner or cleaning fluid*

APPROXIMATE TIME: HOW FAR IS A PLUMBING
SUPPLY HOUSE?

- ☐ *1.* Remove all clothes from sagging hangrod.
- ☐ *2.* Lift hangrod from holding brackets at side (Fig. 35A). If rod does not come away easily, it may be necessary to remove one bracket with hammer claw or screwdriver (Fig. 35B).
- ☐ *3.* Take old wooden hangrod to plumbing supply house or hardware store that stocks pipes. Have pipe cut to exact dimensions of original hangrod.
- ☐ *4.* Home again, install pipe hangrod where the poor soul was before.

    *Note:* It will be necessary to remove oil coating from new hangrod with paint thinner to prevent damage to clothing.

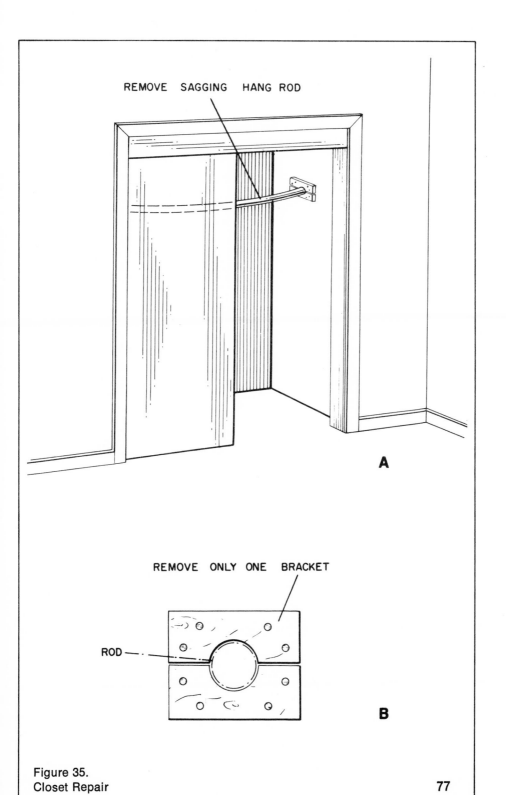

REMOVE SAGGING HANG ROD

**A**

REMOVE ONLY ONE BRACKET

ROD

**B**

Figure 35.
Closet Repair

## 36. CONDENSATION ON EXTERIOR WALLS

Painting the exterior of a wood frame house is an expensive under-taking, even if you do it yourself. And it is particularly frustrating when the paint begins to blister and peel after just a few months. The cause: poor ventilation between the interior and exterior structures allows condensation to form on the newly applied paint. The result: unsightly peeling. Let your walls dry out, per-form this procedure (this recipe is not for brick or stucco build-ings).

UTENSILS
*Pencil*
*Ruler*
*Hand or electric drill*
*1-inch wood bit*
*Caulking gun*
*Hammer*
*Small block of wood*

INGREDIENTS
*Caulking compound or putty*
*Sufficient number of 1-inch*
  *louvers to be inserted*
  *around house exterior*
  *(use 6 louvers for*
  *every 4 feet)*

APPROXIMATE TIME: 5 TO 10 MINUTES PER LOUVER

☐ *1.* Starting at any point on the exterior, measure off marks 16 inches on center (from center of one mark to center of next is called *on center,* as shown in Figure 36A. Precaution: Avoid making marks where later drilling will penetrate interior framing. The procedure for avoiding interior framing is as follows:

☐   a. Mark one spot, starting from your left at any corner of house.

☐   b. Drill into the void between interior and exterior partition.

☐   c. If the drill strikes interior frame, move 3 or 4 inches to the right, mark off the spot, and drill in as before. Errors in drilling may be rectified by inserting dummy louvers later on.

☐   d. Once you have drilled into a spot that does not make contact with interior frame, you may begin measuring 16 inches on center from that point all the way around the periphery of the house.

☐ *2.* Make sure all marks are the same height from the ground so your job will look professional on completion.

☐ *3.* Drill holes at marks all the way around house.

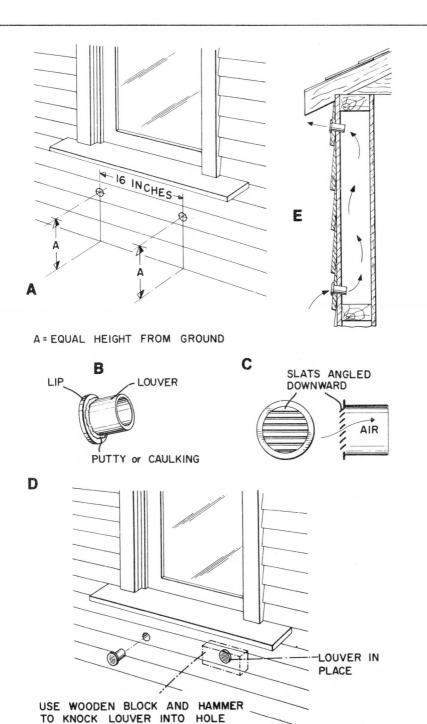

16 INCHES

A

A

A

A = EQUAL HEIGHT FROM GROUND

E

**B**
LIP  LOUVER
PUTTY or CAULKING

**C**
SLATS ANGLED DOWNWARD
AIR

**D**

LOUVER IN PLACE

USE WOODEN BLOCK AND HAMMER TO KNOCK LOUVER INTO HOLE

Figure 36.
Installing Louvers

79

☐ *4.* Apply putty by hand or caulking compound with caulking gun to lip of louver (Fig. 36B).

☐ *5.* Insert louver into drilled hole with slats angled downward to prevent rain from entering structure (Fig. 36C).

☐ *6.* Bang louver securely into place with hammer and wooden block (Fig. 36D).

☐ 7. Make a series of parallel marks 6 inches down from eaves or face of structure, and repeat steps 2 through 6. The purpose of two rows of louvers is to insure proper ventilation (Fig. 36E).

*Note:* There are two types of louvers: plastic and aluminum. Aluminum is preferable, as it contains tighter louver slats and sometimes even a screen to keep out insects.

## 37. LOOSE INSULATION

Heating bills up in winter? Did you just install a new furnace, and the kid's upstairs room is *still* cold? Or is that new air-conditioning unit failing to do the trick? If your heating and cooling equipment is in good shape, then the culprit is loose or fallen insulation within walls or ceilings.

It is an enormous job to get to insulation behind walls, and this should be left to a professional. But you can easily correct this problem in attics and other exposed areas.

UTENSILS
*Scissors*
*Staple gun*
*Small saw*
*Hammer*

INGREDIENTS
*Roll of insulation*
*Roll of tar paper*
*Wooden furring strips*
*Few pounds of 1½-inch
4-penny box nails*

APPROXIMATE TIME: 30 MINUTES FOR SMALL JOB

☐ *1.* Locate area(s) in need of new insulation (Fig. 37A).

☐ *2.* Cut insulation from roll to fit area(s) in need.

☐ *3.* Secure in place with staple gun (Fig. 37B).

☐ *4.* Cut sections of tar paper to fit over insulation.

☐ *5.* Staple tar paper into place by stapling through it into wall or ceiling joists (Fig. 37C).

□ *6.* Cut furring strips to fit across newly insulated area.
□ *7.* Nail furring strips perpendicular to joists 16 inches on center (*on center* means measuring 16 inches from the center of one strip to the center of the next strip), as shown in Figure 37D. This completes the job and will prevent insulation from falling again.

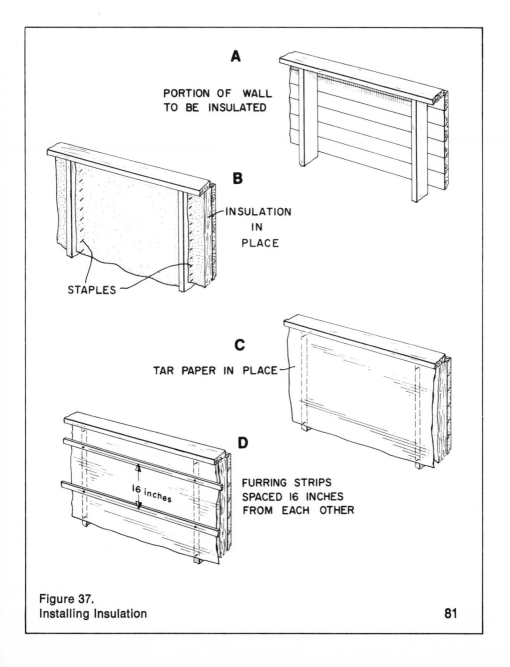

Figure 37.
Installing Insulation

## 38. HANGING LIGHTWEIGHT PICTURE FRAME OR MIRROR

What could be easier than hanging a picture? Hardly anything. But if you want to avoid having to hang the same picture every other week, check out this recipe. Once your picture or mirror is up, only an earthquake will shake it down.

| UTENSILS | INGREDIENTS |
|----------|-------------|
| *Ruler* | *Roll of masking tape* |
| *Pencil* | *1 nail, 1½ or 2 inches long* |
| *Hammer* | *White polyvinyl glue* |

APPROXIMATE TIME: 5 TO 15 MINUTES

- ☐ *1.* Establish exact location on the wall where you wish picture or mirror to be hung. Mark the spot lightly with a pencil or fingerprint.
- ☐ *2.* Make a cross over the spot with two strips of masking tape (Fig. 38A).
- ☐ *3.* Gently hammer nail into center of the cross at an angle of approximately 45 degrees, allowing ½-inch protrusion (Fig. 38B).
- ☐ *4.* If nail is secure, you may hang the picture or mirror (Fig. 38C).
- ☐ *5.* If nail is not secure, remove it and dip it into white glue. Hammer the glued nail into the same hole, still allowing a ½-inch protrusion.
- ☐ *6.* Let glue dry, then hang picture.

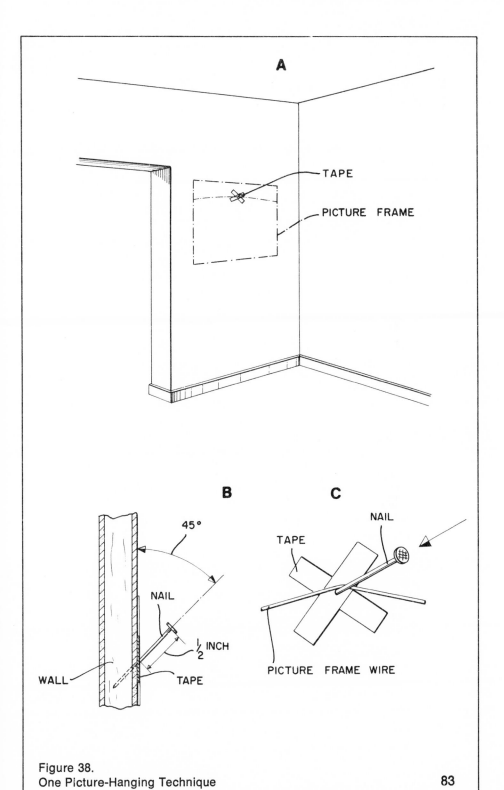

Figure 38.
One Picture-Hanging Technique

83

## 39. HANGING HEAVY PICTURE FRAME OR MIRROR

The principle for hanging a heavy picture frame or mirror is the same as that applied in hanging a lighter object. But there is one essential difference: weight. If you hang a 50-pound gilt mirror on a wall that can't stand the tension, the wall will do exactly what humans do when they can't stand the tension: fall apart. Follow these steps carefully to avoid accidents.

UTENSILS
*Tape measure*
*Hammer*
*Spirit level*
*Medium-heavy flat blade*
  *screwdriver*

INGREDIENTS
*¼-inch by 12-inch piece of*
  *plywood, 3 or 4 inches*
  *shorter than the horizontal*
  *dimension of the frame to*
  *be hung*
*1 dozen 1½-inch common*
  *nails with heads*
*2 1½-inch wood screws with*
  *round heads*

APPROXIMATE TIME: 40 TO 75 MINUTES

- ☐ 1. With tape measure, mark off spot on wall where you wish picture or mirror hung.
- ☐ 2. Center the plywood over spot and drive one nail diagonally through it and into the wall.
- ☐ 3. Level plywood (Fig. 39A). See Recipe 11 on How to Use a Spirit Level.
- ☐ 4. Drive several more nails into plywood until it is secure.
- ☐ 5. Now begin the process of locating studs or beams in the wall behind the plywood:
- ☐   a. Starting from the right, under the plywood, drive a nail into the wall. If you feel the nail sink into wood, you know you've located the stud (Fig. 39B). If this is the case, mark up with level a line from that hole onto the face of plywood (Fig. 39B). If you have missed the stud, nail into wall 1 inch to the left of previous hole. Repeat until stud is located.
- ☐   b. Once stud is located, measure 16 inches to the left and drive in another nail (Fig. 39C). It, too, will be embedded in a stud. Measure up line onto face of plywood.

- ☐ 6. Using lines as guides, drive two nails through plywood into studs.
- ☐ 7. Once this is done, the plywood is secure, and you must now mark off two locations for the wood screws that will carry the weight of the picture frame or mirror (Fig. 39D). Spacing of the screws depends on how your particular frame must be hung. Some frames hang on a wire, others by hooks.
- ☐ 8. Drive screws into place.
- ☐ 9. Now you may safely hang picture or mirror.

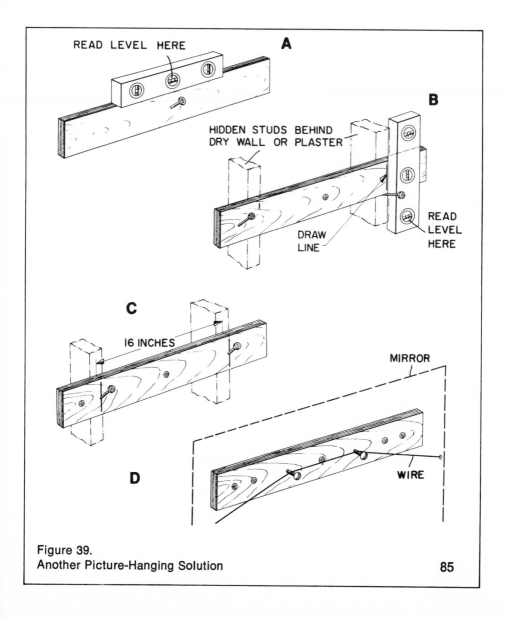

READ LEVEL HERE **A**

**B**

HIDDEN STUDS BEHIND DRY WALL OR PLASTER

READ LEVEL HERE

DRAW LINE

**C**

16 INCHES

MIRROR

**D**

WIRE

Figure 39.
Another Picture-Hanging Solution

## 40. REMOVING A BROKEN SCREW FROM WOOD

Occasionally a screw will break off as it is being driven into wood (Fig. 40A). If you have been frustrated by your inability to deal with this problem, fear no more. This procedure is practically foolproof. No offense intended.

UTENSILS
*Soldering iron*
*Pliers*

INGREDIENTS
*None*

APPROXIMATE TIME: 15 MINUTES

☐ 1. Heat soldering iron until tip is bright orange.
☐ 2. Place iron on embedded screw and heat for several minutes Fig. 40B).
☐ 3. Once wood is burned away, grasp the screw with pliers and turn counterclockwise until screw is removed (Fig. 40C).
☐ 4. If screw is still not dislodged, reheat as necessary.

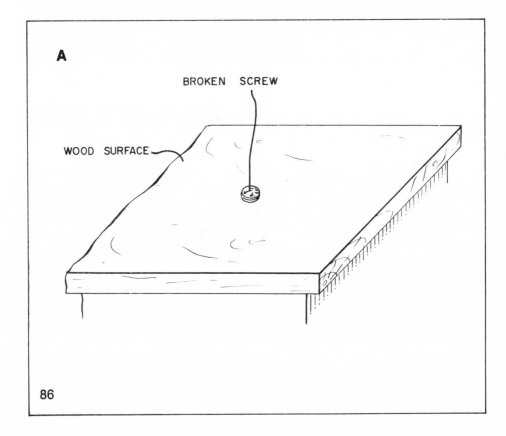

A

BROKEN SCREW

WOOD SURFACE

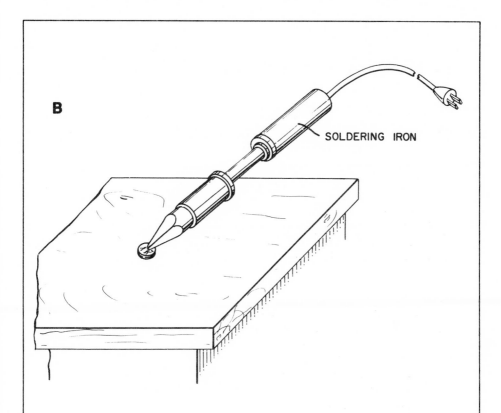

**B**

SOLDERING IRON

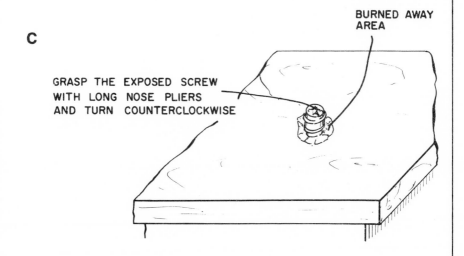

**C**

BURNED AWAY
AREA

GRASP THE EXPOSED SCREW
WITH LONG NOSE PLIERS
AND TURN COUNTERCLOCKWISE

Figure 40.
Broken Screw in Wood

87

## 41. REMOVING A BROKEN SCREW FROM METAL

Though slightly more involved than the preceding recipe, this procedure for removing a broken screw lodged in metal (Fig. 41A) works on much the same principle.

UTENSILS
*Hacksaw*
*Small propane torch*
*Small, thin screwdriver or*
*    screwdriver to match sawcut*
*    and screw*

INGREDIENTS
*Penetrating oil*

APPROXIMATE TIME: 25 MINUTES

☐  *1.* Cut a slot in broken screw with hacksaw (Fig. 41B).
☐  *2.* Squirt a few drops of penetrating oil on screw and let stand for a few hours.
☐  *3.* Heat area slightly with torch.
☐  *4.* Placing screwdriver in new screw slot, attempt to remove screw, turning counterclockwise. Do not overturn, as the screw will break again.
☐  *5.* If screw still cannot be dislodged, reheat with torch. Apply oil. Let stand. Try to remove again.
☐  *6.* Repeat as necessary.

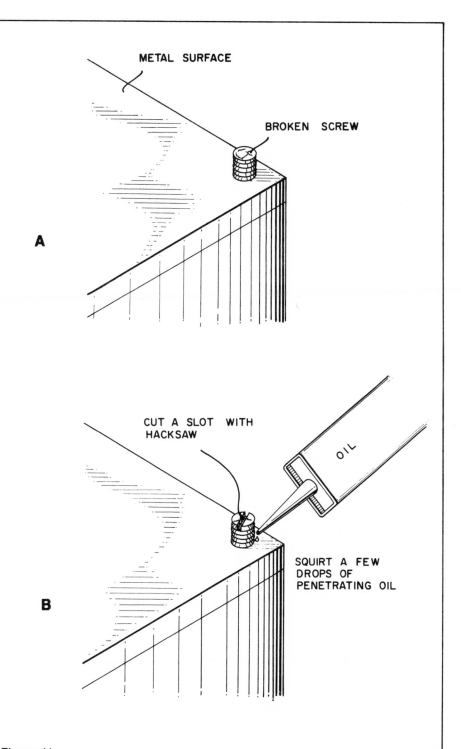

METAL SURFACE

BROKEN SCREW

A

CUT A SLOT WITH HACKSAW

OIL

SQUIRT A FEW DROPS OF PENETRATING OIL

B

Figure 41.
Broken Screw in Metal

## 42. TAPING AND SPACKLING CRACKS

We've heard dry-wall finishers and plasterers do a lot of praising and cursing over the relatively new appearance of perforated paper tape. They love it because it makes wall finishing easier than it ever was; they hate it because it takes less time, and wall finishers usually get paid by the hour.

For the amateur, it is nothing less than a miracle. With just a little care, virtually anyone can do a smooth and professional job on a wall.

UTENSILS
*Ladder*
*2½ - or 3-inch spackle knife,*
  *slanted blade*
*Hammer*
*12-inch smooth trowel*
*Scissors*

INGREDIENTS
*Taping compound, ready mixed*
*Perforated paper tape*
*#2 sandpaper, open coat*

APPROXIMATE TIME: DEPENDS ON LEVEL OF
PROFESSIONALISM

☐ 1. Scratch away all loose plaster with spackle knife (Fig. 42A).
☐ 2. Hammer in any popping nails.
☐ 3. Scrape away or bang away plaster lumps with putty knife and hammer.
☐ 4. Lay a mound of taping compound on trowel with putty knife.
☐ 5. Spread compound into crack and onto 2-inch adjacent area (Fig. 42B).
☐ 6. Cut tape to fit and place over crack (Figs. 42C and 42D). It should adhere to surface.
☐ 7. Holding one end of tape in place, run trowel over length of taping, forcing out excess compound from beneath and at the same time covering the outer surface of the tape with compound (Fig. 42C).
☐ 8. Now run trowel over tape with a steady, even swipe.
☐ 9. If heads of nails are showing, cover with compound and smooth out.
☐ 10. For smooth job, allow compound to dry, sandpaper surface (Fig. 42E), and reapply compound (Fig. 42D). For truly professional results, sandpaper second application, run the compound a third time, let dry, and sandpaper once more.

☐ *11.* Scrape putty knife and trowel against one another to remove built-up compound. Wash in warm water to clean.
☐ *12.* Cover compound can securely.

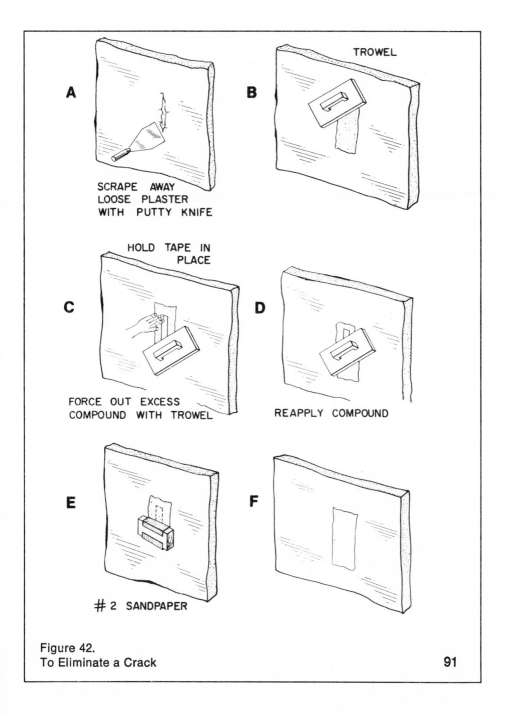

Figure 42.
To Eliminate a Crack

## 43. PATCHING LARGE HOLES IN PLASTERBOARD

Repairing holes in plasterboard, otherwise known as dry wall or sheetrock, is a little trickier than ordinary plaster walls. Still, there's nothing to get uptight about. We've got it all worked out for you. But we'd like to pass along a little anecdote about the current trend in building construction and the feelings some people have about those thin plasterboard walls. We saw a bumper sticker on an auto recently that read: "Keep New York Plastered."

UTENSILS
*Ruler*
*Hand cutter with razor blade*
*Keyhole saw*
*12-inch steel trowel*
*Hammer*

INGREDIENTS
*Piece of plasterboard the same*
  *thickness as existing wall*
  *and slightly larger than the*
  *hole to be patched*
*An extra piece of plasterboard*
  *for strips*
*Taping compound*
*Paper joint tape*
*Sheet of 1/0 sandpaper, open*
  *coat (see Abrasives Chart)*
*1 lb. box 1½-inch flathead nails*

APPROXIMATE TIME: 45 MINUTES

☐ *1.* With ruler or straight edge, mark off a perfectly square or rectangular area around periphery of hole. See Figure 43A.
☐ *2.* Cut strips of plasterboard approximately 2 inches wide with razor cutter.
☐ *3.* Cut out rectangle or square marked off in step 1 with razor cutter or keyhole saw.
☐ *4.* Dab compound at ends of strips and insert behind plasterboard as shown in Figure 43B. Strips may be vertically inserted if there is framing obstruction. Squeeze tightly in position. The more strips you can insert, the stronger the patch will be.
☐ *5.* Let dry overnight.
☐ *6.* Cut piece of new plasterboard approximately ⅛ inch smaller than the hole in wall on all dimensions.
☐ *7.* Now place dabs of taping compound on the strips already in place.
☐ *8.* Fit in new section over strips until flush with wall. Don't use hammer.

□ 9. Trowel on taping compound over joints of new section as shown in Figure 43C. See Recipe 42 for proper technique.
□ 10. Using paper joint tape, tape over joints and trowel compound over tape, squeezing out all excess compound with trowel.
□ 11. Let dry and reapply compound, making a smooth run.
□ 12. Let dry once again.
□ 13. Sandpaper surface smooth in preparation for paint.

*Note:* Additional support may be given the new patch if you happened to notice a stud or beam behind the plasterboard patch. If such a stud is there, drive a few nails through the patch into the stud. The nails should "dimple" the board. The nails must then be spotted with compound, allowed to dry, and sanded smooth. Wash all tools in warm water.

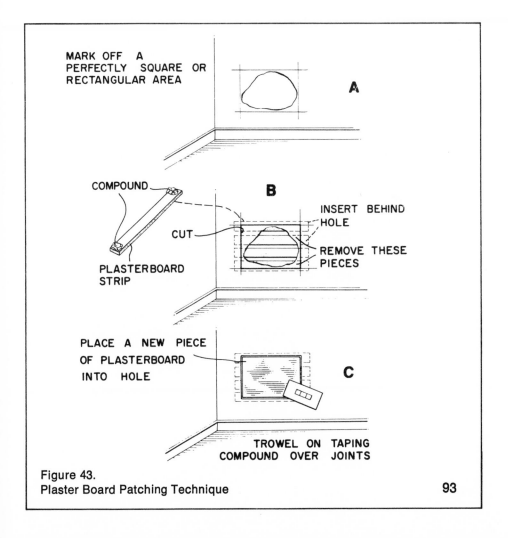

Figure 43.
Plaster Board Patching Technique

## 44. PLASTER PATCHING LARGE HOLES IN WALLS AND CEILINGS

In this recipe we specify "large" holes (Fig. 44A) because they are the most troublesome, though not especially difficult to patch. Essentially, the same procedure is followed as for patching smaller holes; the only real difference is that you do not have to use newspaper as filler for smaller holes.

UTENSILS
*Mixing pan*
*Paintbrush, 3 to 4 inches*
*Spackling knife, 1 to 1½ inch*
*12-inch steel trowel*

INGREDIENTS
*Newspaper*
*Spackle or plastering mix,*
  *not plaster of paris*
*Premix taping compound*
*Sandpaper (see Abrasives*
  *Chart)*

APPROXIMATE TIME: 45 MINUTES

□ *1.* Fill in large hole with wads of newspaper (Fig. 44B).
□ *2.* Mix quantity of Spackle or plaster mix.
□ *3.* Dip brush into water and wet down newspaper and broken periphery of hole.
□ *4.* Apply Spackle to entire periphery of hole, applying some of the mixture onto the newspaper wads as well (Fig. 44C).
□ *5.* Repeat process until edges of hole and newspaper are entirely covered with Spackle mixture. Make no attempt at this point to fill in the entire hole.
□ *6.* Allow to dry overnight.
□ *7.* In the morning, prepare enough Spackle to fill in rest of hole.
□ *8.* Apply Spackle onto 12-inch trowel and spread into hole until flush with existing surface.
□ *9.* Dip paintbrush into water and wet down patched area.
□ *10.* Retrowel to create smooth surface.
□ *11.* Let dry.
□ *12.* Apply taping compound as final coat, using a 12-inch trowel for a really smooth surface (Fig. 44D).
□ *13.* Sand surface smooth with sandpaper to prepare for painting.

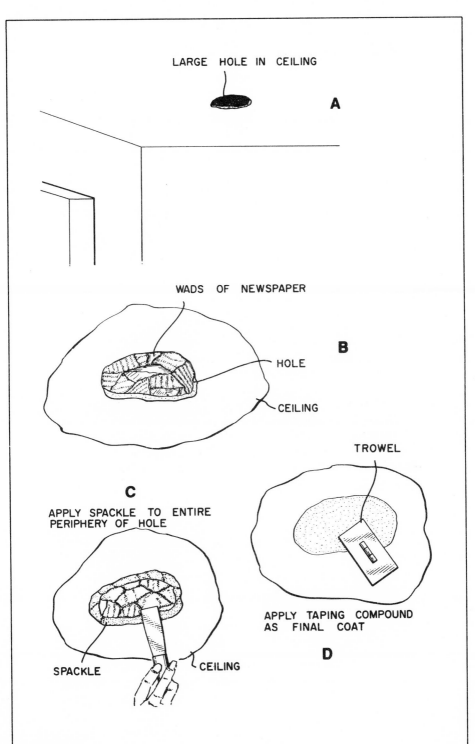

LARGE HOLE IN CEILING

**A**

WADS OF NEWSPAPER

**B**

HOLE

CEILING

**C**

APPLY SPACKLE TO ENTIRE
PERIPHERY OF HOLE

SPACKLE

CEILING

TROWEL

APPLY TAPING COMPOUND
AS FINAL COAT

**D**

Figure 44.
Patching with Plaster

## 45. TORN SCREENING

If you have screen windows and screen doors, it is only a matter of time before a section is punched out. Usually, it is the tendency of the average person to rush out and buy a whole new section of screening and then begin work on what is a tedious project. We offer you a time- and money-saving alternative.

UTENSILS
*Household shears or scissors*

INGREDIENTS
*Section of screening, 36 inches by 24 inches (only a small part of this will be used, but keep the rest for later repairs)*

APPROXIMATE TIME: 15 MINUTES

☐ *1.* From new screening, cut an even square or rectangular piece 2 inches larger in width and length than the damaged area.
☐ *2.* Create a frayed edge in this piece by removing wire strands ½ inch all around as shown in Figure 45A.
☐ *3.* Bend this frayed edge all around, making sure all edges are bent in the same direction (Fig. 45B).
☐ *4.* From the unused section of new screening, pull one length (36 inches) of wire to be used as sewing thread.
☐ *5.* Making close, tight stitches, sew on patch over damaged area as shown in Figure 45C.

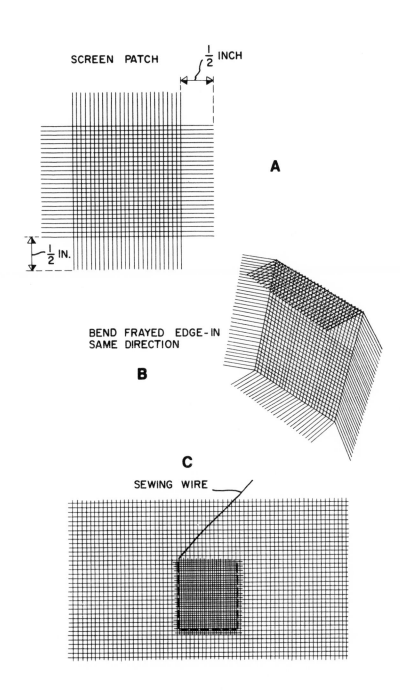

SCREEN PATCH

$\frac{1}{2}$ INCH

**A**

$\frac{1}{2}$ IN.

BEND FRAYED EDGE-IN
SAME DIRECTION

**B**

**C**

SEWING WIRE

Figure 45.
Patching a Screen

97

## 46. SMALL HOLES IN SCREEN

If you think the preceding recipe was novel, you haven't seen anything yet. Try this one for smaller holes and tears.

UTENSILS
*Ice pick or awl*

INGREDIENTS
*Clear nail polish*

APPROXIMATE TIME: 5 TO 15 MINUTES

☐ *1.* Straighten strands of torn area with ice pick or awl (Fig. 46A).
☐ 2. Apply a dab of nail polish over the small hole (Fig. 46B).
☐ 3. Let dry.
☐ *4.* Repeat application several times, allowing each coat to dry until hole is too small for an insect to penetrate.

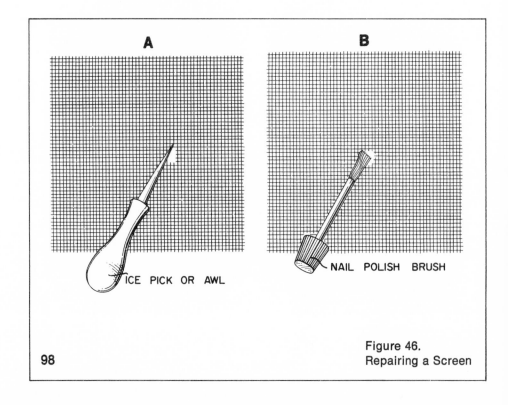

**A**

**B**

ICE PICK OR AWL

NAIL POLISH BRUSH

Figure 46.
Repairing a Screen

## 47. SMALL TEAR IN SCREENING

And here is the pièce de résistance. It combines techniques established in the two preceding recipes and should be used on
medium-sized holes or tears in screening.

UTENSILS
*Ice pick or awl*

INGREDIENTS
*Long strand of nylon thread
   or fishing line
Clear nail polish*

APPROXIMATE TIME: 5 TO 15 MINUTES

- [ ] *1.* Smooth out torn area with ice pick or awl (Fig. 47A).
- [ ] *2.* Darn the area to be repaired in rotating fashion as shown
  in Figure 47B.
- [ ] *3.* Pull stitches snugly but not tightly.
- [ ] *4.* Once hole or tear is completely stitched, apply nail polish
  to sewn area (Fig. 47C).
- [ ] *5.* Let dry.
- [ ] *6.* Repeat application of nail polish to insure adhesion.

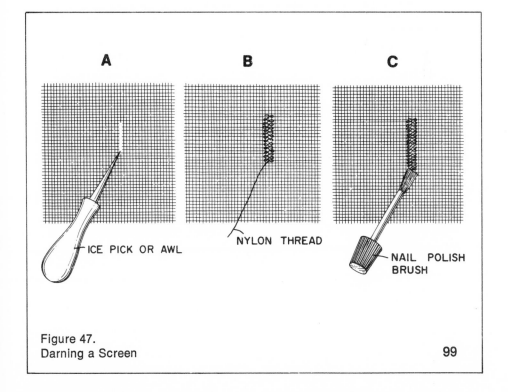

Figure 47.
Darning a Screen

## 48. REMOVING ASPHALT TILE WITH CRACKED ICE

Removing and replacing a broken asphalt tile (Fig. 48A) was always a pain-in-the-neck sort of job—but that was before this recipe came along. We like to call it "The Iceman Cometh." Not since the frozen daiquiri has cracked ice been put to such ingenious use!!

UTENSILS
*12-inch-diameter aluminum pot*
*Hammer*
*1½-inch cold chisel*

INGREDIENTS
*Cracked ice or ice cubes*
*Water*
*Rock or table salt*

APPROXIMATE TIME: 20 MINUTES FOR 4 TILES

- ☐ *1.* Fill pot half with ice and half with water.
- ☐ *2.* Pour liberal amount of salt into pot.
- ☐ *3.* Stir the solution well.
- ☐ *4.* Place pot on tile you wish to remove (Fig. 48B).
- ☐ *5.* Let pot stand for 5 minutes.
- ☐ *6.* Remove pot and tap tile with hammer. The tile will shatter like glass.
- ☐ *7.* Remove any tile remnant with hammer and chisel.
- ☐ *8.* Repeat procedure for all tiles you wish removed.

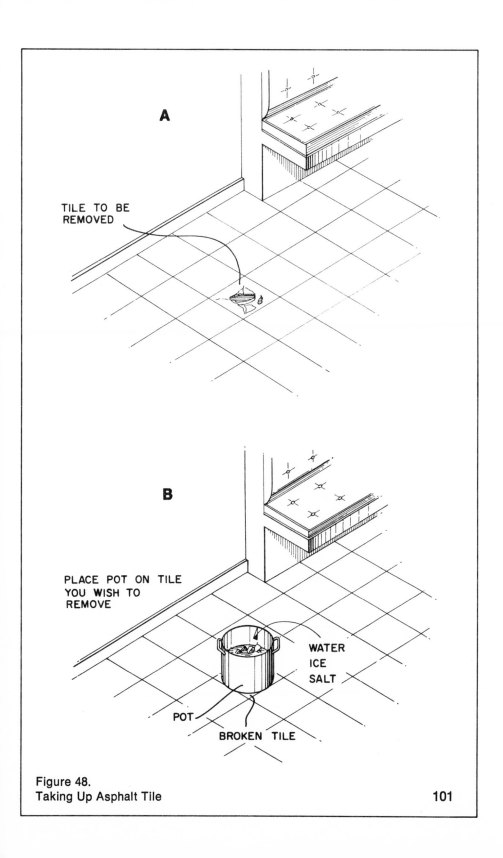

A

TILE TO BE
REMOVED

B

PLACE POT ON TILE
YOU WISH TO
REMOVE

WATER
ICE
SALT

POT

BROKEN TILE

Figure 48.
Taking Up Asphalt Tile

101

## 49. REPLACING BROKEN FLOOR TILES

You want to lay floor tile. First things first. Check Recipe 48 on Removing Asphalt Tile with Cracked Ice, and then you'll be ready to begin work here. We'd like to entertain you as you work with an introduction on the ins and outs of the job, but actually there's not much to say about it.

UTENSILS
*Small putty knife*
*Steel straight edge*
*Ice pick*
*Serrated spreading trowel*

INGREDIENTS
*Plaster of paris*
*1 quart of floor-tile mastic*
*Matching floor tiles*
*Clean cloth*
*Mastic solvent*

APPROXIMATE TIME: 5 MINUTES PER TILE (MINIMUM TIME 30 MINUTES)

- ☐ *1.* Clean work area thoroughly.
- ☐ *2.* If there are holes in tile bed, they can be filled with plaster of paris mixture and smoothed flush with floor surface (Fig. 49A).
- ☐ *3.* Lay tiles into place, without mastic at this time.
- ☐ *4.* If tiles are too large for the space, mark excess on the face of the tile.
- ☐ *5.* Using straight edge and ice pick, score the portion to be eliminated deeply three times (Fig. 49B).
- ☐ *6.* Break off scored edge carefully (Fig. 49C).
- ☐ *7.* Lay in tiles once again. If they fit, the worst is over.
- ☐ *8.* Removing one tile at a time, spread a smooth coat of mastic on the rear of each tile with putty knife and replace in position (Fig. 49D).
- ☐ *9.* Repeat with all additional tiles.
- ☐ *10.* Remove excess mastic from tile face with clean cloth and solvent.
- ☐ *11.* Clean tile face thoroughly and the job is done.

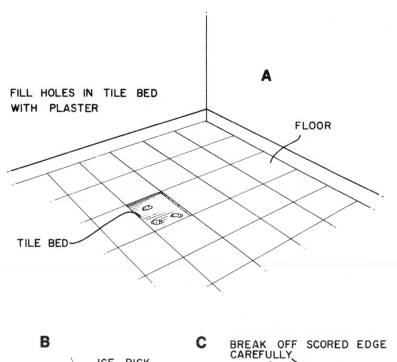

A

FILL HOLES IN TILE BED
WITH PLASTER

FLOOR

TILE BED

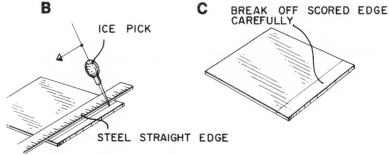

B

ICE PICK

STEEL STRAIGHT EDGE

C

BREAK OFF SCORED EDGE
CAREFULLY

SCORE THE PORTION TO BE
ELIMINATED DEEPLY THREE TIMES

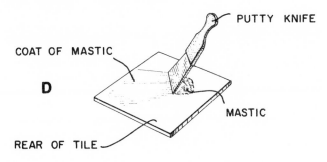

PUTTY KNIFE

COAT OF MASTIC

D

MASTIC

REAR OF TILE

Figure 49.
Laying Floor Tiles

103

## 50. REGROUTING TILES

Grout, in the event you're unfamiliar with the word, is the matrix in the joints between tiles, or between inlaid stones. We refer here only to ceramic tiles, although the procedure is roughly applicable to other regrouting jobs. This is what you will need:

UTENSILS
*Ice pick*
*Large baking pan*
*Putty knife*
*Large sponge*

INGREDIENTS
*Scouring powder*
*Clean soft cloth*
*5-pound bag of dry grout*
*Can of waterproof silicone*
*spray*

APPROXIMATE TIME: DEPENDS ON SIZE OF JOB

- ☐ *1.* Wash down all tile with scouring powder.
- ☐ *2.* Rinse thoroughly so all soap film is gone.
- ☐ *3.* With ice pick, scratch out all loose grout from between tiles as shown in Figure 50. It is advisable to work an entire vertical line, top to bottom, then horizontally.
- ☐ *4.* Using just a minimal amount of water, rinse away loose debris.
- ☐ *5.* Mix sufficient quantity of grout in baking pan as directed on the package. Consistency must be smooth.
- ☐ *6.* Apply grout to sponge with putty knife and squeeze grout into tile joints, rubbing up and down, across, and circularly.
- ☐ *7.* Rinse sponge in cold water and wring dry before wiping excess grout from tile face.
- ☐ *8.* Repeat process several times until joints are filled in and a slight haze forms over face of tiles.
- ☐ *9.* Corner tiles, which are tough to get to, can be grouted with finger, but make sure you remove excess.
- ☐ *10.* Let dry for a few hours.
- ☐ *11.* Wipe away with clean dry cloth until all tile is polished and all joints are smooth and clean.
- ☐ *12.* Spray all corners and tile joints with waterproof silicone spray. This will extend the longevity and beauty of the tile.

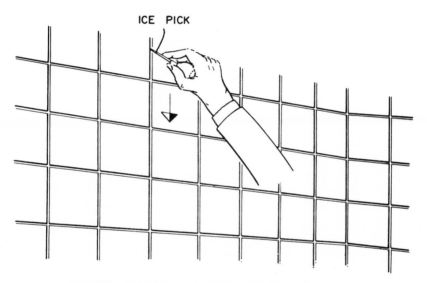

ICE PICK

SCRATCH OUT ALL LOOSE GROUT
FROM BETWEEN TILES

Figure 50.
Repairing Grouting

## 51. REPLACING LOOSE BATHROOM TILE SET IN CEMENT

A ceramic tile bathroom is a much coveted thing in these days of prefabricated construction materials. Still, time and humidity in a bathroom can loosen the best tiles and create unsightly holes in the wall. And if moisture comes, can mildew be far behind?

UTENSILS
*Putty knife, 1½-inch blade*
*Cold chisel, ½-inch blade*
*Small hammer*
*Straight 2 by 3, 3 to 4*
  *feet long*
*Box of round toothpicks*

INGREDIENTS
*New tiles if necessary*
*Few tubes of bathroom silicone*
  *tile adhesive*
*Dry or ready-mix grout*

APPROXIMATE TIME: 30 MINUTES

- ☐ *1.* Remove all loose tiles with putty knife or cold chisel (Fig. 51A).
- ☐ *2.* Check all tiles by tapping gently with hammer handle. If loose, remove. Remember—tap gently.
- ☐ *3.* Clean tiles thoroughly with putty knife or chisel.
- ☐ *4.* Check old tile beds for loose or uneven cement. Remove all loose material and chisel down any protrusions.
- ☐ *5.* Spread silicone adhesive on the back of each tile you removed, as shown in Figure 51B.
- ☐ *6.* Press tiles into position.
- ☐ *7.* Place 2 by 3 over replaced tiles and tap gently with hammer until newly replaced tiles are flush with old ones.
- ☐ *8.* Place toothpicks into tile joints as shown in Figure 51C. This will insure even spacing of joints.
- ☐ *9.* Permit to dry overnight.
- ☐ *10.* Remove toothpicks.
- ☐ *11.* Regrout as directed in Recipe 50 on Regrouting Tiles.

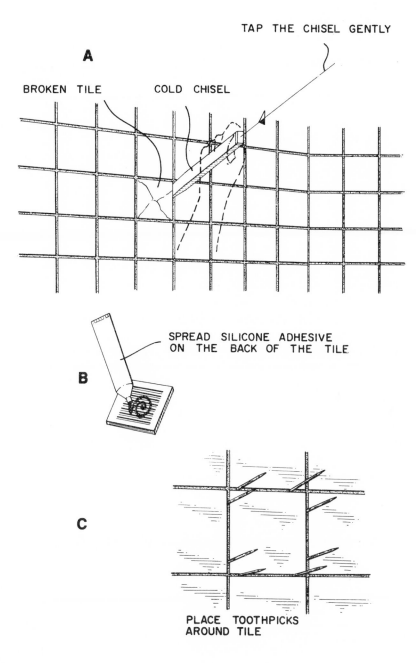

**A**

TAP THE CHISEL GENTLY

BROKEN TILE       COLD CHISEL

SPREAD SILICONE ADHESIVE
ON THE BACK OF THE TILE

**B**

**C**

PLACE TOOTHPICKS
AROUND TILE

Figure 51.
Replacing Ceramic Tiles

107

## 52. REPLACING BATHROOM TILES THAT HAVE FALLEN AWAY FROM PLASTERBOARD

Although this repair must be made over a period of a couple of days, the actual work involved is hardly more than a half hour. So what's a few days when you can get rid of these ugly holes?

UTENSILS
*Putty knife, 1½-inch blade*
*Cold chisel, ½-inch blade*
*Small hammer*
*Straight 2 by 3, 3 to 4*
  *feet long*
*Box of round toothpicks*

INGREDIENTS
*5 to 10 pounds of plaster*
  *of paris*
*Strips of newspaper*

APPROXIMATE TIME: 30 MINUTES

☐ 1. Remove tiles carefully with putty knife or cold chisel.
☐ 2. Check all tiles by tapping gently with hammer handle (Fig. 52A). If loose, remove.
☐ 3. Clean away old plaster from tiles with chisel or putty knife.
☐ 4. Cut away all sections of rotted plasterboard from tile beds.
☐ 5. If there are large holes in the tile beds, mix a quantity of plaster, adding to the mixture several strips of newspaper to give the plaster a thick, workable consistency. Work fast.
☐ 6. Apply mixture into holes with putty knife (Fig. 52B). Beds must be recessed ½ inch from face of tile.
☐ 7. Now prepare a mixture of plaster without newspaper strips and apply to beds. Smooth carefully.
☐ 8. Allow to dry overnight.
☐ 9. Next day, apply silicone adhesive to the back of each tile and set in position.
☐ 10. Place 2 by 3 over newly replaced tiles and tap gently with hammer handle until new tiles are flush with existing ones (Fig. 52C).
☐ 11. Place toothpicks into joints as shown in Recipe 51 on Replacing Loose Bathroom Tile Set in Cement.
☐ 12. Permit adhesive to dry overnight.
☐ 13. Remove toothpicks the next day.
☐ 14. Regrout as directed in Recipe 50 on Regrouting Tiles.

CHECK ALL TILES BY TAPPING GENTLY WITH
HAMMER HANDLE

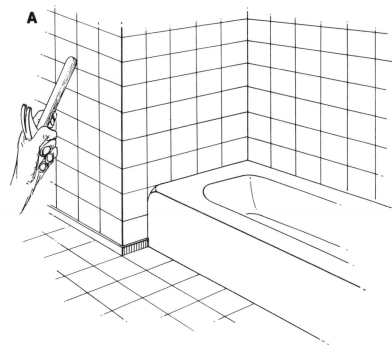

FILL OUT HOLES IN TILE BED

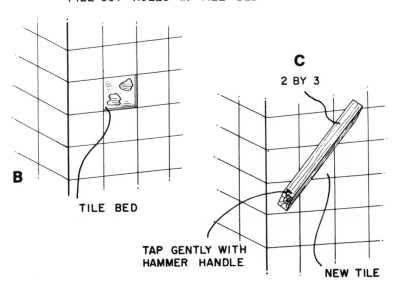

Figure 52.
Another Procedure for Tiles

## 53. CAULKING

When were you last out on a windy day and a vital seam split wide open? Such drafts are common in a house and open seams on a structure will let the wind enter and work havoc, not only on your body temperature, but also on heating bills.

UTENSILS
*Chisel*
*Wire brush*
*Heating pad*
*Pocketknife*
*Medium flat blade screwdriver*
*Cartridge caulking gun*
*Old rags*
*Ladder, if necessary*

INGREDIENTS
*Caulking cartridges as needed*
*Can of solvent*
*Roll or bundle of oakum*

APPROXIMATE TIME: YOU TELL US

☐ *1.* Check exterior walls of structure for loose caulking or where caulking has never been applied. Places to check: window frames, doorjambs, all trim, and generally wherever wood and masonry, wood and metal, or metal and masonry, come together.
☐ *2.* Remove all loose caulking with chisel.
☐ *3.* Clean area(s) thoroughly with wire brush.
☐ *4.* Working one area at a time, apply undercoating as indicated in caulking chart.
☐ *5.* Heat caulking cartridge in heating pad, or place beside water heater before use.
☐ *6.* With pocketknife, cut off a bit of cartridge tip at approximately a 45-degree angle. See Figure 53A.
☐ *7.* Insert screwdriver blade into tip and press in until cartridge seal is broken.
☐ *8.* Remove and clean screwdriver with solvent.
☐ *9.* Insert cartridge into cartridge gun.
☐ *10.* Holding gun comfortably, place cartridge tip against area to be caulked. See Figure 53B.
☐ *11.* Pull trigger slowly and easily while moving the tip along caulking area. Do not squeeze excessively.

**A**

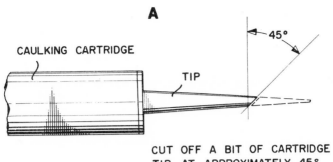

CAULKING CARTRIDGE

TIP

45°

CUT OFF A BIT OF CARTRIDGE
TIP AT APPROXIMATELY 45°

**B**

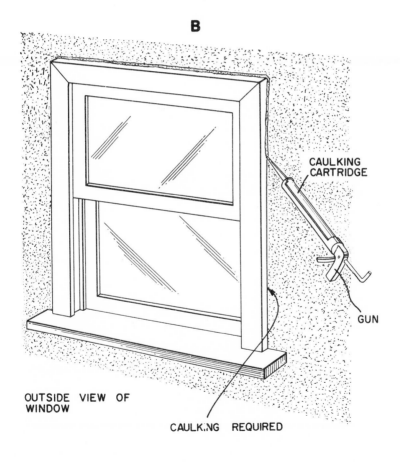

CAULKING
CARTRIDGE

GUN

OUTSIDE VIEW OF
WINDOW

CAULKING REQUIRED

Figure 53.
Caulking Procedure

111

☐ *12.* If you must caulk a large hole, first cut several strips of oakum with pocketknife.

☐ *13.* Stuff strips into hole.

☐ *14.* Repeat as necessary.

*Note:* Always keep a rag with solvent handy to wipe away caulking compound immediately.

# PART III

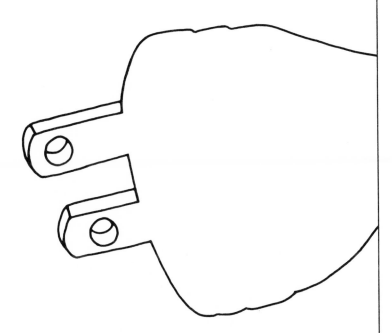

# Electricity

Ignorance may be bliss but not with electricity. Most people fear electricity because they do not understand it. While we have no intention here of giving you a crash course in the principles of electricity, we do wish to calm some of your fears by explaining one simple precept.

Electricity flows *from* a source, through a conductor (wire), and, finally, to an outlet (light bulb or motor). If you wish to avoid electrical "shocks," you need remember only one thing: Always shut down the source of electrical current (wall switch, fuse, or circuit breaker), before beginning work.

If you are working with an electrical appliance, all that is necessary is the act of unplugging it from the wall outlet. After that is done, electrical flow to the appliance is impossible.

If you are working on a wall outlet or switch or ceiling fixture, you must first locate your fuse box or circuit-breaker box. Locate the fuse that controls the area you are working on by trial and error (see Recipe 54 on Changing Blown Fuses). Once you have located the proper fuse or circuit breaker, unscrew the fuse and/or throw the arm of the circuit breaker, whichever applies in your case. This will prevent electrical flow to the area where you are working. A final test for the presence of "hot" wires (those actually carrying current), can be made with a "tester." The final and absolute measure you can take to insure against hot wires is to shut down the power for the entire house. This control is located in your basement.

The following items, though not a complete list, will be adequate for all your household electrical work.

*Set of Screwdrivers (see Recipe 2 on How to Use a Screwdriver)*
*Long-nosed pliers, Linemen's pliers, Adjustable pliers*
*Assortment of sheet metal screws, nuts, bolt*
*Pocketknife*
*Diagonal cutters*
*Assortment of wire nuts*
*Assortment of fuses, if necessary*

*Soldering iron, medium-small point*
*Voltage tester with light*
*Small hand drill with assortment of bits*
*Wire strippers*
*Roll of electrical tape*
*Coil of solder, resin core*
*Solder paste or flux (non-acid)*

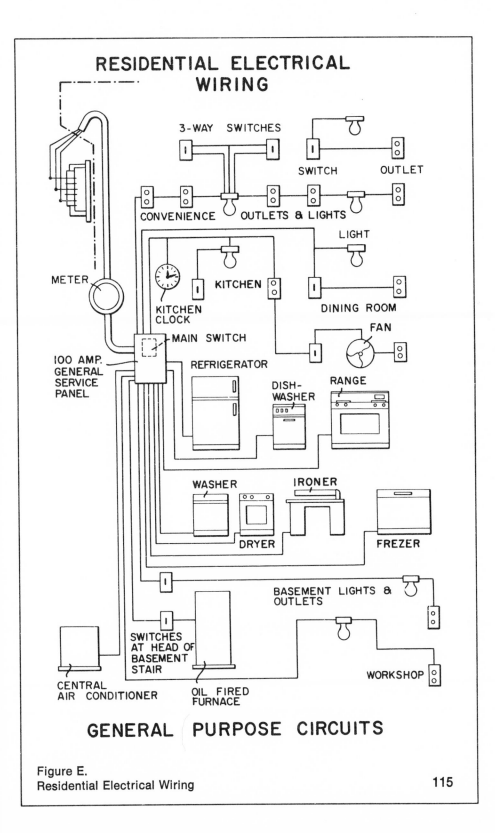

# RESIDENTIAL ELECTRICAL WIRING

3-WAY SWITCHES

SWITCH    OUTLET

CONVENIENCE    OUTLETS & LIGHTS

LIGHT

KITCHEN

KITCHEN CLOCK

DINING ROOM

METER

MAIN SWITCH

FAN

IOO AMP. GENERAL SERVICE PANEL

REFRIGERATOR

DISH-WASHER

RANGE

WASHER

IRONER

DRYER

FREZER

BASEMENT LIGHTS & OUTLETS

SWITCHES AT HEAD OF BASEMENT STAIR

CENTRAL AIR CONDITIONER

OIL FIRED FURNACE

WORKSHOP

## GENERAL PURPOSE CIRCUITS

Figure E.
Residential Electrical Wiring

115

## 54. CHANGING BLOWN FUSE OR RE-SETTING CIRCUIT BREAKERS

Because the "blowing" of a fuse results from the overloading of an electrical circuit, many people think that the fuse box is a dangerous area to approach, as it controls the flow of so much electricity. Nothing could be further from the truth. Of course, it is always advisable to approach electrical apparatus with caution; but there should be no fear whatsoever attached to the common chore of changing a burnt fuse.

We would, however, like to give you a few pointers before we begin the actual procedure for that simple task. As far as fuses are concerned, the cardinal rule is Be Prepared. That is to say, you should make a list of all the different types and sizes of fuse in your fuse box, and make sure you have three or four of each on hand at all times. Because, if one "blows" on Sunday, you'll be whistling in the dark till Monday.

Now, if you really want to be secure when working around your fuse box, take our humbly offered advice, and make the following chart:

☐ 1. Make a diagram of your fuse or circuit breaker box, as shown in Figure 54A.
☐ 2. Number each fuse or circuit breaker, both on the chart and beside each in the box, making sure that your numbers correspond exactly with one another.
☐ 3. Turn on all the lights in your apartment or house.
☐ 4. Now, one at a time, unscrew each fuse or trip circuit breaker and see which lights go off.
☐ 5. Mark down beside each fuse or circuit breaker in your chart the area of the house or apartment each controls. See Figure 54B.
☐ 6. Once you have completed this, tape your chart beside the box in plain site.
☐ 7. From then on, if the power fails in your bedroom, say, you will know exactly which fuse or circuit breaker has disconnected and must be corrected by consulting the chart.

# FUSE BOX DIAGRAM

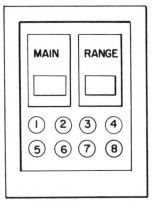

A

| | | | |
|---|---|---|---|
| I | BEDROOMS | 5 | GARAGE |
| 2 | BATHROOM | 6 | BASEMENT |
| 3 | LIVING-ROOM | 7 | |
| 4 | KITCHEN | 8 | |

# BREAKER BOX DIAGRAM

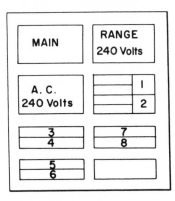

B

| | | | | | |
|---|---|---|---|---|---|
| I | BEDROOMS | 5 | GARAGE | 9 | |
| 2 | BATHROOM | 6 | BASEMENT | IO | |
| 3 | LIVING-ROOM | 7 | | II | |
| 4 | KITCHEN | 8 | | I2 | |

Figure 54.
Fuse and Circuit Breaker Box Diagrams

117

## Procedure for Re-setting Fuse or Circuit Breaker

UTENSILS

*A wooden platform (for the homeowner whose panel box may be in the basement where floors are often wet) made of three 2 by 6 by 24-inch planks to be set on the floor beneath the box and covered with a rubber mat 18 by 24 inches.*
*Flashlight*

☐ *1.* When current fails in a section of your house, consult the chart prepared above.

☐ *2.* While standing on platform, unscrew that fuse and examine with flashlight. You will see a deep, gray "cloud" on the surface of the fuse.

☐ *3.* Replace fuse with one of identical amperage. Never, never, under any circumstances, replace one fuse with another of higher amperage. It is the greatest fire hazard.

☐ *4.* If a circuit-breaker needs to be re-set, trip it to the "off" position and then to "on" position. Power should be restored.

☐ *5.* If fuses and circuit breakers repeatedly disconnect, consult a competent electrician.

## 55. LOOSE ELECTRICAL PLUG

The patient's heartbeat is becoming faint. Scalpel in hand, the surgeon prepares to make his first incision on our hero. The breath is labored, the pulse bleeps across the scope, and tension builds . . . then BLOOP! The television goes black. It's that electrical plug again—always falling out of the wall receptacle!

If you know that scene and want to change it in no time at all, read on.

UTENSILS
*Pliers*

APPROXIMATE TIME: 1 MINUTE (BELIEVE IT?)

☐ *1.* With pliers grasp tip end of one of the plug prongs (Fig. 55A).
☐ *2.* Twist prong one-eighth of a counterclockwise revolution (Fig. 55B).
☐ *3.* Repeat with second prong.
☐ *4.* Replace plug in receptacle, and it will hold firmly. (Whatever happened to our hero on the operating table?)

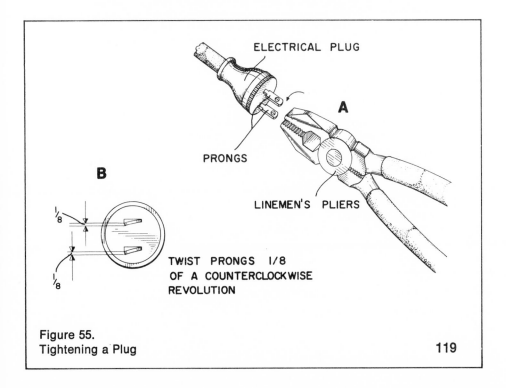

ELECTRICAL PLUG

A

PRONGS

B

LINEMEN'S PLIERS

TWIST PRONGS 1/8
OF A COUNTERCLOCKWISE
REVOLUTION

Figure 55.
Tightening a Plug

119

## 56. DEFECTIVE MALE PLUG

In the course of time, a male electrical plug will become worn from constant use. Ask yourselves, Is there anything that goes in and out of something all the time that won't someday fall apart? At any rate, a faulty plug can shoot off sparks, and worn cord insulation may release enough heat to cause a fire. If you haven't checked your appliance plugs recently, do so immediately. If they are in need of repair, get to it now. Do not be afraid. A plug, once removed from a wall outlet, carries no electrical current.

UTENSILS
*Diagonal cutters*
*Pocketknife*
*Wire stripper*
*Soldering iron*
*Medium flat blade screwdriver*
*Long-nosed pliers*

INGREDIENTS
*Soldering flux (non-acid)*
*Coil of solder, resin core*
*2- or 3-pronged heavy-duty*
 *plug with fiber cover*

APPROXIMATE TIME: 25 MINUTES

□  1. Cut off defective plug and 2 inches of cord with diagonal cutters.
□  2. Slit cord insulation (if fabric) with pocketknife and strip back 3 to 4 inches, baring the inner insulation (Fig. 56A). Note: When there is no outer insulation, 1 inch of the plastic or rubber-covered wire should be removed with knife.
□  3. Remove 1 inch of inner insulation on all wires with wire stripper, taking care not to damage inner strands.
□  4. Twist loose wire strands tightly together, once bared.
□  5. Dip bare wire into soldering flux or paste.
□  6. Heat each wire with soldering iron (Fig. 56B).
□  7. Apply end of solder coil and let run freely through strands, sealing them.
□  8. Feed the sealed wires through rear of new male plug (Fig. 56C).
□  9. Tie underwriter's knot as shown in Figure 56D.
□ 10. Tug insulated portion of wire cord until knot catches in plug.
□ 11. Loosen terminal screws as far as they will go, but do not remove.
□ 12. With long-nosed pliers, form a hook at the end of each wire (Fig. 56E).

□ *13.* Wrap hooks tightly around terminals in clockwise direction.
□ *14.* Tighten screws over hooks with screwdriver in a clockwise direction, and cut off excess wire with diagonal cutters.
□ *15.* If you are working with a 3-pronged plug, hook up the wires as follows: white wire to silver terminal; black wire to brass terminal; green wire to U-shaped terminal.
□ *16.* Place fiber cover over prongs (Fig. 56F).
□ *17.* Test appliance by plugging into wall outlet.

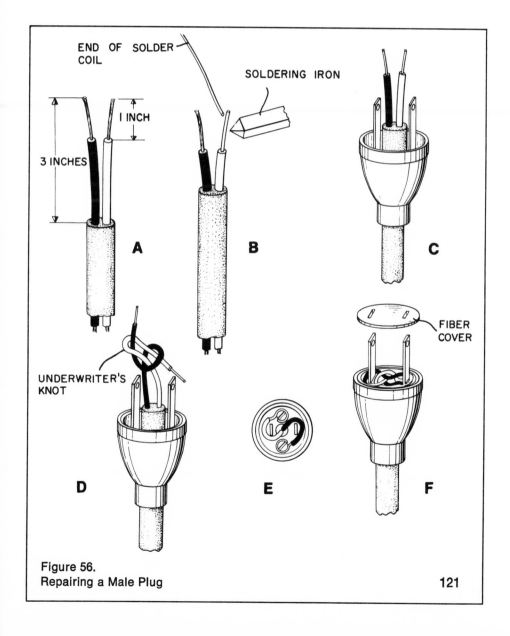

Figure 56.
Repairing a Male Plug

## 57. INSTALLING AND REPLACING FEMALE EXTENSION PLUG

With an extension cord, as in romance, it "takes two to tango." The male end is worthless without the female. Here is a simple recipe, very similar to the preceding one, for the speedy repair of a female extension plug.

UTENSILS
*Diagonal cutter*
*Pocketknife*
*Wire stripper*
*Medium flat blade screwdriver*
*Long-nosed pliers*

INGREDIENTS
*Soldering flux (non-acid)*
*Coil of solder, resin core*
*2- or 3-pronged heavy-duty*
    *female plug*

APPROXIMATE TIME: 25 MINUTES

☐  *1.* Unplug male end from wall outlet and unplug all appliances from female end.

☐  *2.* Cut off defective plug and 2 inches of cord with diagonal cutters.

☐  *3.* Slit cord insulation (if fabric) with pocketknife and strip back 2 to 4 inches, baring inner insulation. Note: When there is no outer insulation, 1 inch of the plastic or rubber-covered wire should be removed with pocketknife.

☐  *4.* With wire stripper, remove 1 inch of inner insulation on all wires, taking care not to damage inner strands.

☐  *5.* Twist loose wire strands together, once bared (Fig. 57A).

☐  *6.* Dip bared wire into soldering flux or paste.

☐  *7.* Heat each wire with soldering iron (Fig. 57B).

☐  *8.* Apply end of solder coil and let run freely through strands, sealing them.

☐  *9.* Disassemble female plug (Fig. 57C). The plug is held together by two screws. Once apart, screws and face section should be put aside.

☐ *10.* Take hold of the terminal section (the one with screws, plug prongs, and occasionally a clamp).

☐ *11.* Feed sealed wires through rear of terminal section of plug.

☐ *12.* Tie underwriter's knot, as shown in Figure 57D.

☐ *13.* Tug insulated portion of wire cord until knot catches in plug.

☐ *14.* Loosen terminal screws as far as they will go, but do not remove.

☐ *15.* With long-nosed pliers, form a hook at the end of each wire

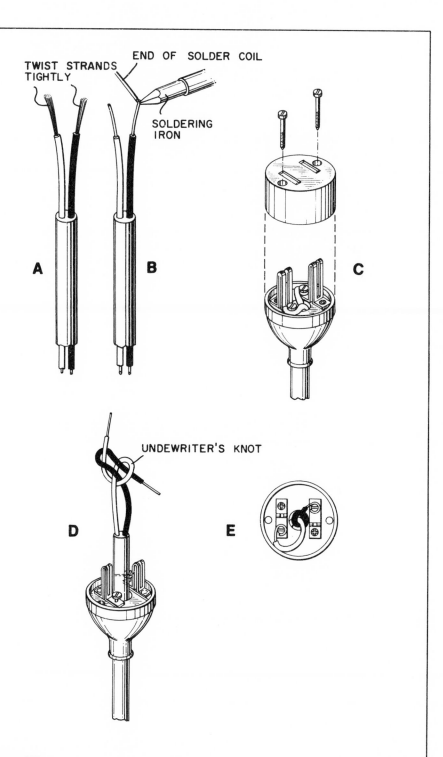

Figure 57.
Female Extension Plug Replacement

123

and wrap hooks tightly under terminal screws in clockwise direction (Fig. 57E).

☐ *16.* Tighten screws over hooks and cut off excess wire with diagonal cutters.

☐ *17.* If you are working with a 3-pronged plug, hook up the wire as follows: white wire to silver terminal; black wire to brass terminal; green wire to U-shaped terminal.

☐ *18.* Reset face section of plug onto terminal section, making sure that screw holes are in line with screws and that prongs penetrate properly.

☐ *19.* Screw all screws tightly into position. Do not overtighten.

☐ *20.* Test your new extension cord by plugging male end into wall outlet and inserting a male plug from an electrical appliance into your new female extension plug. Energize the appliance. All systems should be "go."

☐ *21.* If system is not operational, plug appliance directly into wall outlet. If appliance operates, you'll have to reexamine your own wiring job.

## 58. FEMALE APPLIANCE PLUG

To show that all things are equal, we now turn our attention to the defective female plug. Because these plugs come in all shapes and sizes, it will be necessary for you to take the broken one along with you to the hardware store so that it can be matched perfectly with a new one.

UTENSILS
Diagonal cutters
Pocketknife
Wire stripper
Soldering iron
Small flat blade screwdriver
Medium flat blade screwdriver
Long-nosed pliers

INGREDIENTS
Soldering paste or flux
    (non-acid)
Coil of solder, resin core
New female plug (buy one
    with wire protector spring)

APPROXIMATE TIME: 30 MINUTES

□  1. Remove male plug from wall outlet.
□  2. With diagonal cutters, cut away old female plug and 2 or 3 inches of cord.
□  3. With pocketknife, cut away about ¾ inch of outer fabric insulation, baring inner insulation.
□  4. With wire strippers, strip away ¾ inch of inner insulation, baring the wires. Do not cut off strands.
□  5. Twist strands tightly in clockwise direction.
□  6. Dip twisted ends into soldering paste.
□  7. Heat twisted ends with soldering iron.
□  8. Apply end of solder coil and let run through strands.
□  9. Let cool.
□ 10. With small screwdriver, remove screw in center of new plug and disassemble. Some plugs have two screws, others have a screw on one side and a nut on the other (Fig. 58A).
□ 11. Also disassemble interior unit (Fig. 58B).
□ 12. You will now see two contacts (Fig. 58B), each of which has a screw. Loosen screws with medium screwdriver but do not remove.
□ 13. With long-nosed pliers, form hooks of the twisted wire ends.
□ 14. Place hooks around contact screws in clockwise direction.
□ 15. Tighten screws in clockwise direction with medium screwdriver. Cut away excess wire with diagonal cutters.
□ 16. Place contact prongs into slot of plug.

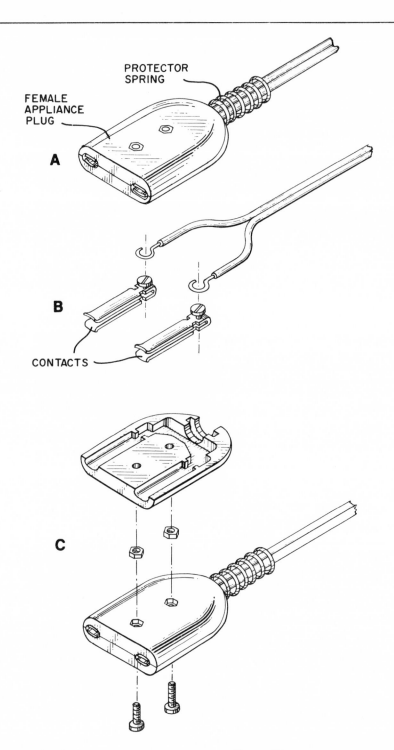

PROTECTOR
SPRING

FEMALE
APPLIANCE
PLUG

A

B

CONTACTS

C

Figure 58.
Repairing Female Appliance Plug

☐ *17.* Place protector spring in position.
☐ *18.* Reassemble two halves of plug. Holding the nut on the bottom of the plug, insert screw and tighten with small screwdriver (Fig. 58C).
☐ *19.* Insert female plug into appliance, plug male end into wall, and test.

## 59. REPLACING A LAMP SOCKET

The lamp socket, found in all lamps and occasionally in ceiling fixtures, comes in four basic types: no switch, chain switch, turn switch, and push switch. Each is installed virtually identically. The type you choose depends solely on your personal preference. The following procedure applies to all four types and includes some advice on how to handle special problems with ceiling fixture types.

UTENSILS
*Medium screwdriver*
*Test light*
*Diagonal cutters*
*Wire stripper*
*Soldering iron*
*Long-nosed pliers*

INGREDIENTS
*New lamp socket*
*Soldering paste (non-acid)*
*Coil of solder, resin core*

APPROXIMATE TIME: 60 MINUTES

☐ *1.* If it is a ceiling fixture that needs a new lamp socket, it is advisable to cut off power supply by finding and unscrewing the appropriate fuse, or by tripping the appropriate circuit breaker, or by disconnecting the main switch for the entire house. If it is a lamp you are working on, just pull plug from the wall.
☐ *2.* To insure that power is off on ceiling fixture, touch one lead of the test light to an inner side of the socket and the other to the bottom terminal inside the socket. If the test light doesn't respond, electrical power is off.
☐ *3.* Disassemble new socket by inserting screwdriver into base

cover and snapping it open. It comes apart in four sections: socket cover, insulation cover, base of socket, and base cover. See Figure 59A.

*Note:* If, when removing old socket, you notice any broken wires, it is advisable to test with test light for possible flow of current (ceiling fixtures only).

☐ 4. With diagonal cutters, cut wire away from old socket, and with wire stripper, strip back each wire ¾ inch until bared.
☐ 5. Twist strands of wire ends clockwise and dip into solder paste.
☐ 6. Heat each wire end with soldering iron.
☐ 7. Apply end of solder coil until it melts and runs through strands.
☐ 8. Let cool.
☐ 9. Reinsert wires through base cover.
☐ 10. Tie underwriter's knot, as shown in Figure 59B.
☐ 11. Form a hook at the end of each wire with long-nosed pliers.
☐ 12. Unscrew—but do not remove—screws at base of socket.
☐ 13. Place wire hooks beneath screws in clockwise direction and tighten securely. Cut away excess wire with diagonal cutters.
☐ 14. Once insulation cover is replaced over socket base, force both into socket cover.
☐ 15. Make sure all grips are in position.
☐ 16. Screw in bulb.
☐ 17. Restore power.
☐ 18. Switch on lamp or ceiling fixture to test.

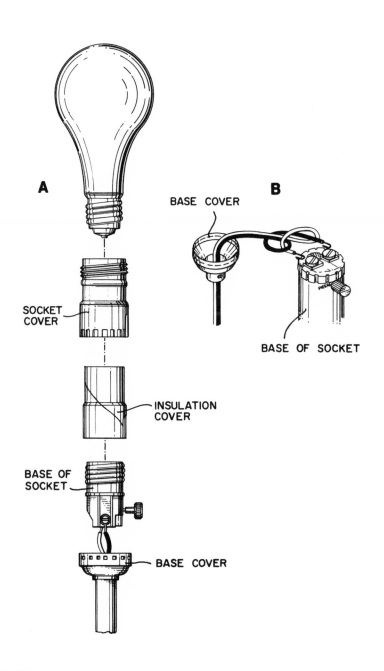

A

B

BASE COVER

SOCKET COVER

INSULATION COVER

BASE OF SOCKET

BASE OF SOCKET

BASE COVER

Figure 59.
Lamp Socket Assembly

## 60. REMOVING BROKEN LIGHT BULB

If the cat knocks the lamp from the table, or if your kids love to kick field goals in your living room, chances are good for a light bulb shattering in its socket. We offer this cautious and unique procedure for its swift and safe removal.

UTENSILS
*Pocketknife*
*Hammer*

INGREDIENTS
*Newspaper*
*Light bulb*
*6- to 8-inch piece of wood,*
*½ inch square*

APPROXIMATE TIME: 15 MINUTES

### Simple Procedure

☐ *1.* Turn off current.
☐ *2.* Using a folded section of newspaper for protection, grasp the broken bulb (Fig. 60A) and turn from socket in counterclockwise direction.
☐ *3.* Replace with new light bulb.

> *Note:* The above procedure is normally sufficient. Often, however, there is nothing left of the broken bulb that can be grasped. If this is the case, follow these alternate directions.

### Surmounting Complications

☐ *1.* Carve a point at the end of the stick with pocketknife.
☐ *2.* Insert stick into broken bulb (Fig. 60B) and wedge it there by gently tapping blunt end of stick with hammer.
☐ *3.* When stick is secure, turn it in a counterclockwise direction. This will remove what remains of the broken bulb.
☐ *4.* Install new bulb.

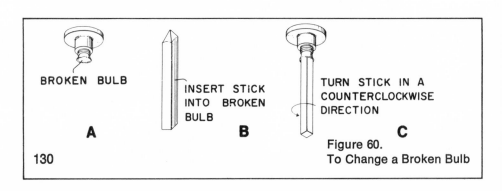

BROKEN BULB

**A**

INSERT STICK INTO BROKEN BULB

**B**

TURN STICK IN A COUNTERCLOCKWISE DIRECTION

**C**

Figure 60.
To Change a Broken Bulb

## 61. DEFECTIVE LIGHT SWITCH

In a turned on world, a defective light switch is definitely not what should be happenin', baby. If you want to restore that sweet light of lights, carry on.

UTENSILS
*Pocketknife*
*Medium flat blade screwdriver*
*Hammer*
*Diagonal cutters*
*Wire stripper*
*Linemen's pliers*
*Long-nosed pliers*

INGREDIENTS
*New toggle switch*
*New faceplate*
*2 #8 wire nuts*
*2 6-inch lengths of #14*
  *insulated wire*
*2 #6 sheet metal screws,*
  *1 inch in length*

APPROXIMATE TIME: 60 MINUTES

☐ 1. Cut off power by removing fuse or tripping circuit breaker that controls junction box.
☐ 2. Making a deep score with the knife, cut the paint from around the old faceplate.
☐ 3. Remove screws from faceplate. If screw slots are filled with paint, chip away with screwdriver and then remove screws.
☐ 4. Place screwdriver at edge of faceplate, tap with hammer, and faceplate will come away.
☐ 5. Remove the 2 screws from the bar plate that secured switch to junction box.
☐ 6. Pull switch out of box and remove wires from switch by turning screws counterclockwise. See Figure 61A.
☐ 7. If junction box is dusty or dirty, clean with vacuum cleaner.
☐ 8. If wires are frayed or uninsulated, cut away defective portion with diagonal cutters and restrip insulation with wire stripper.
☐ 9. Attach wires with newly stripped ends to the old wires by twisting both together with linemen's pliers in clockwise direction (approximately four turns).
☐ 10. Screw wire nuts onto newly spliced ends. See Figure 61A.
☐ 11. Form a hook at the end of each wire with long-nosed pliers (Fig. 61B).
☐ 12. On many new toggle switches, you'll find 2 terminal screws on one side of the switch. Other switches have a single screw on each side. Regardless, loosen screws in counterclockwise direction, but do not remove.
☐ 13. Hook wires to terminal screws in clockwise direction.

☐ *14.* Tighten screws over hooks in clockwise direction (Fig. 61A).
☐ *15.* At either end of bar strip, there are 2 extensions called horns. If these interfere with easy replacement of switch into junction box, break them off with long-nosed pliers.
☐ *16.* Push wires into junction box with screwdriver handle.
☐ *17.* Line up elongated holes of bar plate with screw holes in junction box, making sure that the "off" position shows when the switch is down and screw into place (using sheet metal screws if original screws no longer hold). Make sure bar plate is even with wall at top and bottom.
☐ *18.* Replace faceplate.
☐ *19.* Figures 61C and 61D are typical circuitry for toggle switches.

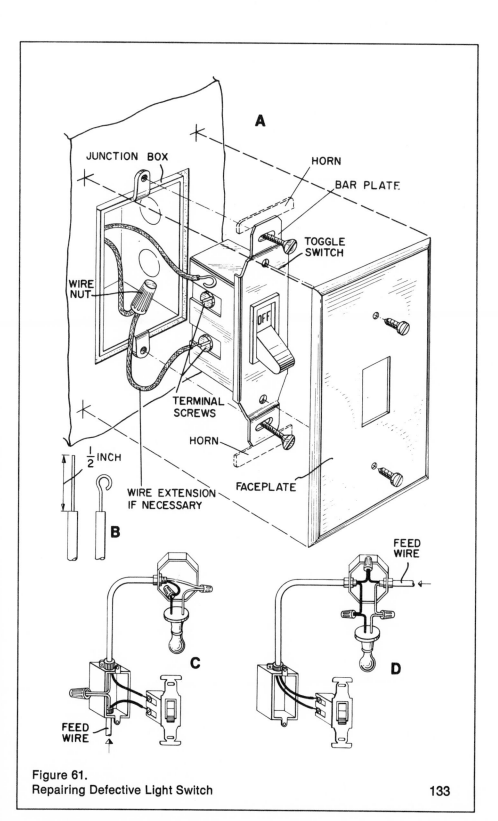

A

JUNCTION BOX

HORN

BAR PLATE

TOGGLE SWITCH

WIRE NUT

OFF

TERMINAL SCREWS

HORN

½ INCH

WIRE EXTENSION IF NECESSARY

FACEPLATE

B

FEED WIRE

C

D

FEED WIRE

Figure 61.
Repairing Defective Light Switch

133

## 62. DEFECTIVE WALL OUTLET

If sparks fly in your house every time you stick a plug in the wall, it's time to replace that old outlet with a new one. Or maybe the outlet no longer supplies current, doesn't hold a plug securely, or is falling out of the wall. In any event, it's time for a change. This recipe is a bit complicated, but if you take the necessary precautions and follow directions carefully, you'll do a beautiful job. Ready?

UTENSILS
*Pocketknife*
*Medium flat blade screwdriver*
*Hammer*
*Test light*
*Diagonal cutters*
*Wire stripper*
*Linemen's pliers*
*Long-nosed pliers*

INGREDIENTS
*Grounded duplex receptacle*
*New faceplate to match*
*2 #8 wire nuts*
*2 6-inch lengths of #12*
  *insulated wire*
*2 #6 sheet metal screws, 1*
  *inch long*

APPROXIMATE TIME: 60 MINUTES

☐ 1. Cut off power by removing fuse or tripping circuit breaker that controls junction box.
☐ 2. Making a deep score with the knife, cut the paint from around old faceplate.
☐ 3. Remove screws from faceplate. If screw slots are filled with paint, chip away with screwdriver and then remove screws.
☐ 4. Place screwdriver at edge of faceplate, tap with hammer, and faceplate will come away.
☐ 5. Remove the 2 screws from the bar plate that secures the old outlet to junction box.
☐ 6. Pull outlet from box and unscrew the 2 screws attached to it in a counterclockwise direction.
☐ 7. If junction box is dusty or dirty, clean with vacuum cleaner.
☐ 8. If wires are frayed or uninsulated, cut away defective portion with diagonal cutters and restrip insulation with wire stripper.
☐ 9. Attach wires with newly stripped ends to the old wires by twisting both together with pliers in a clockwise direction (approximately four turns).
☐ 10. Screw wire nuts onto newly spliced ends.

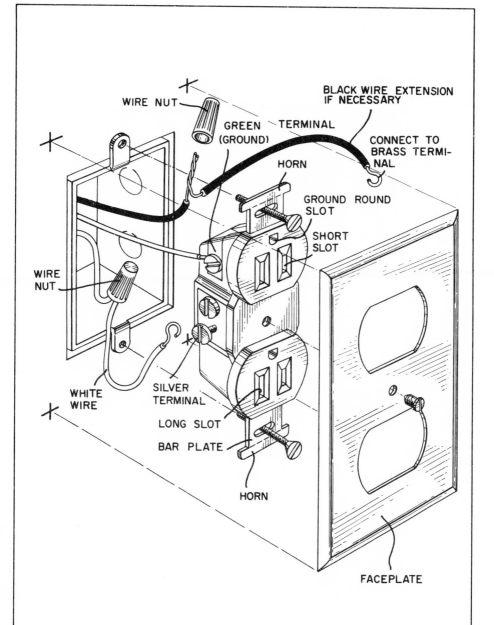

WIRE NUT

GREEN (GROUND) TERMINAL

BLACK WIRE EXTENSION IF NECESSARY

CONNECT TO BRASS TERMINAL

HORN

GROUND ROUND SLOT

SHORT SLOT

WIRE NUT

WHITE WIRE

SILVER TERMINAL

LONG SLOT

BAR PLATE

HORN

FACEPLATE

Figure 62.
Repairing Wall Outlet

135

☐ *11.* Form a hook at the end of each wire with long-nosed pliers.

☐ *12.* There are 2 screws on each side of the new outlet (Fig. 62). Unscrew 1 screw on each side but do not remove.

☐ *13.* Hook up wires to terminals in clockwise direction as follows: white wire to silver terminal; black wire to brass terminal; and connect green ground, if provided.

☐ *14.* Tighten screws over hooks in clockwise direction.

☐ *15.* At either end of bar strip, there are 2 extensions called horns. If these interfere with replacement of outlet into junction box, they can be easily broken off by twisting with pliers.

☐ *16.* Push wires into junction box with screwdriver handle.

☐ *17.* Line up elongated holes of bar strip with screw holes in junction box and screw into position (using sheet metal screws if original screws no longer hold). Make sure bar strip is even with wall, top and bottom.

☐ *18.* Fit new faceplate over outlet and install screws into original holes. Do not overtighten.

☐ *19.* Turn on power and test ground with test light as follows:

☐      a. Insert 1 prong of tester into long slot and 1 into short slot; tester should light up.

☐      b. Now repeat with prongs in short slot to ground round slot; tester should light up.

☐      c. Repeat with prongs in long slot and ground slot; tester should not light.

☐      d. If your test light does not function as we've indicated, turn off current again, go back to step 13, and reverse wires.

*Note:* If the fuse "blows," or a circuit breaker disconnects once the power is restored, do what all electricians do: start over.

## 63. INSTALLING A 3-PRONGED GROUNDED ADAPTER

A grounded adapter is a must for power tools and appliances in order to prevent the possibility of electrical shocks. If your wall outlet does not have a 3-pronged receptacle, it is essential that you install a grounded adapter.

UTENSILS
*Medium flat blade screwdriver*
*Voltage tester or*
  *test light*

INGREDIENTS
*Grounded adapter with 2-*
  *pronged male plug and*
  *grounded lead at one end*
  *and 3-pronged female*
  *connection at other*

APPROXIMATE TIME: 15 TO 30 MINUTES

### To Install the Adapter

☐ *1.* Unscrew center screw of wall outlet in counterclockwise direction (Fig. 63A).
☐ *2.* Scrape away all paint from around and under screw.
☐ *3.* Place outlet center screw through lug end of adapter's pigtail lead. See Figure 63A.
☐ *4.* Screw back into wall outlet.
☐ *5.* Plug adapter into wall outlet.
☐ *6.* Insert leads of test light into slots of plug. The light should light. If not, remove plug and test wall outlet directly with test light to see if current is flowing. It usually is. If not, check your fuses. And, if that's not the cause, you may have to replace wall outlet or call an electrician.
☐ *7.* Replug adapter and insert test leads into short slot and the "U" or "O"-shaped ground slot of the adapter (Fig. 63A). Light should light.
☐ *8.* If not, unplug adapter and reverse position of prongs in the wall outlet. Test with light. Light should light. If not, this means that the adapter is not grounded and must be grounded at once for safe operation of power tools in that outlet.

## Procedure for Remote Grounding of Adapter

UTENSILS
*Small adjustable wrench*
*Pipe grounding bracket*
*Soldering iron*
*Wire stripper*
*Long-nosed pliers*

INGREDIENTS
*Length of #14 stranded*
*insulated wire to reach*
*from water pipe to electrical*
*outlet*
*Coil of solder, resin core*
*Soldering flux (non-acid)*
*⅛-inch machine screw with*
*round head, ½ inch long,*
*and nut*

☐ 1. Connect grounding bracket to nearest water or steam pipe, as shown in Figure 63B.
☐ 2. Strip back ½ inch of insulation from both ends of #14 wire with wire stripper.
☐ 3. Twist the open strands of wire together and dip bared wire ends into soldering flux.
☐ 4. Heat one fluxed end with soldering iron.
☐ 5. Apply end of solder coil to heated end and let run freely through strands, sealing them. Repeat for other end.
☐ 6. Form hook at soldered ends with long-nosed pliers.
☐ 7. Wrap one hook around screw on grounding bracket in clockwise direction and screw firmly into place.
☐ 8. Insert machine screw through lug in adapter's pigtail lead (Fig. 63C).
☐ 9. Hook other end of #14 wire around machine screw, and screw nut and machine screw securely together with wrench and screwdriver (Fig. 63C).
☐ 10. Repeat steps 5 through 8 for test procedure.

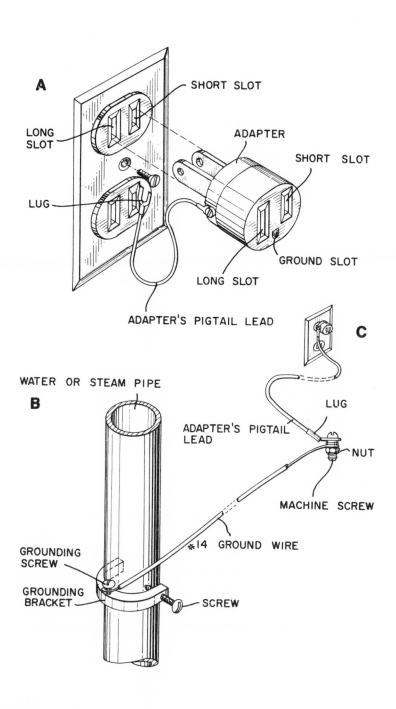

**A**

SHORT SLOT

LONG SLOT

ADAPTER

SHORT SLOT

LUG

GROUND SLOT

LONG SLOT

ADAPTER'S PIGTAIL LEAD

**C**

WATER OR STEAM PIPE

**B**

ADAPTER'S PIGTAIL LEAD

LUG

NUT

MACHINE SCREW

*14 GROUND WIRE

GROUNDING SCREW

GROUNDING BRACKET

SCREW

Figure 63.
Procedure for 3-Pronged Adapter

139

# 64. REPLACING PORCELAIN CEILING FIXTURES

It doesn't take much to smash an old porcelain ceiling fixture, and we have found this to be the most common disaster for this piece of equipment. But whatever the cause of the malfunction of your fixture, it will have to be replaced. The job is a bit complicated, but nothing to worry about. You can pull it off. Be careful on the ladder.

UTENSILS
*Medium flat blade screwdriver*
*Diagonal cutters*
*Pliers*
*Soldering iron*
*Hammer*
*Wire stripper*

INGREDIENTS
*2 lengths of #14 stranded insulated wire, one black and one white, 5 inches long*
*2 #8 wire nuts*
*Lightweight porcelain fixture*
*2 8/32-inch machine screws, 1, 1½, or 2 inches as necessary*
*Bar strap may or may not be required*
*Coil of solder*
*Soldering flux (non-acid)*

APPROXIMATE TIME: 30 MINUTES

☐ 1. Turn off power by disengaging appropriate fuse or circuit breaker.
☐ 2. Turning counterclockwise, remove 2 screws from both sides of old fixture (Fig. 64A). Pull fixture away gently to avoid breaking plaster.
☐ 3. You will notice 2 wires connected to fixture from ceiling box (Fig. 64B). Unscrew old wire nuts, if any. If wires are soldered or taped, cut away uninsulated portions. See Figure 64B.
☐ 4. Strip back ½ inch of insulation with wire stripper and bare wires in ceiling box.
☐ 5. Strip back ½ inch of insulation at both ends of the new lengths of #14 wire.
☐ 6. Twist strands of #14 wire together in clockwise direction.
☐ 7. Solder ends of strands together.
☐ 8. Form a hook at one end of each wire.
☐ 9. Now disassemble new ceiling fixture. See Figure 64C.

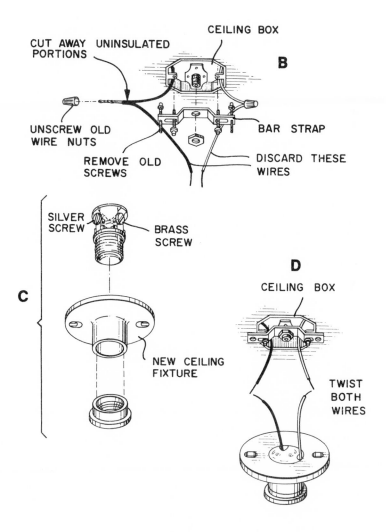

SCREW — SCREW

**A**

CUT AWAY UNINSULATED PORTIONS

CEILING BOX

**B**

UNSCREW OLD WIRE NUTS

BAR STRAP

REMOVE OLD SCREWS

DISCARD THESE WIRES

SILVER SCREW — BRASS SCREW

**C**

NEW CEILING FIXTURE

**D**

CEILING BOX

TWIST BOTH WIRES

Figure 64.
Procedure with Porcelain Ceiling Fixture

☐ *10.* Place hook of black wire under brass screw in fixture and tighten securely in clockwise direction.

☐ *11.* Place hook of white wire under silver screw and tighten as above.

☐ *12.* Reassemble fixture.

☐ *13.* Twist ends of wires from new fixture to ends of wires from ceiling box: black to black, white to white. See Figure 64D.

☐ *14.* Screw wire nuts onto these connections and push wires back into ceiling box.

☐ *15.* Secure new fixture to ceiling box with screws. See Figure 64A.

☐ *16.* Screw in bulb.

☐ *17.* Turn on current at fuse box.

☐ *18.* Energize.

*Note:* If fixture you have purchased is not the same type as described in this recipe, see the two recipes that follow.

## 65. INSTALLING CEILING FIXTURE WITH BAR STRAP

What happens when the screw holes in the new ceiling fixture you want to install do not match up with the old ones? Easy. Introducing the bar strap! The procedure for making this installation is virtually identical with the preceding recipe. It will just take a few minutes longer to install the bar strap.

UTENSILS
*Medium flat blade screwdriver*
*Adjustable pliers*
*Drill*
*Bits*
*Soldering iron*
*Long-nosed pliers*
*Wire stripper*

INGREDIENTS
*Ceiling fixture*
*Fixture stud, if none exists*
  *in ceiling box*
*Assortment of sheet metal*
  *screws*
*1 to 2 extension nipples*
*Bar strap to match holes*
  *in new fixture*
*Lock nut to match stud or*
  *nipples*
*Coil of solder, resin core*
*Soldering flux (non-acid)*
*2 #8 wire nuts*
*2 8/32-inch machine screws,*
  *1, 1½, or 2 inches long,*
  *as necessary*

APPROXIMATE TIME: 30 TO 45 MINUTES, DEPENDING ON SIZE AND WEIGHT OF NEW FIXTURE

☐ *1.* Turn off current by disengaging appropriate fuse or circuit-breaker.
☐ *2.* Remove old fixture by unscrewing screws in counterclockwise direction. Pull fixture away gently so as not to break plaster. Disconnect wires.
☐ *3.* Examine ceiling box. If there is no stud, install one (as shown in Fig. 66A) by drilling into ceiling box and securing stud with sheet metal screws. Four holes and four screws will be necessary.
☐ *4.* Place center hole of bar strap over stud. If it does not reach, it will be necessary to install 1 or 2 nipples to the stud.
☐ *5.* With stud (or nipple) protruding through center hole of bar

strap, install lock nut as shown in Figure 65A. Tighten with pliers in clockwise direction, but do not overtighten.

☐ 6. If wires from ceiling box have been soldered or taped together, cut those sections away.

☐ 7. Strip back ½ inch of insulation from the ends of wires from ceiling box and from fixture, with wire stripper, exposing the inner strands.

☐ 8. Twist strands together in clockwise direction.

☐ 9. Solder each wire end and let cool.

☐ 10. Connect wires from ceiling box to wires from fixture: black to black and white to white. If both wires from the ceiling box are white, then they may be connected arbitrarily to the wires from the fixture (Fig. 65B).

☐ 11. Place wire nuts over exposed ends.

☐ 12. Stuff wires into ceiling box.

☐ 13. Screw fixture into bar strap using machine screws.

☐ 14. Insert bulb.

☐ 15. Turn on current and energize fixture.

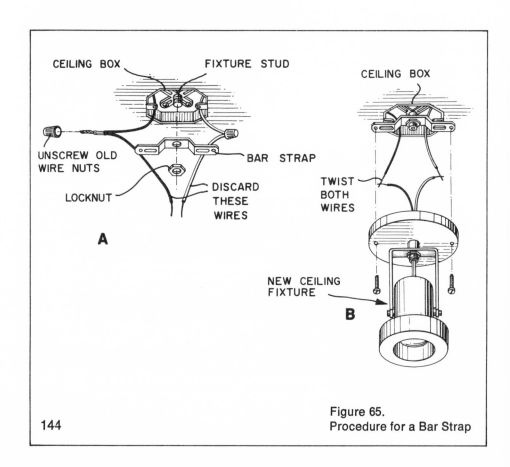

Figure 65.
Procedure for a Bar Strap

## 66. INSTALLING CANOPY CEILING FIXTURE

A canopy or chandelier fixture is much heavier than the porcelain fixture previously described. Because it will exert a greater pull on the ceiling, it is necessary to add support. This is a chore, but hang with it.

UTENSILS
*Medium flat blade screwdriver*
*Diagonal cutters*
*Wire strippers*
*Drill*
*Bits*
*Pliers*
*Soldering iron*
*Hammer*

INGREDIENTS
*Fixture stud, if necessary*
*Short metal screws*
*Hickey*
*New ceiling fixture*
*Several assorted nipples*
 *including extension nipples*
*2 #8 wire nuts*
*2 8/32-inch machine screws*
 *1, 1½, or 2 inches, as*
 *necessary*
*Coil of solder*
*Soldering flux (non-acid)*

APPROXIMATE TIME: 60 MINUTES, DEPENDING ON SIZE
AND WEIGHT OF FIXTURE

☐ *1.* Turn off power by disengaging appropriate fuse or circuit breaker.
☐ *2.* Turning counterclockwise, remove screws holding old fixture in place. Pull fixture away gently to avoid breaking plaster.
☐ *3.* You will notice 2 wires connected to fixture from ceiling box (Fig. 66A). Unscrew old wire nuts, if any. If wires are soldered or taped, cut away uninsulated portions.
☐ *4.* Strip back ½ inch of insulation and bare wires with wire stripper.
☐ *5.* Now examine interior of ceiling box to see if there is a stud. If not, you will have to buy one and install, as shown in Figure 66B, with drill, bit, and short metal screws, as in Recipe 65.
☐ *6.* Now screw hickey into newly installed stud (Fig. 66C). Bottom of hickey should be flush with bottom of box. If not, install nipple between stud and hickey until hickey is flush.

☐ 7. Install short nipple, which comes with new fixture, into bottom of hickey (Fig. 66C).

☐ 8. Working with fixture on a table, disconnect chain support from chain of fixture (Fig. 66C).

☐ 9. Screw chain support onto nipple at bottom of hickey at ceiling box.

☐ 10. Remove locknut from chain support.

☐ 11. Place canopy over entire ceiling box. You will notice the threads of the chain support peeking through.

☐ 12. To see if chain support is long enough, try to screw locknut onto chain support so that it holds canopy to ceiling. If you cannot do so, you will have to add an extension nipple between the hickey and the stud.

☐ 13. Now remove locknut and pull away canopy from chain support.

☐ 14. Slide the locknut down over the chain, and then slide the canopy down over the chain.

☐ 15. Weave wires of fixture through chain up to and through chain support. Occasionally, the wires must be run through nipple and out of hickey.

☐ 16. Resecure chain to chain support (Fig. 66C).

☐ 17. Once fixture is hanging from ceiling box, pull up on wires, through hickey, eliminating all slack.

☐ 18. Now cut off all but 6 inches of fixture wire with diagonal cutter.

☐ 19. Strip back ½ inch insulation with wire stripper, and twist bared strands in clockwise direction. Solder.

☐ 20. Connect fixture wires to ceiling wires—black to black, white to white (if no color, connect arbitrarily).

☐ 21. Screw wire nuts onto connected ends.

☐ 22. Push all wires into ceiling box.

☐ 23. Slide canopy up over chain onto chain support, covering ceiling box.

☐ 24. Slide locknut up over chain and screw onto chain support in clockwise direction.

☐ 25. Turn on power, energize new fixture.

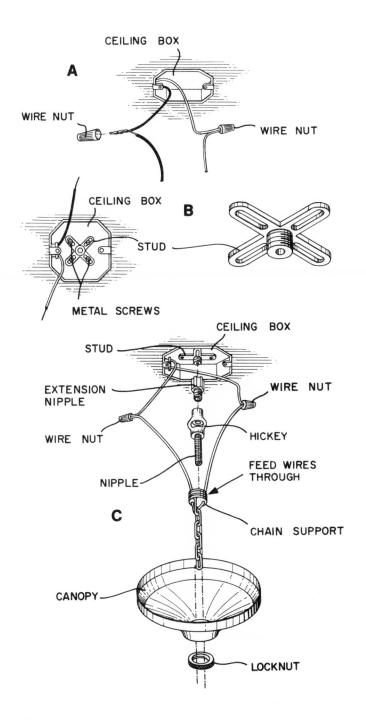

CEILING BOX

**A**

WIRE NUT

WIRE NUT

CEILING BOX

**B**

STUD

METAL SCREWS

CEILING BOX

STUD

EXTENSION
NIPPLE

WIRE NUT

WIRE NUT

HICKEY

FEED WIRES
THROUGH

NIPPLE

**C**

CHAIN SUPPORT

CANOPY

LOCKNUT

Figure 66.
Procedure for a Chandelier

147

## 67. BROKEN DOORBELL BUTTON

Did you ever wonder why nobody ever seems to visit you anymore? Maybe it's because your doorbell button doesn't work, and your would-be visitors turn away from your door, disappointed that you're not at home. To reactivate the old social life, try this. And don't be afraid of electric current—voltage is negligible.

UTENSILS
*Small thin screwdriver*
*Wire stripper*
*Long-nosed pliers*
*Awl*

INGREDIENTS
*Roll of plastic friction tape*
*New doorbell button*

APPROXIMATE TIME: 30 MINUTES

☐ *1.* Remove old doorbell button with screwdriver.
☐ *2.* Unscrew the 2 connecting wires and straighten ends (Fig. 67A).
☐ *3.* Clean away dirt.
☐ *4.* If wires are broken, strip both back with wire stripper ½ inch.
☐ *5.* If wires are frayed, tape frayed areas with friction tape (Fig. 67A).
☐ *6.* With long-nosed pliers, form hooks of wire ends (Fig. 67B).
☐ *7.* Unscrew terminal screws on new doorbell but do not remove (Fig. 67C).
☐ *8.* Place hooks around terminal screws in clockwise direction and tighten screws in clockwise direction, making sure wires do not touch (Fig. 67D).
☐ *9.* Push wires back into wall hole.
☐ *10.* Place new doorbell button against door where old button was removed.
☐ *11.* With awl, punch holes in door through screw holes in the doorbell button plate (Fig. 67A).
☐ *12.* Insert screws and drive into place.
☐ *13.* Press button, and bell, buzzer, or chimes will sound.

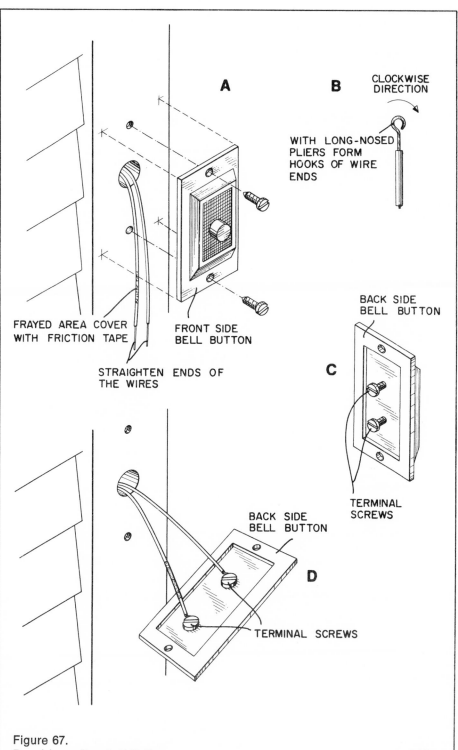

**A**

**B** CLOCKWISE DIRECTION

WITH LONG-NOSED PLIERS FORM HOOKS OF WIRE ENDS

FRAYED AREA COVER WITH FRICTION TAPE

FRONT SIDE BELL BUTTON

STRAIGHTEN ENDS OF THE WIRES

BACK SIDE BELL BUTTON

**C**

TERMINAL SCREWS

BACK SIDE BELL BUTTON

**D**

TERMINAL SCREWS

Figure 67.
Repairing a Doorbell Button

149

## 68. BROKEN DOOR BUZZER OR CHIME

What can we possibly say about a broken buzzer? Fix it, so you'll know people are outside waiting to get in!

UTENSILS
*Small thin screwdriver*
*Wire stripper*
*Long-nosed pliers*
*Awl*

INGREDIENTS
*Plastic friction tape*
*New buzzer, 6 or 12 volt*
*½-inch #4 sheet metal screws,*
*   round head*

APPROXIMATE TIME: 30 MINUTES

□  *1.* Remove old buzzer with screwdriver.
□  *2.* Clean area with brush or vacuum cleaner.
□  *3.* Unscrew the 2 connecting wires and straighten ends.
□  *4.* If wires are broken or frayed, strip back with wire stripper ½ inch, and strip ends so that bare wire is exposed ½ inch.
□  *5.* With long-nosed pliers, form hooks of the ends.
□  *6.* Unscrew terminal screws on new buzzer (Fig. 68), but do not remove.
□  *7.* Place hooks around terminal screws in clockwise direction.
□  *8.* Tighten screws in clockwise direction, making sure the wires do not touch.
□  *9.* Let the new buzzer hang by its wires.
□ *10.* Test the new buzzer by pressing doorbell button. It should work.
□ *11.* Holding the buzzer in place on the wall, punch holes with awl through screw holes in buzzer plate.
□ *12.* Insert sheet metal screws and drive securely into wall.
□ *13.* Install new buzzer cover, which comes with buzzer assembly.

150

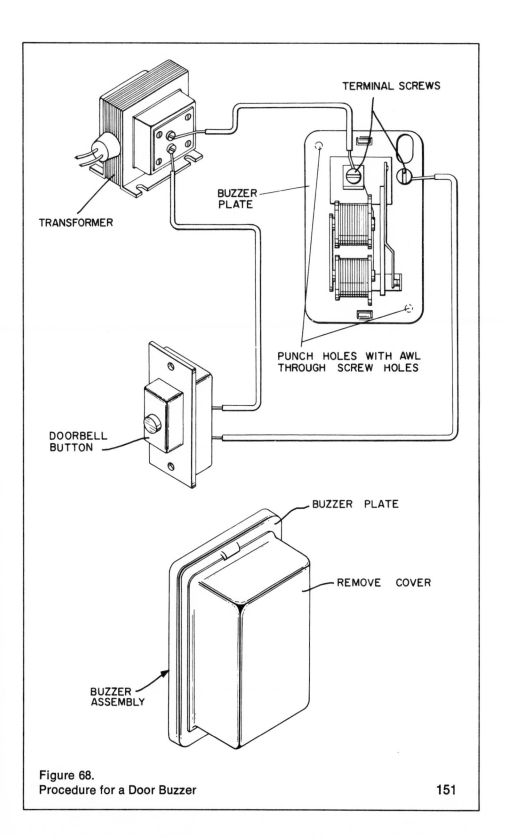

TERMINAL SCREWS

BUZZER PLATE

TRANSFORMER

PUNCH HOLES WITH AWL THROUGH SCREW HOLES

DOORBELL BUTTON

BUZZER PLATE

REMOVE COVER

BUZZER ASSEMBLY

Figure 68.
Procedure for a Door Buzzer

151

## 69. THERMOSTAT READING

The prime requirement for success in this simplest of recipes is your personal understanding of comfort. If you know what room temperature is comfortable for you, we'll tell you how to get it.

A thermostat is a temperature control device that comes in two basic types: temperature Fahrenheit (range 50 to 90 degrees) and arbitrary comfort gradation (range 0 to 10, *not* degrees). See Figure 69 for details.

If your home or apartment has a thermostat with arbitrary temperature gradations, it is essential that you install a Fahrenheit thermometer on an interior wall of the structure, 5 feet from the floor.

The conventional temperature settings thermostat comes equipped with its own thermometer.

Two recipes for thermostat reading follow below; select the appropriate one for yourself.

### Thermostat with Temperature Settings

☐ *1.* Set thermostat at 72 degrees and do not move setting for a few hours.

☐ 2. Now check thermometer. Thermostat setting and thermometer reading should be virtually identical. In any event, the differential must not be greater than 2 or 3 degrees. If differential is greater than that, thermostat is not functioning properly and may have to be replaced.

☐ *3.* If you are too cold, push thermostat setting one-half of one degree higher. If you are too warm, lower setting by one-half degree.

☐ *4.* Wait a few hours before changing temperature settings again.

☐ *5.* Repeat until you have found your personal comfort range. The following table is a general seasonal comfort range:

| SEASON | DAYTIME | NIGHTTIME |
|--------|---------|-----------|
| Winter | 64°–74° | 66°–72° |
| Summer | 72°–78° | 70°–76° |

*Note:* The thermostat does not work like an automobile accelerator. Pushing it far up or down will not speed the warming or cooling of a room.

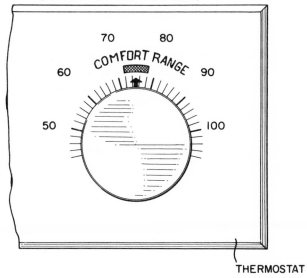

① TEMPERATURE FAHRENHEIT
(RANGE: 50 - 90 DEGREES )

THERMOSTAT

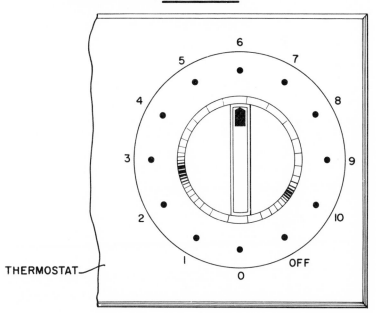

② ARBITRARY COMFORT GRADUATION
(RANGE: 0-10, NOT DEGREES )

THERMOSTAT

Figure 69.
Two Types of Thermostats

153

## 70. THERMOSTATS THAT DON'T HAVE TEMPERATURE SETTINGS

We have certain feelings about cheaply manufactured equipment, and now is a good time to expose them. How difficult, for example, would it be for a manufacturer of air conditioners to install a temperature control graduated in Fahrenheit degrees rather than one with dots, dashes, letters, numbers, or other confusing symbols? In point of fact, a great many heating and cooling units come equipped with these abstractly graduated thermostats. And if you want a specific temperature setting, it is necessary for you to buy a thermometer and then go through the following rigmarole.

UTENSILS
*Hammer*
*Awl*
*Medium flat blade screwdriver*
*Marking pen*

INGREDIENTS
*½-inch #4 sheet metal*
*  screw*
*Fahrenheit wall*
*  thermometer*

APPROXIMATE TIME: QUITE A WHILE

☐ *1.* Punch a small hole with hammer and awl 5 feet from the floor on an interior wall of house or apartment (Fig. 70A).

☐ *2.* Line up screw hole on thermometer plate with hole.

☐ *3.* Insert sheet metal screw and drive into hole in clockwise direction.

☐ *4.* Now set thermostat at middle marking (it could be a dot or a number or a letter). This will activate the heating or cooling unit. After some time the unit will either shut down or, in the case of a window air conditioner, the compressor will deactivate itself. This you will hear.

☐ *5.* When this occurs, take a thermometer reading and mark down that temperature beside the middle marking of the thermostat (Fig. 70B).

☐ *6.* If it is an air conditioner you are running, and the room temperature is too high, reset thermostat at next highest graduation mark; if a heating unit, and the room is too warm, reset thermostat to next lowest graduation mark.

☐ *7.* Wait an hour and read thermometer again.

☐ *8.* Write in temperature beside new thermostat setting.

☐ *9.* Repeat until you have established temperatures for each of the settings.

154

☐ *10.* Now turn to preceding recipe (Recipe 69 on Thermostat Reading) for procedure on finding comfort range.

*Note:* It would be advisable, when writing in temperature readings, to mark those in the comfort range with a different color ink. Or perhaps you can mark those settings with a heavier hand.

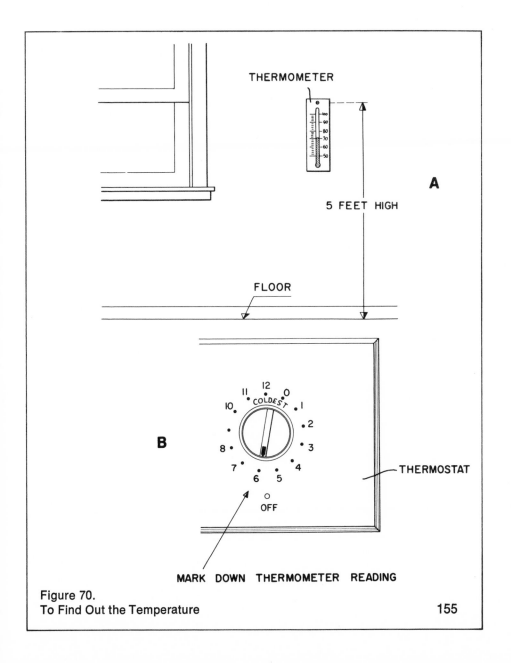

THERMOMETER

**A**

5 FEET HIGH

FLOOR

**B**

12
11 0
COLDEST
10 1
2
8 3
7 4
6 5

THERMOSTAT

O
OFF

MARK DOWN THERMOMETER READING

Figure 70.
To Find Out the Temperature

155

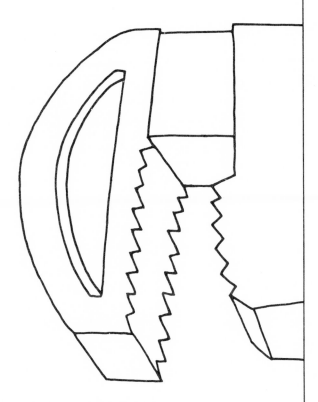

# PART IV

# Plumbing

Remember those old movies of the twenties and thirties when some oaf of a plumber turned his wrench a little too hard and got blasted in the face with a torrent of water? Well, it's a big laugh in the movies, but not a very funny reality.

If you can remember one rule, you'll be on your way to understanding enough about plumbing to avoid dangerous mistakes. Like electricity, water flows *from* a source, *through* a conductor, and, finally, *to* an outlet. If you want to avoid a splash in the face, the first thing you must do before beginning any plumbing work is to shut down the source. This is a simple process, and it involves the clockwise turning of a valve beneath the fixture on which you wish to perform a repair, or the identical closing of the main water valve in your basement. Once this is done, you may proceed without fear of flood or tidal wave.

Most plumbing jobs require the assistance of an expert. There are many, however, that the homeowner or apartment dweller may perform alone at tremendous savings. The following items, although they by no means represent a complete list, should be acquired for your permanent collection.

| | |
|---|---|
| *1 plunger* | *Assortment of rubber washers* |
| *1 Stillson wrench, 10 inches* | *Assortment of screws* |
| *1 end wrench* | *Roll of 1-inch adhesive tape* |
| *1 pair adjustable pliers* | *Coil of solder, resin core* |
| *Set of screwdrivers (see* | *Soldering paste or flux* |
| *Chapter 2 on How to Use a* | *(non-acid)* |
| *Screwdriver)* | *Lampwick* |
| *Set of 5 socket wrenches* | *Petroleum jelly* |
| *Soldering iron* | *Stiff wire or snake* |

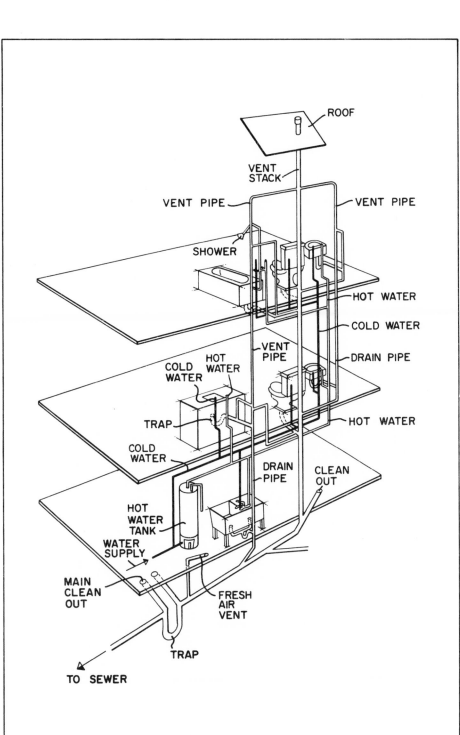

ROOF

VENT
STACK

VENT PIPE

VENT PIPE

SHOWER

HOT WATER

COLD WATER

VENT
PIPE

DRAIN PIPE

COLD
WATER

HOT
WATER

TRAP

HOT WATER

COLD
WATER

DRAIN
PIPE

CLEAN
OUT

HOT
WATER
TANK

WATER
SUPPLY

MAIN
CLEAN
OUT

FRESH
AIR
VENT

TRAP

TO SEWER

Figure F.
Basic Water Supply and Waste Piping for a Two
Story House

159

## 71. RESCUING LOST VALUABLES FROM SINK TRAP (OR BLOCKED TRAP)

There is probably more treasure in the New York sewer system than in half-a-dozen sunken Spanish galleons. This is due primarily to the fact that when you see a ring or other item of value go down the drain, you give it up for lost. Belay! Just seeing things disappear is salvation itself! Here's how to effect the rescue.

UTENSILS
*Dishpan or pot*
*Adjustable wrench*
*Stiff wire or snake (for blockage)*

INGREDIENTS
*Petroleum jelly*
*Cotton thread*

APPROXIMATE TIME: 20 MINUTES

☐ 1. Do not turn on water faucet until procedure is completed.
☐ 2. Under sink you will see a U-shaped pipe known as the *trap*. At the bottom is a thin, circular, threaded fitting or plug (Fig. 71A). Place dishpan beneath the trap to catch escaping water.
☐ 3. Remove the plug with wrench, turning counterclockwise. Once plug is removed, the water and the lost item swimming in it will flow out into the dishpan.
☐ 4. If there is no plug on your trap, the trap itself will have to be removed, as shown in Figure 71B.
☐ 5. Clean plug thoroughly and lubricate with petroleum jelly.
☐ 6. Replace plug or trap, whichever applies to you. Tighten carefully.
☐ 7. Turn on water faucet and then allow water to run while you check for leaks beneath the sink. Pipes should be dry if you have replaced plug well.
☐ 8. If there is a leak, do not attempt to overtighten plug, as this will strip the threads.
☐ 9. Remove plug or trap and wind some cotton thread around the threaded sections.
☐ 10. Smear cotton thread with petroleum jelly and reinsert plug or trap.
☐ 11. Check again for leaks. There won't be any. If there are, however, check the index for fixing leaky pipes.

*Note:* Identical procedure may be followed to remove blockage in sink trap, except that trap interior must be reamed with wire or snake.

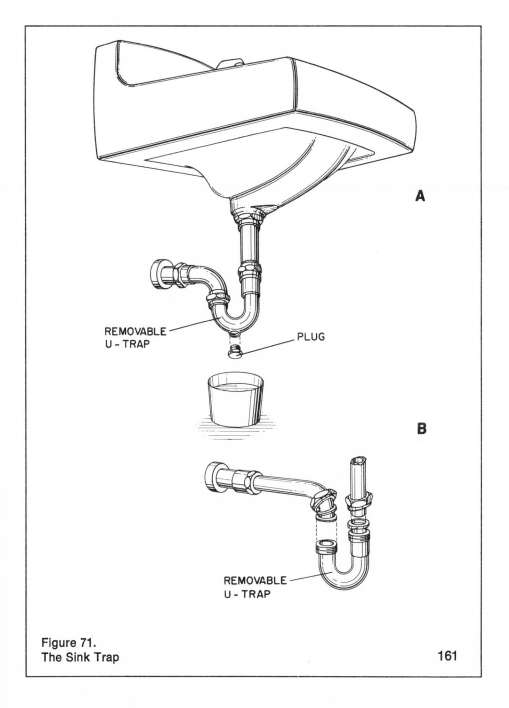

REMOVABLE
U - TRAP

PLUG

A

B

REMOVABLE
U - TRAP

Figure 71.
The Sink Trap

## 72. LEAKY FAUCET: DEFECTIVE WASHER

If you can live with the constant plink-plink of a leaky faucet, you have no need of this recipe. But if you find that the sounds of eternal dripping have the same effect on your mind as the ancient Chinese water torture, then follow these easy steps and tranquility will again be yours. The faucet pictured in Fig. 72 is one of many common types. It appears old, but its mechanism is as modern as any manufactured today.

UTENSILS
*Masking tape*
*Phillips screwdriver*
*Medium screwdriver, flat blade*
*Smooth-jawed wrench*

INGREDIENTS
*Box of assorted screws and washers*

APPROXIMATE TIME: 30 TO 45 MINUTES

- ☐ *1.* Shut off water supply beneath fixture or in basement.
- ☐ *2.* Tape hexagonal nut to prevent damage by wrench jaws.
- ☐ *3.* Remove hexagonal nut with wrench, turning counterclockwise. While doing so, make sure the faucet (Fig. 72) is slightly open. This will release spindle shaft, a metal rod in center of faucet.
- ☐ *4.* Remove spindle shaft.
- ☐ *5.* Remove the screw on the underside of shaft, turning counterclockwise.
- ☐ *6.* Remove washer held in place by screw, edging it from its seat with either flat blade or Phillips screwdriver.
- ☐ *7.* Clean all dirt from washer seat.
- ☐ *8.* Select a washer (hot or cold as specified on assortment box) that fits most snugly into seat.
- ☐ *9.* Select a new screw to fit and tighten washer into place until it bulges slightly. Only then will it be really secure and the "whistling faucet" syndrome averted.
- ☐ *10.* Reassemble faucet.
- ☐ *11.* Turn on water.
- ☐ *12.* If leak persists, please see next recipe.

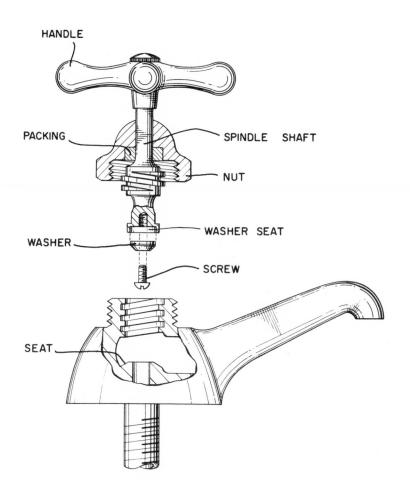

HANDLE

PACKING

SPINDLE SHAFT

NUT

WASHER SEAT

WASHER

SCREW

SEAT

Figure 72.
Replacing a Defective Washer

163

## 73. LEAKY FAUCET: GRINDING VALVE SEAT

Readers with still leaky faucets, we apologize for having put you through unnecessary labor. In the preceding recipe we told you that the leak in your faucet was caused by a defective washer; now, when the leak is still there after you've gone through the entire procedure, we're telling you the cause is a corroded valve seat, and that you've got to take the whole faucet apart again. Don't be angry—for long. This recipe for grinding a defective valve seat is a brief and simple one and will usually do the trick.

UTENSILS
*Valve seat grinder (you will
  have to measure the inside
  diameter of the valve to
  purchase correct size)
Smooth or flat-jaw
  adjustable wrench
Masking tape
Flashlight*

APPROXIMATE TIME: 30 TO 45 MINUTES

- [ ] *1.* Cut off water supply at valve stop beneath fixture or in basement.
- [ ] *2.* Remove faucet handle.
- [ ] *3.* Tape cap nut to avoid damage by wrench jaws.
- [ ] *4.* Remove cap nut under screw stem and lift out.
- [ ] *5.* Insert valve seat grinder and tighten in place, either with cap nut or tightening device, which comes with grinder (Fig. 73).
- [ ] *6.* With gentle, downward pressure, turn grinder in continuous clockwise direction until valve seat is smooth. The surface of the seat should be shiny. Inspect with flashlight. Note: You should purchase a grinder with finest cutter available.
- [ ] *7.* Reassemble faucet.
- [ ] *8.* Turn on water. Leak will have disappeared.

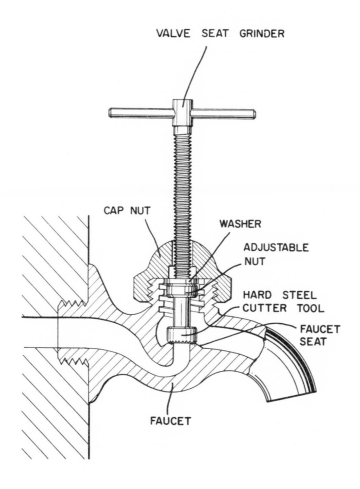

VALVE SEAT GRINDER

CAP NUT

WASHER

ADJUSTABLE
NUT

HARD STEEL
CUTTER TOOL

FAUCET
SEAT

FAUCET

Figure 73.
Stopping the Leak

## 74. BATHTUB OR SHOWER SHUTOFF VALVE

If you're not a plumber now, you will be one after this! You know the problem: the shower head leaks all the time, or the tub faucet is always dripping. Both are maddening. You must get behind the wall to fix this one. First, check the temperature of the water leaking from faucet or shower head. If it's hot, then that is the valve body you must disassemble. If cold, then disassemble the cold. Finally: hang in there.

UTENSILS
*Medium flat blade screwdriver
   and/or Phillips head
Hammer
Adjustable wrench
Pliers
Set of socket wrenches
Small cold chisel
Penknife
Flashlight*

INGREDIENTS
*Can of penetrating oil
Necessary washers (seat,
   "O" ring, bonnet)
Can of putty*

APPROXIMATE TIME: 60 MINUTES

☐  *1.*  Shut off water supply either in the bathroom or at the main cutoff valve in the basement.

☐  *2.*  Turn faucet handle to "open" position and allow water to drain.

☐  *3.*  Remove faucet handle screw, turning counterclockwise. Sometimes screw is located beneath snap-on cover, and this cover must be pried off with screwdriver or knife.

☐  *4.*  Pull off handle. If handle is corroded and stuck to stem within, apply several drops of penetrating oil and allow to sit for a few minutes. Then tap handle slightly with handle of hammer until it loosens. Do this gently!

☐  *5.*  Remove escutcheon, turning counterclockwise. If there is a set screw at the side or bottom of escutcheon, this will have to be loosened to allow removal of escutcheon.

☐  *6.*  Examine inside of escutcheon ring and scrape away old putty.

☐  *7.*  Remove stem sleeve by placing a cloth or rag over it, grasping it with pliers, and turning counterclockwise.

☐  *8.*  Remove bonnet or stem nut.

☐  *9.*  If bonnet is hexagonally shaped, select a socket wrench (Fig. 74A) to fit and remove by turning counterclockwise.

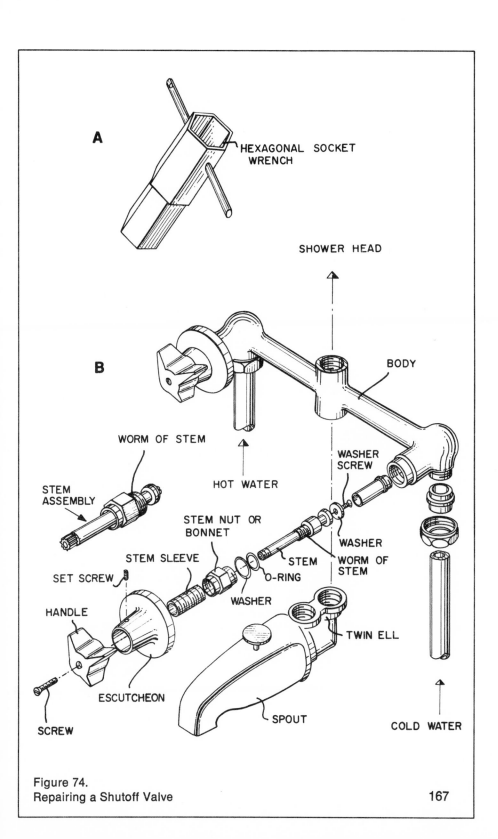

**A** HEXAGONAL SOCKET WRENCH

**B**

SHOWER HEAD

BODY

WORM OF STEM

STEM ASSEMBLY

WASHER SCREW

HOT WATER

STEM NUT OR BONNET

WASHER

STEM SLEEVE

STEM

O-RING

WORM OF STEM

SET SCREW

WASHER

HANDLE

SCREW

ESCUTCHEON

SPOUT

TWIN ELL

COLD WATER

Figure 74.
Repairing a Shutoff Valve

167

□ *10.* If wrench will not fit around bonnet because of surrounding tile and plaster, it will be necessary to remove enough of the plaster to allow wrench to fit around bonnet. Use cold chisel and hammer.

□ *11.* If bonnet is not hexagonal but has two flat sides, try to fit either pliers or wrench around flat sides and turn out in counterclockwise direction.

□ *12.* Examine washer on the shoulder of bonnet. If worn, replace.

□ *13.* At the very bottom of bonnet, there is an "O" ring washer. Remove and examine. If worn, replace.

□ *14.* Place faucet handle onto valve stem and remove by turning either clockwise or counterclockwise as may be the case.

□ *15.* Unscrew screw at bottom of stem by turning counter-clockwise.

□ *16.* Examine washer held in place by screw, and, if worn, replace.

□ *17.* If worm section of stem is worn, the entire stem should be replaced. When ordering new parts, it is advisable to take all old parts to the hardware store so you will get perfectly matched replacements.

□ *18.* Examine inside of valve body with flashlight. If valve seat is etched and worn, it may be necessary to regrind the seat. See Chapter 73 on Leaky Faucet: Grinding Valve Seat. If valve seat is made of plastic, do not disturb.

□ *19.* After all steps have been completed and all new parts and washers have been replaced, reassemble entire valve body, as shown in Figure 74B. Tighten parts by turning in the opposite direction as when you disassembled the unit. Make sure all fittings are tight and snug, but do not overtighten, as this will damage valve body.

□ *20.* Fill escutcheon ring with putty and fit over valve stem and stem sleeve. Then press escutcheon ring against wall until putty oozes out from the edges. This will prevent leakage from tub into walls.

□ *21.* Reset escutcheon in place.

□ *22.* Clean away putty from tiles.

□ *23.* Place valve handle on valve stem and screw into position.

□ *24.* Turn on water supply and test for leakage.

## 75. SINGLE HANDLE VALVE: BALL FAUCET

This is a relatively new plumbing device and is found in homes built in the last decade. It is modern, simple to work, but prone to the same malfunctions as other valves. It is our suggestion that, whenever this faucet begins to leak, you disassemble the entire valve body and check the entire thing out. In this way, you will be replacing worn parts that, if not causing your present trouble, will cause some new trouble in the near future. So stay with this one. It will not take long. (Note: Though the ball faucet pictured in Figure 75 is just one of many modern types, it is one of the more common varieties.)

UTENSILS
*Screwdriver*
*Pliers*
*Set of Allen wrenches*

INGREDIENTS
*Seat assembly with springs*
*    if valve leaks*
*New ball, if leakage is there*
*New "O" rings if leaks occur*
*    from top or bottom of valve*
*    assembly*

APPROXIMATE TIME: 60 MINUTES

☐  *1.* If faucet leaks from under handle, unscrew set screw under handle and remove handle (Fig. 75A).
☐  *2.* Tighten adjusting ring until water stops leaking (Fig. 75B). This should be done with water supply on. Adjust ring until leakage ceases, turning clockwise.
☐  *3.* If faucet drips at spout, turn off water supply.
☐  *4.* Disassemble handle as in step 1.
☐  *5.* Remove adjusting ring cap assembly turning counter-clockwise (Fig. 75B).
☐  *6.* Pull up on ball stem to remove cam and ball assembly (Fig. 75C).
☐  *7.* Check ball assembly for sharp edges, especially around the two small holes. Replace if this is the condition.
☐  *8.* Lift rubber seat and spring out of the body of the valve, and replace if necessary and reassemble (Fig. 75D).
☐  *9.* Replace adjusting ring cap assembly. Do not replace handle assembly yet.
☐ *10.* Turn on water and tighten adjusting ring until leak ceases.
☐ *11.* Replace handle assembly.
☐ *12.* If water leaks from either top or bottom of spout assembly,

turn off water supply and disassemble mechanism, as in step 1 through step 6.

☐ *13.* Lift up spout and examine "O" rings. Replace both "O" rings if they are worn or frayed or broken (Fig. 75E).

☐ *14.* Reassemble mechanism but do not reinstall handle.

☐ *15.* Turn on water, and tighten adjusting ring until leak ceases.

☐ *16.* Reinstall handle and check operation.

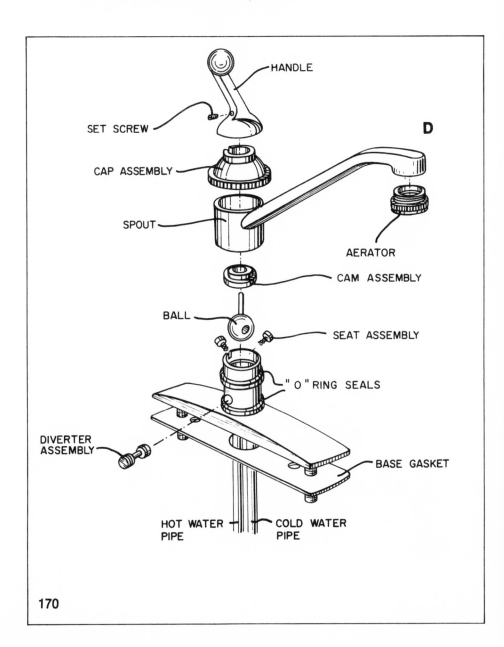

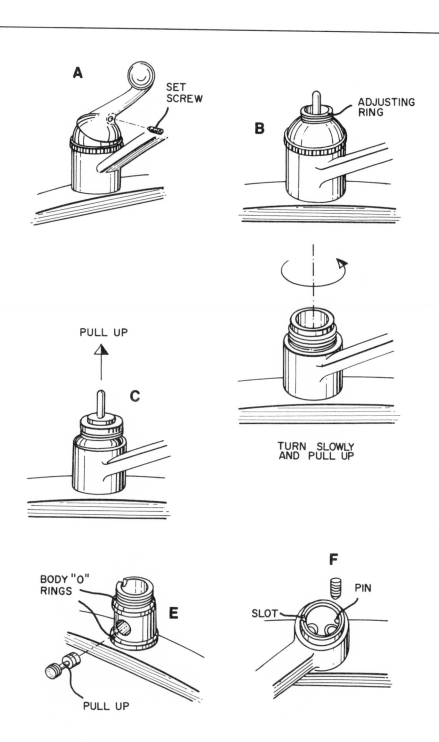

A — SET SCREW

B — ADJUSTING RING

TURN SLOWLY AND PULL UP

C — PULL UP

E — BODY "O" RINGS / PULL UP

F — PIN / SLOT

Figure 75.
Repairing a Ball Faucet

171

## 76. CLOGGED DRAINS

As far as we're concerned, the plunger is such an ingenious tool it should have been invented by Rube Goldberg. Herein we instruct on the truly proper technique for handling a plunger for greatest efficiency. Learn it now, and it will stand you in good stead for many a clog.

UTENSILS

*Plunger, 3-, 4-, or 5-inch diameter, whichever is most suitable*

INGREDIENTS

*Petroleum jelly*

APPROXIMATE TIME: 20 MINUTES

- ☐ *1.* Lubricate the under circumference of plunger with petroleum jelly (Fig. 76A). Apply liberally with fingers.
- ☐ *2.* Place your hand in the standing sink water, locate drain, and wipe away dirt or food residue collected there.
- ☐ *3.* If your sink has an overflow, which may be at front or back of sink (Fig. 76B), place one hand firmly over opening.
- ☐ *4.* Place plunger directly over drain.
- ☐ *5.* Depress plunger slowly until it completely seals off drain.
- ☐ *6.* Once the plunger is firmly in place, jerk up rapidly. This will create a vacuum in the drainpipe.
- ☐ *7.* Repeat as necessary until clog has been broken.
- ☐ *8.* Clean plunger thoroughly with soap and water after use.

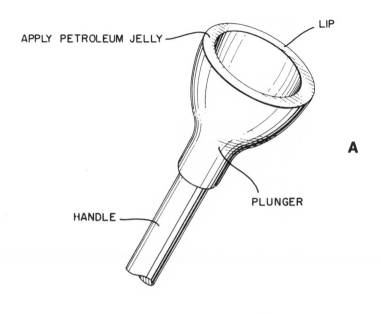

APPLY PETROLEUM JELLY

LIP

**A**

PLUNGER

HANDLE

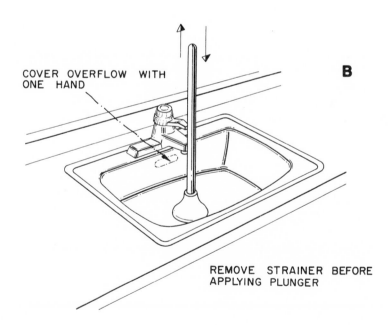

**B**

COVER OVERFLOW WITH ONE HAND

REMOVE STRAINER BEFORE APPLYING PLUNGER

Figure 76.
Unclogging a Sink

173

## 77. CLOGGED TOILET BOWL

Toilet bowls, like all other drains, often become clogged. An excessive amount of toilet tissue or a diaper accidentally flushed can be the culprit. We know of an absentminded young mother who did a double reverse. Her son, it seems, had soiled his diaper. Off came the lad's trousers, then the diaper. With her boy's unclean garments in hand, mama walked into the bathroom, threw the diaper into the hamper, and flushed the trousers down the toilet! Anyway, we're sure you'll find this recipe unique.

UTENSILS
*Large water kettle*
*Ball-type plunger*

INGREDIENTS
*Liquid bleach*
*Powdered soap*
*Petroleum jelly*

APPROXIMATE TIME: 20 TO 30 MINUTES

- ☐ *1.* Fill kettle with hot tap water.
- ☐ *2.* Pour water into toilet bowl.
- ☐ *3.* Repeat two or three times.
- ☐ *4.* Refill kettle and set on stove to boil.
- ☐ *5.* While water is heating, pour 2 to 3 cups of bleach and 1 cup of soap powder into bowl and let stand until kettle boils.
- ☐ *6.* Pour boiling water into bowl and let stand. In a short time, the chemical action of the soap and bleach will break the clog.
- ☐ *7.* If clog is not entirely broken, a plunger must be used.
- ☐ *8.* Lubricate entire lip circumference of plunger with petroleum jelly as shown in Figure 77A.
- ☐ *9.* Depress plunger slowly and jerk up rapidly (Fig. 77B).
- ☐ *10.* Repeat as necessary.
- ☐ *11.* After use, clean plunger thoroughly.

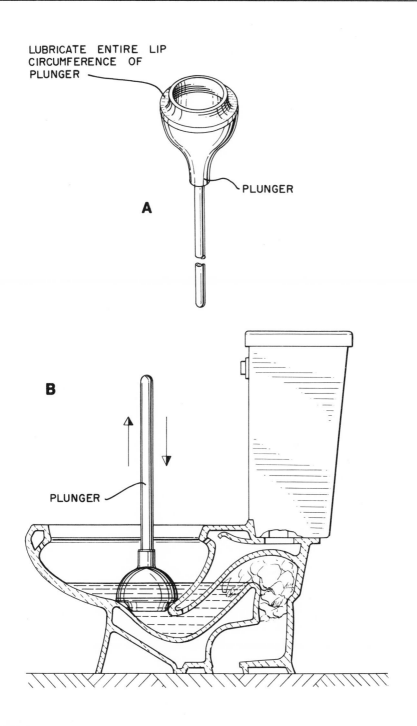

LUBRICATE ENTIRE LIP
CIRCUMFERENCE OF
PLUNGER

PLUNGER

A

B

PLUNGER

Figure 77.
Using a Plunger

## 78. REMOVING AND REPLACING OLD TOILET SEAT

Though the job of changing a toilet seat is a simple one, there are times, as described below, when the task takes on a new dimension, due to the fact that the seat bolts are virtually welded in place and must be sawed off before the new seat can be installed.

UTENSILS
*Adjustable pliers*
*Hacksaw with fine-tooth*
  *blade*
*Roll of masking tape*

INGREDIENTS
*Petroleum jelly*
*New toilet seat*

APPROXIMATE TIME: 30 TO 45 MINUTES

- ☐ 1. Note first that the seat is held in place by two bolts at rear.
- ☐ 2. With pliers, loosen the nuts on these bolts.
- ☐ 3. If nuts are frozen and will not turn, follow this alternate procedure before continuing, beginning with the bolt on your right.
- ☐   a. Raise seat.
- ☐   b. Clean hacksaw blade thoroughly and tape right side of blade.
- ☐   c. Smear the tape with a coat of petroleum jelly. (The tape and lubricant will insure against damage to the fixture.)
- ☐   d. Lay the blade flat, taped side down (Fig. 78A), saw through bolt (Fig. 78B), and remove.
- ☐   e. Remove tape and clean the blade.
- ☐   f. Now place strip of tape on left side of blade and lubricate as before.
- ☐   g. Cut away and remove bolt.
- ☐ 4. Once the bolts have been removed, clean area thoroughly.
- ☐ 5. Remove nuts and washers from bolts on new seat.
- ☐ 6. Lubricate new bolts with petroleum jelly.
- ☐ 7. Insert bolts through seat holes.
- ☐ 8. Once the bolts are through, place a washer on each.
- ☐ 9. Screw nuts onto bolts by hand in clockwise direction, and then using pliers, tighten a half turn. Do not overtighten—you never know when you'll need to remove them again.

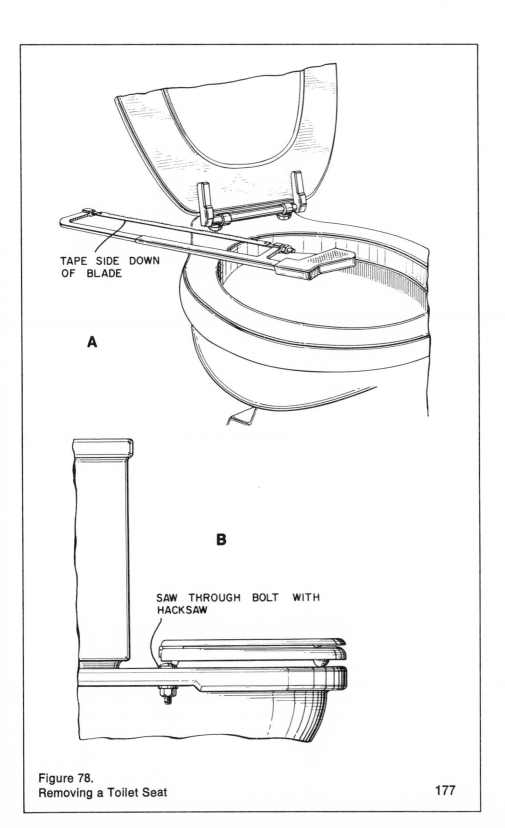

TAPE SIDE DOWN
OF BLADE

A

B

SAW THROUGH BOLT WITH
HACKSAW

Figure 78.
Removing a Toilet Seat

177

## FLUSH TANKS

Like any other mechanism with a number of moving parts, the flush tank is subject to a variety of disorders. Most of the common maladies, however, are simple to correct. And part of the simplicity of the work is due to the easy accessibility of the malfunctioning parts. That is one of the beauties of the flush tank—all one must do to diagnose a problem is to raise the tank cover and look inside.

But because "looking" does not always constitute "seeing"—particularly for the inexperienced eye—we have included a Diagnostic Chart listing the most common flush tank disorders. Here's how to read it: first establish what seems to be going wrong with your own flush tank; then proceed to the "symptom" column of the chart and match your flush tank's disorder symptoms with the ones which most resemble them in the chart. Now read across to the "diagnosis" column, and, finally, to the "cure." In most instances, we have provided a detailed recipe—in the pages which follow the chart—for the speedy repair of the disorder.

## FLUSH TANK DIAGNOSTIC CHART

| SYMPTOM | DIAGNOSIS | RECIPE CURE |
|---|---|---|
| Water runs and will not stop | 1. Overflows through overflow tube. | 1. a. Bend float rod down slightly. See Recipe 79.<br>b. Replace float if it no longer floats. |
| | 2. Water runs under stopper ball. | 2. a. Realign stopper ball guide bracket and lift rod.<br>b. Replace ball.<br>c. Clean ball seat with sandpaper.<br>d. Install new flapper stop ball. |
| | 3. Inlet valve body leaks. | 3. a. Replace plunger washer.<br>b. Replace ball-cock washer.<br>c. Replace ball-cock.<br>d. Reset action rod.<br>e. Regrind valve seat. |

| | | |
|---|---|---|
| | 4. Flush handle stuck. | 4. a. Lubricate all connecting points.<br>b. Loosen flush handle nut.<br>c. Reset flush handle nut. |
| Does not flush | 1. No water in tank.<br><br>2. Flush handle loose. | 1. Open shutoff valve under tank.<br>2. a. Reconnect trip arm lever.<br>b. Reconnect upper lift wire.<br>c. Reconnect lower lift wire.<br>d. Reconnect handle connection. |
| Water flushes but does not stop | 1. Water runs under ball stop. | 1. a. Realign stopper ball guide.<br>b. Clean ball seat with fine sandpaper or steel wool. |
| Does not flush enough water | 1. Tank does not fill to proper level. | 1. Bend float rod up slightly. See Recipe 79. |
| Not enough water in bowl after flush | 1. Refill tube not set into overflow pipe.<br>2. Refill tube missing or broken. | 1. Reset refill tube into overflow pipe.<br>2. Replace refill tube. |
| Tank leaks under cover | 1. Refill tube leaks.<br><br>2. Ball-cock plunger leaks. | 1. Repair or replace refill tube.<br>2. Replace all washers in ball-cock mechanism. |
| Tank leaks at flush handle | 1. Flush handle nut loose.<br>2. Flush handle washer is worn. | 1. Tighten flush handle nut.<br>2. Replace flush handle washer. |
| Water leaks under tank | 1. Shank locknut loose.<br>2. Shank washer worn.<br>3. Ball seat locknut loose.<br>4. Ball seat tank washer worn. | 1. Tighten shank locknut.<br>2. Replace shank washer.<br>3. Tighten ball seat locknut.<br>4. Replace ball seat tank washer. |
| Tank sweats | 1. Cold water in tank. | 1. Insulate inside of tank with ½-inch sheet styrofoam. See Recipe 82. |

## 79. TOO MUCH WATER OR NOT ENOUGH FOR FLUSH

There are essentially two things that can go wrong with a float rod in a flush tank: either the rod sits too low in the tank, causing an insufficient amount of water (allowed) into the tank for the next flush, or the rod is too high, which results in an overflowing of water through the overflow tube and a constant gurgling and bubbling in the toilet bowl.

UTENSILS
*None*

INGREDIENTS
*None*

APPROXIMATE TIME: 10 MINUTES

### Insufficient Water for Flush

☐ *1.* Remove cover from flush tank.
☐ *2.* Grasp float rod in both hands as shown in Figure 79.
☐ *3.* Bend slightly upward.
☐ *4.* Permit tank to fill.
☐ *5.* You will notice that there is a water-level mark in tank. If water does not reach proper level, bend rod once again.
☐ *6.* Flush tank and let fill again. Repeat bending of rod until proper level is achieved.

### Excessive Water Flow in Tank

☐ *1.* Remove cover from flush tank.
☐ *2.* Pull up gently on float rod. If water shuts off, this is an indication that the float rod must be bent slightly downward.
☐ *3.* Grasp float rod with both hands as shown in Figure 79 and bend slightly downward.
☐ *4.* Flush the tank and allow to refill.
☐ *5.* Check level mark and repeat bending as necessary until water reaches proper level.
☐ *6.* If this procedure does not correct condition, it may be necessary to replace float. Unscrew old float in counter-clockwise direction. Screw on new float in clockwise direction.

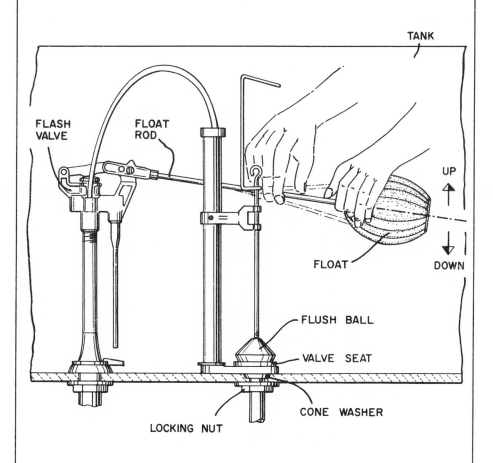

Figure 79.
Adjusting Water for Flush Toilet

181

## 80. FLUSH BALL DOES NOT FIT PROPERLY

This is both an annoying and potentially embarrassing problem. Not only must you put up with the constant trickling of water in the toilet bowl, but you will have no water in the tank when you need a good flush. This, like the previous procedure, is a two-part recipe.

UTENSILS
*Screwdriver*

INGREDIENTS
*Steel wool or sandpaper*
*New rubber mechanism,*
*    if necessary*

APPROXIMATE TIME: 30 MINUTES

- ☐ *1.* Turn off water supply and empty tank by flushing.
- ☐ *2.* Remove cover on tank.
- ☐ *3.* Check flush ball guide and make sure it is in line with center of the flush ball seat (Fig. 80A). Adjust by loosening screws on bracket of guide and realign.
- ☐ *4.* Straighten flush ball lift wire (Fig. 80A). This wire must be perfectly straight. If there are any bends in it, it must be replaced. Simply unscrew old unit, and rescrew new one.
- ☐ *5.* With steel wool or sandpaper, clean flush ball seat of any residue to form a perfect surface.
- ☐ *6.* If the above procedure does not correct condition, it will be necessary to replace flush ball with new all-rubber mechanism, as shown in Figure 80B.
- ☐ *7.* To install new unit:
- ☐     a. Remove old ball stopper guides, linkage wire, and lift wire.
- ☐     b. Pull refill tube out of overflow pipe.
- ☐     c. Slide new ball stopper down overflow pipe until it is in contact with ball seat.
- ☐     d. Lift chain and connect to trip arm. Make sure that trip arm is in down position and there is no slack in pull chain.
- ☐     e. Turn on water and allow tank to fill to proper level.
- ☐     f. Trip handle to check position of flush ball. Lengthen or shorten chain as necessary for a good fit of the ball on the ball seat.
- ☐ *8.* Reset refill tube in overflow pipe.
- ☐ *9.* Replace cover on tank.
- ☐ *10.* Flush tank.

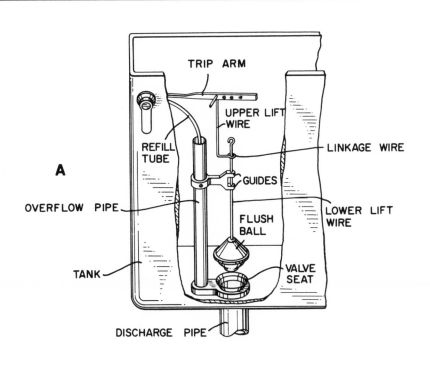

**A**

TRIP ARM

UPPER LIFT WIRE

LINKAGE WIRE

REFILL TUBE

GUIDES

OVERFLOW PIPE

LOWER LIFT WIRE

FLUSH BALL

TANK

VALVE SEAT

DISCHARGE PIPE

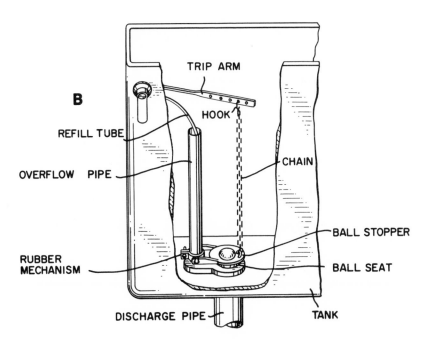

**B**

TRIP ARM

HOOK

REFILL TUBE

OVERFLOW PIPE

CHAIN

BALL STOPPER

BALL SEAT

RUBBER MECHANISM

DISCHARGE PIPE

TANK

Figure 80.
To Replace a Flush Ball

## 81. WATER CONTINUES TO FLOW

You've noticed by now that one symptom of a flush tank malady may have one or several possible causes. Repair is often performed on a trial-and-error basis. Sorry about that, folks—but this is the only way you can be sure of correcting the condition once and for all.

In this particular case, the cause for continuous water flow may be worn washers in plunger valve.

UTENSILS

*Small and medium flat
blade screwdrivers*
*Pliers*
*Adjustable wrench*

INGREDIENTS

*Plunger washer*
*Seat washer*
*New seat washer screw,
if necessary*

APPROXIMATE TIME: 30 MINUTES

☐ 1. Turn off water supply and empty tank by flushing.
☐ 2. Disassemble plunger valve linkage by turning wing screws in counterclockwise direction (Fig. 81A). If regular screws, use screwdriver.
☐ 3. Lift plunger from valve. If this is difficult, turn out gently with pliers.
☐ 4. Take plunger to hardware store and have the salesperson give you a new plunger washer and seat washer to match your plunger exactly. The same holds for the new seat washer screw, if one is necessary for your plunger.
☐ 5. Home again, unscrew old seat washer screw (if you have one) and remove seat washer (Fig. 81B). If your plunger does not have a screw, simply pry out the old washer with a screwdriver. (Chances are, the person at the hardware store will already have removed it for you.)
☐ 6. Install new seat washer securely.
☐ 7. The plunger washer fits into a groove in the side of the plunger. It is a split washer, made of leather or rubber. Remove it.
☐ 8. Install new plunger washer.
☐ 9. Reassemble entire valve body and readjust linkage and float arm as necessary.

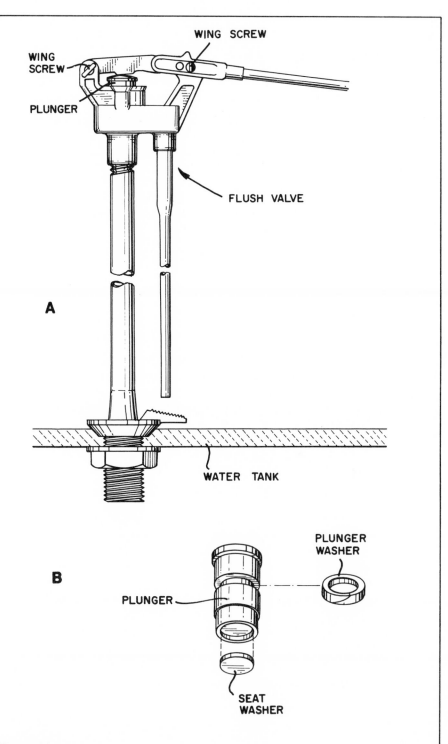

Figure 81.
Worn Washers in Plunger Valve

185

## 82. FLUSH TANK SWEATS

Condensation will often form on the outside face of your flush tank when the temperature of the water in the tank is considerably below room temperature. This is an annoying problem at best. We suggest a small insulation job that is extremely effective. We'll bet you've never heard of this one before!

UTENSILS
*Pencil*
*Sharp knife*
*Ruler*

INGREDIENTS
*6 square feet of ½ -inch*
  *styrofoam*
*Tube of silicone adhesive*
*Paper pad*

APPROXIMATE TIME: 45 MINUTES

☐   *1.* Remove flush tank cover (Fig. 82A).
☐   *2.* Shut off water supply at valve below tank.
☐   *3.* Flush tank to empty.
☐   *4.* Dry off the inside walls of the tank with a towel and let stand for 1 hour until all moisture is gone.
☐   *5.* With ruler, measure front and rear walls of tank inside, from right to left and from top to bottom. Subtract 1 inch from each dimension and note on piece of paper.
☐   *6.* With ruler, measure side walls of tank from front to back and from top to bottom. Subtract 1 inch from each dimension and mark down on piece of paper.
☐   *7.* Now cut 2 pieces of styrofoam to match the larger measurements.
☐   *8.* Now cut 2 pieces of styrofoam to match the smaller measurements.
☐   *9.* Spread silicone adhesive on the back of the 2 narrow pieces of styrofoam, as shown in Figure 82B, and install into sides of tank (Fig. 82C).
☐ *10.* Repeat process for the 2 larger pieces of styrofoam that will be installed on the rear and front walls of the tank (Fig. 82C). It may be necessary to cut a hole in the styrofoam to fit around flush handle.
☐ *11.* Press all the styrofoam sheets tightly against wall. It is not necessary to have a perfect fit.
☐ *12.* Allow to dry for approximately 2 hours.
☐ *13.* Turn on water supply.
☐ *14.* Replace tank cover. Condensation will be eliminated.

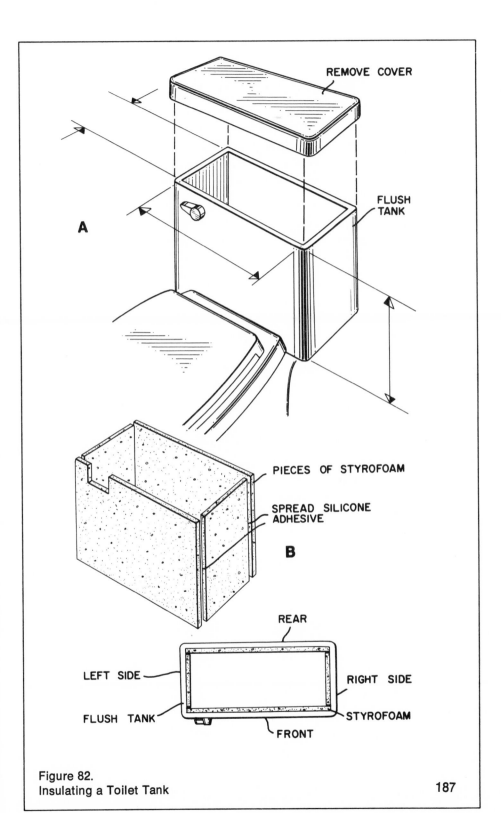

REMOVE COVER

FLUSH TANK

A

PIECES OF STYROFOAM

SPREAD SILICONE ADHESIVE

B

REAR

LEFT SIDE

RIGHT SIDE

FLUSH TANK

STYROFOAM

FRONT

Figure 82.
Insulating a Toilet Tank

187

# FLUSH VALVE DIAGNOSTIC CHART

There are a mutiplicity of potential problems that may develop in a common household flush valve because it is a rather intricate device. But don't let that scare you—they usually happen one at a time.

It would have been too lengthy a task to prepare a recipe for each possible malady, so we have done the next best thing: we have prepared a diagnostic chart that enumerates, in brief, everything that can go wrong with a flush valve, and which provides the most dramatic and recognizable symptoms of each along with the speediest remedy.

Not all homes and apartments utilize the flush valve system. For those of our readers whose homes employ flush tank systems, there is a diagnostic chart of the same order as the one here.

A word now about the flush valve, and its advantage over other toilet systems, would be appropriate.

The greatest advantage of this mechanism is that it makes for what we call "instant flush." That is to say, you can flush as many times as you wish without waiting. This is handy when you've got baby diapers to clean. Right, parents? Second, the flush valve system, as it is almost entirely out of sight, is extremely sanitary. And we cannot stress enough the value of sanitary conditions in the bathroom.

The greatest single drawback of the flush valve system is its noise level. It has been known to wake people sleeping three rooms away! That may be an exaggeration, but, if you have flush valves in your home, you know what we mean.

In any event, flush valves can go awry, and we're here to tell you that they are a breeze to repair. Make use of our diagnostic chart periodically and check to see if any of the symptoms listed apply to your system.

| SYMPTOM | DIAGNOSIS | RECIPE CURE |
|---|---|---|
| Valve will not start to flush | 1. Control stop is shut.<br>2. Tip of operating stem is worn.<br>3. Operating stem is too short. | 1. Open control stop.<br>2. Replace operating stem, now supplied with nylon tip.<br>3. Install correct length stem, indicated in parts listings. |
| Valve starts flushing but closes immediately | 1. Diaphragm is ruptured.<br><br>2. Valve contains an oversized bypass orifice (pinhole).<br><br>3. Tip of operating stem is worn.<br>4. Seat guide is loose. | 1. Replace diaphragm. Good preventive maintenance includes simultaneous replacement of auxiliary valve seat supplied in same kit.<br>2. Install diaphragm with correct bypass size from proper kit. Valves with ¾-inch supply or smaller use larger orifice sizes than valves with 1-inch supply or larger. Replace auxiliary valve seat at same time.<br>3. Replace operating stem.<br>4. Tighten. |
| Valve gives too short a flush or too long a flush | 1. Valve needs regulation.<br><br><br>2. Valve contains an oversized bypass orifice (flush too short).<br><br>3. Bypass orifice is partially blocked (flush too long).<br><br>4. Tip of operating stem is worn. | 1. Remove cover screw. Insert screwdriver and turn regulating screw counterclockwise for shorter flush. If valve is equipped with non-hold open feature, timing must be changed by trial and error of different bypass orifices.<br>2. Install diaphragm with correct bypass size from kit. Replace auxiliary valve seat at same time. Step 1 above should be tried first.<br>3. Clean bypass protecting screen. Hold pinhole up to light. If blocked, pinhole may be cleaned with pin, air hose, or acid solution.<br>4. Replace operating stem. |
| Valve continues to run full force or continues to run but only slightly | 1. Bypass blocked.<br><br>2. Foreign object is blocking, closing action. | 1. Clean as indicated in step 3 immediately above.<br>2. Remove foreign object. Smooth any indentations on underside of diaphragm. If diaphragm is mutilated, replace. |

| SYMPTOM | DIAGNOSIS | RECIPE CURE |
|---|---|---|
| | 3. Leakage is occurring at the auxiliary valve seat due to foreign objects or wearing and pitting of the auxiliary valve. | 3. Remove any foreign objects from number 8 auxiliary valve seat. Examine seating surface for pitting or cutting. Replace as needed with new auxiliary valve. Replace auxiliary valve seat at the same time. |
| | 4. Water pressure and/or volume is insufficient to fill upper chamber of valve and cause valve to close. | 4. Increase pressure and/or volume. If several valves are running at one time, pressure may be built up by shutting off all control stops and then opening them again one by one. |
| | 5. Auxiliary valve head has separated from rod allowing leakage. | 5. Replace auxiliary valve and auxiliary valve seat. |
| | 6. Slight leakage is present at main auxiliary valve seat due to minute foreign objects or very slight wearing and pitting of the auxiliary valve. | 6. Remove any foreign objects. If diaphragm has been scarred at contact point with main valve seat, replace diaphragm. If main valve seat is scored or pitted, replace. Most valves are equipped with renewable main valve seats. |
| | 7. Main valve seat is loose. | 7. Tighten. |
| Water splashes from bowl | 1. The pressure at the fixture is in excess of that set by the fixture manufacturer as an upper limit. | 1. Install a pressure reducing valve in the supply line. Failing this, reduce the volume of water flowing through the flush valve by partially closing the control stop. |
| Valve will not pass enough water to satisfactorily siphon bowl | 1. Control stop not completely open. | 1. Open control stop wide. |
| | 2. Seat guide for valves with ¾-inch supply or smaller has been installed in valve in error. | 2. Replace with seat guide for valves with 1-inch supply or larger. |
| | 3. Insufficient volume of water is being supplied to valve due to low pressure, undersized piping, or both. | 3. Establish volume of water available by removing entire diaphragm operating assembly from flush valve, replacing cover, and flushing valve. This converts valve into a simple elbow. If adequate flush still cannot be obtained, water pressure or pipe sizes, or both, must be increased. |

190

| SYMPTOM | DIAGNOSIS | RECIPE CURE |
|---|---|---|
| Valve goes off by itself | 1. Water in upper chamber of valve has been siphoned out by demand from lower levels. When pressure is restored, valve flushes automatically. | 1. Install diaphragm with nonsiphon bypass, if available. Increase pressure or replace piping. |
| Flushing action is not quiet enough | 1. High pressure causes abnormally high water in supply system. | 1. Install pressure reducing valve in water supply line. |
|  | 2. Flush valve is not quiet type. | 2. Install valve with turn-to-silence equipment. |
|  | 3. Turn-to-silence equipment is not properly adjusted for maximum quietness. | 3. To set for minimum flushing noise, open turn-to-silence wide by turning counterclockwise with screwdriver or wheel handle. Trip the valve and note noise level. While valve is running, begin to close stop and slowly turn-to-silence. Depending on inlet pressure at any given fixture, there is one setting of the stop at which water noise will be hushed. If pressure is low, this optimum setting will be near the wide open stop position. If pressure is high, the setting will be near the closed position. The gallonage demands of the fixture must also be satisfied. Adjustment of the regulating screw in the valve cover may be helpful in this regard. |
|  | 4. Localized roaring noise of fixture may be contributing factor. | 4. Make quick test to isolate fixture noise from any valve noise. Place cardboard under toilet seat all but covering opening of bowl. Valve noise will then be readily identifiable. If fixture is noisy, install quiet action bowl. |

| SYMPTOM | DIAGNOSIS | RECIPE CURE |
|---|---|---|
| Valve leaks at handle | 1. Handle packing is worn. | 1. Tighten packing nut or replace packing. |
| | 2. Valve is fitted with old-style spring-loaded handle. | 2. Replace with modern handle. |
| | 3. Flexer has fatigued and ruptured. | 3. Replace flexer to regain new spring and sealing action. Also replace operating stem. |
| Water leaks from air vents or vacuum breaker | 1. Rubber sleeve has ruptured from fatigue. | 1. Replace rubber sleeve as in recipe to follow. |
| | 2. Vacuum breaker is being subjected to excessive back pressure by restrictive urinal or water closet. | 2. Open up flow control on urinal if such a device is provided. Also, flow rate through valve may be reduced at control stop. If condition persists, contact manufacturer of fixture for corrective action. |

## 83. REPAIR OF DIAPHRAGM ON FLUSH VALVE

While we were told it was good to drive around with a tiger in our tanks, we cannot speak so highly of the lion in our toilet! The roaring ferocity of a torn flushometer diaphragm can be nerve-racking. Here's how the beast malfunctions: you trip the handle; the diaphragm rises inside the valve, roars, and then snaps closed before enough water has passed through. The only way you can get a full flush is to hold the handle until the job is done. And that's a pain. So read on.

UTENSILS
*Smooth or flat-jaw adjustable wrench*
*Roll of masking tape*
*Medium flat blade screwdriver*
*Adjustable pliers*

INGREDIENTS
*Diaphragm Flushometer Kit (Copy the brand name on the flushometer and take with you to the hardware store so you are certain of getting the proper kit)*
*Petroleum jelly*

APPROXIMATE TIME: 30 TO 45 MINUTES

☐ 1. Shut off water supply at stop valve or at main cutoff in basement (Fig. 83A).
☐ 2. Tape jaws of wrench or large cap to prevent damage to fixtures.
☐ 3. Place wrench on large cap of cover assembly, and turn in counterclockwise direction until assembly is removed (Fig. 83A).
☐ 4. Place fingers inside flush valve and find diaphragm. Vulcanized into it is a brass fitting held in place by several rings. This is called the diaphragm operating assembly (Fig. 83B).
☐ 5. Remove assembly.
☐ 6. Examine diaphragm for holes or tears.
☐ 7. Unscrew diaphragm bushing from seat guide in counter-clockwise direction.
☐ 8. Remove diaphragm and replace with new one, making sure that the strainer side of the bleeder valve is next to seat guide holder. See Figure 83B.
☐ 9. Reassemble into flush valve as follows:
☐     a. Place seat guide downward into valve.
☐     b. Place auxiliary valve seat in center.

☐ *10.* Replace cover assembly, first lubricating threads with petroleum jelly. Tighten slowly.

☐ *11.* Turn on water and test.

☐ *12.* After procedure is completed, it may be necessary to adjust the length of the flush as follows:

☐     a. Remove cap nut.

☐     b. Insert screwdriver through top of valve seat assembly and turn in a clockwise and counterclockwise direction until proper flush is achieved. Clockwise turning shortens the flush and counterclockwise turning lengthens the flush.

☐     c. Replace cap nut.

☐     d. Test flush.

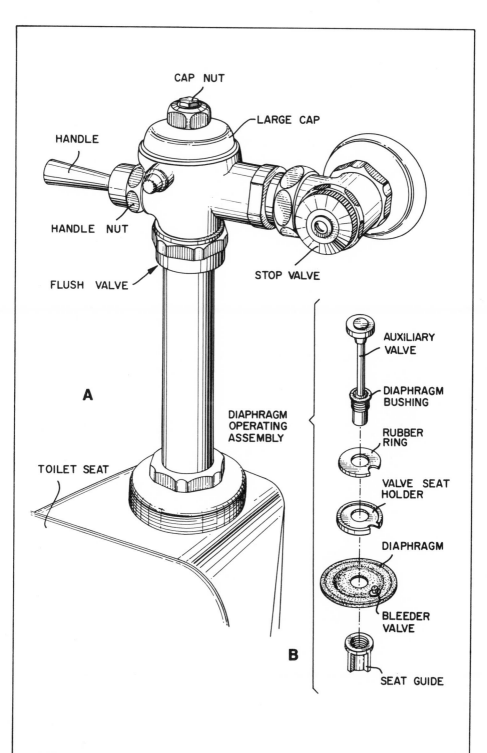

CAP NUT

LARGE CAP

HANDLE

HANDLE NUT

FLUSH VALVE

STOP VALVE

A

DIAPHRAGM
OPERATING
ASSEMBLY

TOILET SEAT

B

AUXILIARY
VALVE

DIAPHRAGM
BUSHING

RUBBER
RING

VALVE SEAT
HOLDER

DIAPHRAGM

BLEEDER
VALVE

SEAT GUIDE

Figure 83.
Repair a Diaphragm on Flush Valve

## 84. VALVE WILL NOT PASS ENOUGH WATER TO FLUSH

There is nothing worse than half a flush when a full flush is what you need. Like the poker four-flush, it doesn't quite make for a winner.

UTENSILS
*Smooth or flat-jaw adjustable*
   *wrench*
*Medium flat blade screwdriver*

APPROXIMATE TIME: 5 TO 10 MINUTES

☐  *1.* Do not cut off water supply.
☐  *2.* Remove nut on top of valve assembly (Fig. 84A).
☐  *3.* Turn screw that is beneath nut in counterclockwise direction, one-fourth turn at a time (Fig. 84B).
☐  *4.* Flush intermittently until proper amount of water is passed through.
☐  *5.* If this doesn't do the trick, go on to the next recipe.

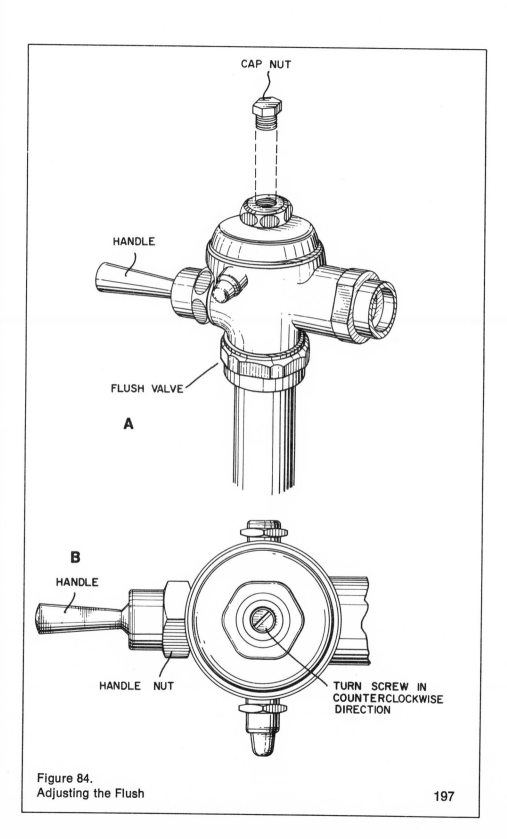

CAP NUT

HANDLE

FLUSH VALVE

A

B

HANDLE

HANDLE NUT

TURN SCREW IN
COUNTERCLOCKWISE
DIRECTION

Figure 84.
Adjusting the Flush

197

## 85. CORRECTING WATER FLOW IN FLUSH VALVE

Sometimes, the length of a flush cannot be corrected by turning the regulating screw as described in preceding recipes. The major symptom we are dealing with here is either a very short, ineffective flush, or no flush at all. This usually indicates a defective operating stem. It's a short and easy job, so don't get nervous about it. You should be nervous about a twenty-dollar plumbing fee, which is the alternative.

UTENSILS
*Smooth or flat-jaw adjustable*
*    wrench*
*Roll of masking tape*
*Medium flat blade screwdriver*

INGREDIENTS
*Operating stem*
*Valve handle washer kit*
*Petroleum jelly*

APPROXIMATE TIME: 20 TO 30 MINUTES

☐ *1.* Shut off water supply at valve stop or at main cutoff in basement.
☐ *2.* Trip valve handle to release water pressure.
☐ *3.* Tape jaws of wrench to prevent damage to fixture.
☐ *4.* With wrench, remove handle nut and then handle assembly, taking care not to lose screws and nuts. If they are worn, replace them.
☐ *5.* Install new operating stem as shown in Figure 85A.
☐ *6.* Reassemble handle assembly as shown in Figure 85B.
☐ *7.* Lubricate all replaced parts with petroleum jelly.
☐ *8.* Adjust length of flush as described in step 12 of Recipe 83.

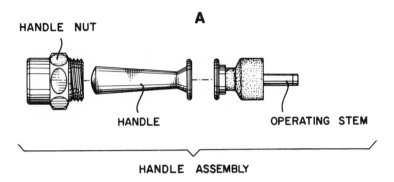

**A**

HANDLE NUT

HANDLE

OPERATING STEM

HANDLE ASSEMBLY

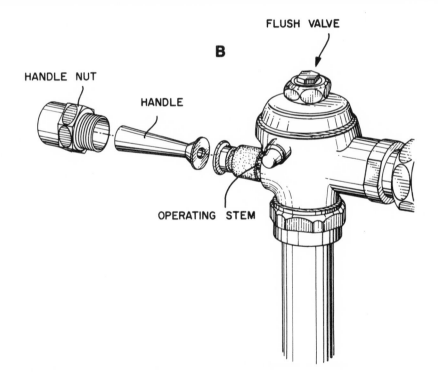

FLUSH VALVE

**B**

HANDLE NUT

HANDLE

OPERATING STEM

Figure 85.
Correcting the Water Flow

## 86. CLOGGED BLEEDER VALVE: WATER CONTINUES TO FLUSH WITHOUT STOPPING

More and more people are coming to love the American country-side. The greenery, the fauna in its natural habitat, the noisy silence of the evening—all do wonders for the urban soul. But everything in its place! It does less to our spirit and more to our nerves when the normally pleasant and contemplative sound of a babbling brook is issuing from a toilet in our apartment. *It will not stop flushing!* But relief is just a pinprick away.

UTENSILS

*Roll of masking tape*
*Smooth or flat-jaw adjustable*
   *wrench*
*Straight pin*
*Medium flat blade screwdriver*

INGREDIENTS

*Petroleum jelly*

APPROXIMATE TIME: 20 TO 25 MINUTES

- ☐ 1. Shut off water supply at valve stop or at main cutoff in basement.
- ☐ 2. Tape jaws of wrench or large cap to prevent damage to fixture.
- ☐ 3. Place wrench on large cap of cover assembly (Fig. 86A) and turn in counterclockwise direction until assembly is removed.
- ☐ 4. Place fingers inside flushometer and remove diaphragm assembly.
- ☐ 5. Examine bleeder valve bypass vulcanized into diaphragm. One side has a screen, the other a small pinhole (Fig. 86B and 86C).
- ☐ 6. Hold assembly up to light. If you cannot see any light through the pinhole, this is an indication that the bleeder valve is clogged.
- ☐ 7. Insert straight pin and punch through.
- ☐ 8. Now hold up to light. The pin should do the trick.
- ☐ 9. Reassemble into flush valve again as follows:
- ☐     a. Place seat guide downward into valve.
- ☐     b. Place auxiliary valve seat in center.
- ☐ 10. Lubricate threads with petroleum jelly and then replace cover assembly, tightening slowly.
- ☐ 11. Turn on water and test.
- ☐ 12. It may be necessary at this point to adjust the length of flush:

☐   a. Remove cap nut.
☐   b. Insert screwdriver through top of valve seat assembly, and turn in counterclockwise and clockwise directions until proper flush is achieved. Clockwise turning shortens the flush; counterclockwise turning lengthens it.
☐   c. Replace cap screw.
☐   d. Test flush.

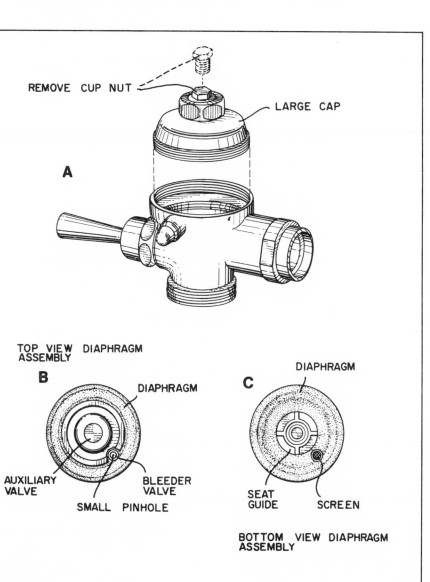

Figure 86.
Unclogging a Bleeder Valve

## 87. CONDENSATION ON COLD WATER PIPES

This simple and effective recipe offers a cure for the all-too-universal problem of sweating water pipes. This invariably occurs in areas of high humidity (usually basement), and particularly during warm weather months. Now, once and for all, clear up this annoying condition with the following antiperspirant!

UTENSILS
*Tape measure*
*Scissors*

INGREDIENTS
*Roll of fiberglass insulation*
*Roll of duct (cloth) tape*
*Roll of aluminum foil*
*Roll of tar paper*

APPROXIMATE TIME: HOW MUCH PIPE?

☐ *1.* Measure circumference of pipe with tape measure (Fig. 87A).
☐ *2.* Cut long strips of fiberglass, the width of each identical to the circumference of the pipe.
☐ *3.* Wrap fiberglass around pipe and tape in place (Fig. 87B).
☐ *4.* Wrap aluminum foil around fiberglass and tape in place (Fig. 87C).
☐ *5.* Now wrap tar paper around foil and tape firmly in place (Fig. 87D).
☐ *6.* No more sweat.

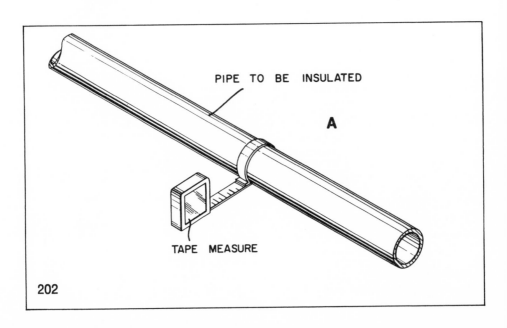

PIPE TO BE INSULATED

A

TAPE MEASURE

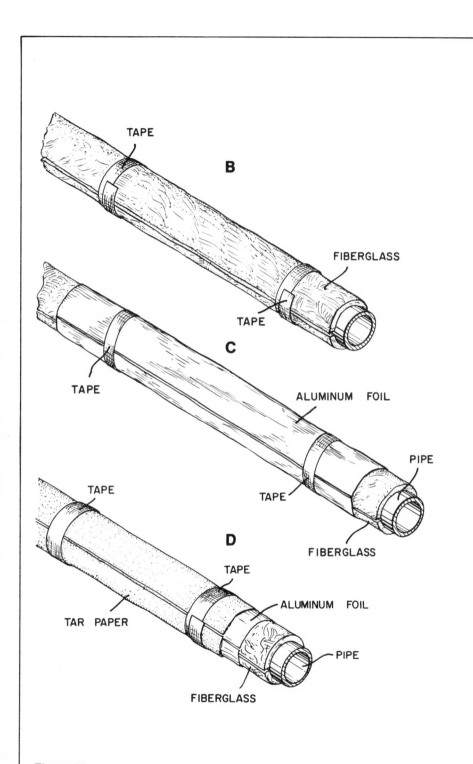

TAPE

**B**

FIBERGLASS

TAPE

**C**

TAPE

ALUMINUM FOIL

PIPE

FIBERGLASS

TAPE

**D**

TAPE

TAPE

ALUMINUM FOIL

TAR PAPER

PIPE

FIBERGLASS

Figure 87.
To Correct Sweating Pipes

## 88. PIPE LEAKS AT THREAD

Pipe leaks, whenever they occur, are messy, unpleasant, and sometimes dangerous affairs. If we were convinced there were humor in the situation, we'd crack a joke about it. But we don't find anything funny about the prices plumbers charge to make emergency repairs, especially on Saturdays, Sundays, and holidays when they are called away from their recreation.

This and the next three recipes offer quick-and-easy emergency measures to be taken when a plumber is not regularly available. They will provide relief and save you money in the bargain. The first of these is a permanent repair, while the others are stopgap procedures to be followed until an expert can be called in.

| UTENSILS | INGREDIENTS |
|---|---|
| *Paintbrush* | *Spool of white cotton thread* |
| *Medium flat blade screwdriver* | *Small amount of house paint* |
| *Hammer* | |

APPROXIMATE TIME: 30 MINUTES

☐ *1.* After locating leak, turn off water supply to pipe.
☐ *2.* Apply a coat of paint to leaking section of pipe.
☐ *3.* Wrap cotton thread around exposed sections of pipe thread in clockwise direction. Use thread liberally and wrap as close to fitting as possible (Fig. 88A).
☐ *4.* Using the point of the screwdriver as a wedge and tapping screwdriver handle gently with hammer, force thread into pipe joint all around (Fig. 88B).
☐ *5.* Apply a coat of paint over wound cotton thread (Fig. 88C).
☐ *6.* Repeat steps 3 and 4.
☐ *7.* Apply another coat of paint on cotton thread.
☐ *8.* Let dry.
☐ *9.* Reopen water supply and test patched area. If leak is not totally sealed, repeat procedure.

*Note:* Epoxy glue may be used instead of paint.

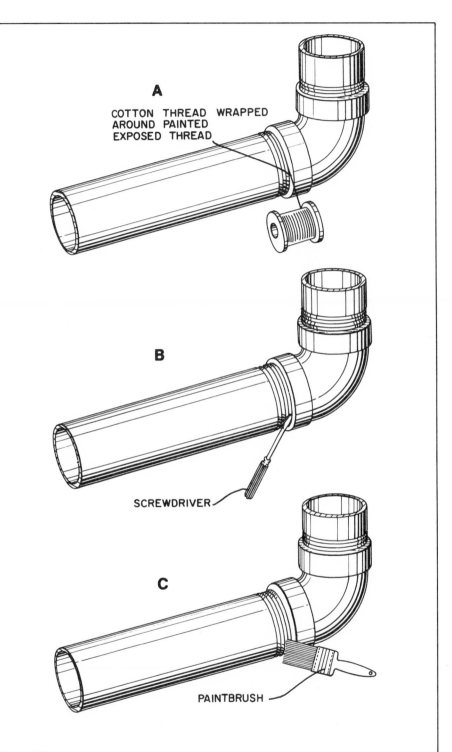

A

COTTON THREAD WRAPPED
AROUND PAINTED
EXPOSED THREAD

B

SCREWDRIVER

C

PAINTBRUSH

Figure 88.
Patching a Leaking Pipe

205

## 89. PINHOLES IN PIPE

This is the least troublesome repair to make on a leaky pipe. A pinhole just can't create a big hassle: a squirt here and there, but certainly not a flood. So be calm as you perform this simple task.

INGREDIENTS
*Box of round toothpicks*

APPROXIMATE TIME: 10 TO 15 MINUTES

☐ *1.* Locate pinhole in pipe (Fig. 89A). It is not necessary, for this recipe, to shut off water supply, though some find it desirable.

☐ *2.* Push toothpick as far as possible into pinhole (Fig. 89B).

☐ *3.* If you have shut off water supply, you may now turn it back on.

☐ *4.* The leak may persist for several moments, but it will cease once the toothpick has expanded in the hole.

☐ *5.* Call plumber when time allows, but not on weekends or holidays.

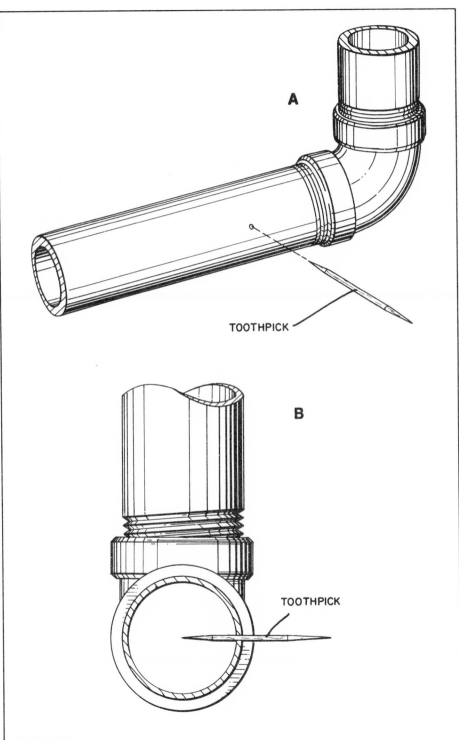

A

TOOTHPICK

B

TOOTHPICK

Figure 89.
To Stop a Small Leak

207

## 90. LEAKY PIPES: SEMIPERMANENT REPAIR

You already know about leaky pipes. But what is a semipermanent repair? It's not quite temporary, but it also should not remain unattended forever. So follow this recipe, and if a plumber happens to stumble by within the next six months, ask the fellow to complete the job in a slightly more professional manner.

UTENSILS
*Paintbrush*

INGREDIENTS
*Coarse sandpaper (see
    Abrasives Chart)*
*½ pint can polyester resin
    and catalyst*
*2-inch-wide strips of fiber-
    glass cloth, in rolls*
*Dry rags*
*Acetone brush cleaner*

APPROXIMATE TIME: 30 TO 40 MINUTES

- ☐ *1.* Shut off main water supply.
- ☐ *2.* Dry off pipe thoroughly.
- ☐ *3.* Sandpaper pipe 6 inches around leakage area (Fig. 90A).
- ☐ *4.* Mix polyester resin and catalyst as described on can. Read directions carefully for exact application and precautions.
- ☐ *5.* Apply mixture to and around leakage area with paintbrush (Fig. 90B).
- ☐ *6.* Wrap fiberglass strip around leakage area, bandage style (Fig. 90C).
- ☐ *7.* Apply second coat of resin mixture over fiberglass cloth.
- ☐ *8.* Wrap second strip of fiberglass over second coat of mixture.
- ☐ *9.* Apply remainder of resin mixture to fiberglass.
- ☐ *10.* Clean brush immediately before polyester resin hardens.
- ☐ *11.* Let dry 6 to 8 hours or overnight.
- ☐ *12.* Turn on water supply again.

*Note:* Epoxy glue may be substituted for polyester resin.

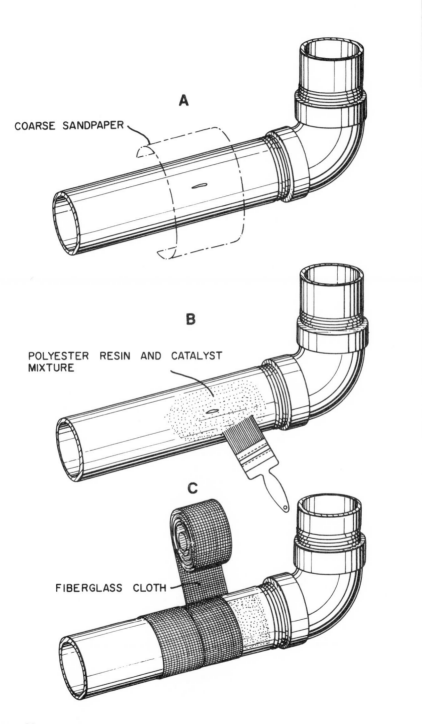

A

COARSE SANDPAPER

B

POLYESTER RESIN AND CATALYST
MIXTURE

C

FIBERGLASS CLOTH

Figure 90.
Another Way to Stop a Leak

## 91. LARGE HOLES IN PIPES OR WATER TANKS

We could never figure out how a torpedoed ship in those good old war movies could stay afloat with a huge section of its hull torn out. But we found out the damage-control procedure, and we'd like to pass it along to you for nonhostile use. Aboard a leaky ship it is impossible to turn off the ocean; but in your home, all you have to do is turn a valve. Do so immediately when a large hole is detected. Note: If there is a flood in your basement, allow water to recede before beginning to work. No need to risk electrocution.

UTENSILS
*Pocketknife*
*Hammer or hatchet*

INGREDIENTS
*Small block of pine or other*
  *soft wood*

APPROXIMATE TIME: 30 TO 60 MINUTES

☐  *1.* Shut off water supply at main valve.
☐  *2.* Having established the location and size of hole to be plugged, carve out a wedge of wood from the block to match it.
☐  *3.* Insert wedge into hole and secure it there by gently tapping with hammer (Fig. 91A).
☐  *4.* Carve out several additional splinter-type wedges from the remaining portion of the block.
☐  *5.* Tap in a few of these wedges to further seal any openings the larger wedge failed to close (Fig. 91B).
☐  *6.* If there is still some leakage, drive additional small wedges into spot(s) from which leak is issuing. The leak will continue until wood expands in hole.
☐  *7.* Call plumber as soon as possible, but don't get him out of bed on Saturdays, Sundays, or holidays.

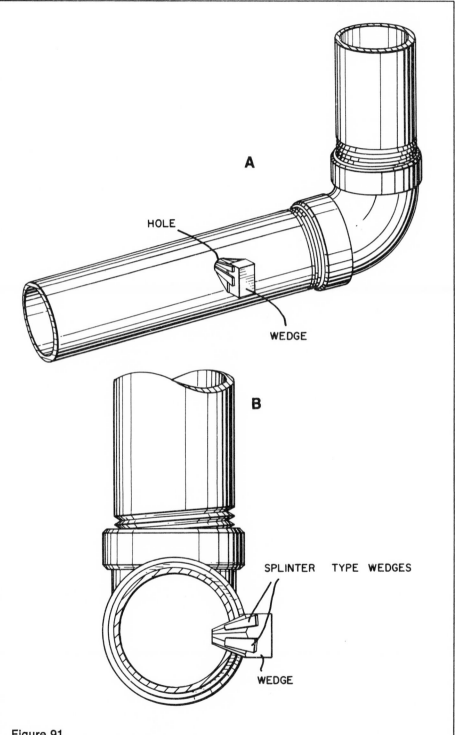

A

HOLE

WEDGE

B

SPLINTER TYPE WEDGES

WEDGE

Figure 91.
To Stop Leak from Large Hole

211

## 92. LEAKS IN WATER TANKS

We frankly offer this recipe with a good deal of reservation. Our feeling is that, should an old ferrous-type water tank, which has neither permanent insulation nor glass lining, develop a large hole, it is far better to buy a new tank than to spend money repairing the old one. However, it is necessary to know emergency alternatives, and so we provide the following procedure.

UTENSILS
*Ice pick or center punch*
*Hammer*
*Wrench*

INGREDIENTS
*Several self-tapping tank*
*plugs of various sizes*
*Ace plugs of various sizes*

APPROXIMATE TIME: 30 MINUTES

- ☐ *1.* Shut off water supply.
- ☐ *2.* Locate leak in tank (Fig. 92A).
- ☐ *3.* If leak is small, insert ice pick or center punch and enlarge slightly.
- ☐ *4.* Insert smallest self-tapping plug (Fig. 92B), turning clockwise with adjustable wrench until washer bulges slightly. Do not overtighten.
- ☐ *5.* If hole is large to begin with, it will be necessary to use a larger self-tapping plug. To find the plug of the right size, it is advisable to start with the smallest and work from there.
- ☐ *6.* Once you have found the right plug, insert as in step 4.
- ☐ *7.* If hole is extremely large, it may be necessary to ream out and then insert a large bolt-type Ace-plug or utility plug (Fig. 92C). But if the hole is really that large, it is best to start shopping for a new tank.
- ☐ *8.* Turn on water and test plugged hole for leakage.

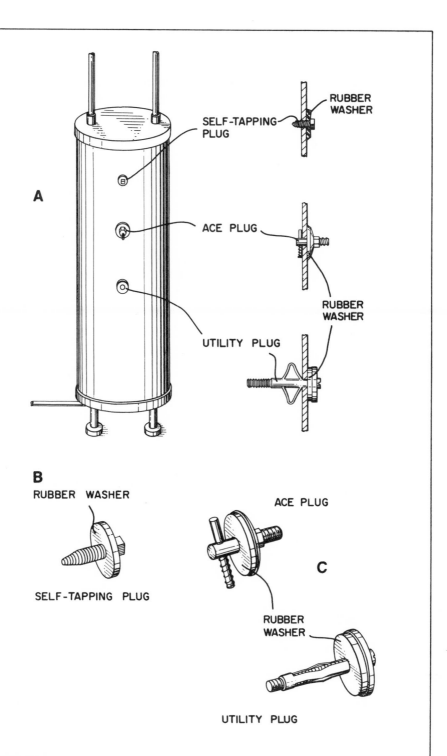

RUBBER WASHER

SELF-TAPPING PLUG

ACE PLUG

RUBBER WASHER

UTILITY PLUG

**A**

**B**

RUBBER WASHER

SELF-TAPPING PLUG

ACE PLUG

**C**

RUBBER WASHER

UTILITY PLUG

Figure 92.
To Repair a Water Tank

213

## 93. REPAIRING LEAKY PIPE WITH COMMERCIALLY MANUFACTURED PIPE CLAMP

We call this a semipermanent repair, but in all truth, it is as close to the perfect repair on a leaky pipe as possible. This clamp, as you will discover, is a fantastic and effective device. It is so convenient to install that it is not even necessary to turn off the water supply if you have a small leak. Still, it is best that you shut down the water source before working.

Another advantage of this device is that it may be used to stop leaks on all pipes, regardless of type or size. The only difficulty (we can hardly call it that) for the layperson is in the ordering. You must first measure the outer diameter of the pipe with a ruler and then subtract ¼ inch when ordering the clamp at the hardware store. If your pipe measures ¾ inch, ask for a ½-inch clamp, and so on.

UTENSILS
*Adjustable wrench*

INGREDIENTS
*Pipe clamp with bolts and
    nuts
Rubber or leather gasket*

APPROXIMATE TIME: 15 MINUTES

☐  1. Place midsection of rubber or leather gasket (Fig. 93A) over leaky section of pipe.
☐  2. Place clamp around gasket onto pipe, making sure that the midsection of the clamp is over the hole. See Figure 93B.
☐  3. Tighten nuts onto bolts with wrench.
☐  4. If leaks persist, tighten bolts uniformly until leaks cease.

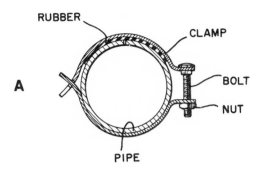

RUBBER

CLAMP

A

BOLT

NUT

PIPE

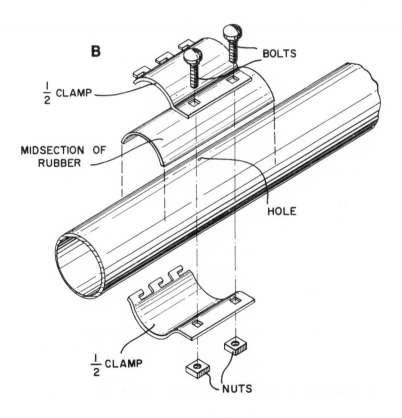

B

BOLTS

$\frac{1}{2}$ CLAMP

MIDSECTION OF
RUBBER

HOLE

$\frac{1}{2}$ CLAMP

NUTS

Figure 93.
Installing a Pipe Clamp

## 94. REPLACING SINK SPRAYER HOSE

This one is a little more difficult than the preceding recipe, but if you follow the steps carefully and pay special attention to the illustrations, the job of replacing a worn or eroded sink sprayer hose will take no more than an hour. Note: We suggest you follow our method of connecting hose. It lasts much longer that way.

UTENSILS
*Adjustable wrench*
*Pliers*
*Screwdriver*
*Small pipe wrench*
*Small paintbrush*

INGREDIENTS
*6-inch length of ⅛-inch*
*brass nipple*
*Ball of lampwick or cotton*
*thread*
*Pipe dope or small can of*
*oil paint*
*⅛-inch brass elbow*
*⅛-inch universal brass*
*coupling*
*New hose*

APPROXIMATE TIME: 60 MINUTES

☐  *1.* Examine the connection of the worn hose beneath the sink valves. If the connection is not as it appears in Figure 94, chances are the hose is broken just below the connecting point because of excess tension placed on it during normal operation.
☐  *2.* With adjustable wrench, unscrew male end of old hose from valve body or fitting beneath counter top in a counter-clockwise direction. If the fittings are the same as in Figure 94, do not disturb them. Disregard nipple and elbow in Ingredients list and proceed directly to step 8.
☐  *3.* Wind lampwick or cotton thread around the male threads at the end of the new nipple.
☐  *4.* Apply pipe dope or paint to the ends of all fittings.
☐  *5.* Screw all fittings together, as shown in Figure 94, including elbow at bottom of nipple.
☐  *6.* Tighten all fittings securely with wrench in clockwise direction.
☐  *7.* When elbow is secure, it must be facing the direction from which the new hose will be coming.
☐  *8.* Insert male end of new hose through hole in sink top or valve body.

216

☐ 9. Wrap threads of male end of hose with several turns of cotton thread. Apply pipe dope or paint with brush.
☐ 10. With jaws of adjustable wrench firmly around male end of new hose, screw male end into elbow, turning a clockwise direction until snug.
☐ 11. Turn water on at valve body to test connection.

> *Note:* It is sometimes necessary to remove sprayer head before connecting hose. See Recipe 95 for removal procedure.

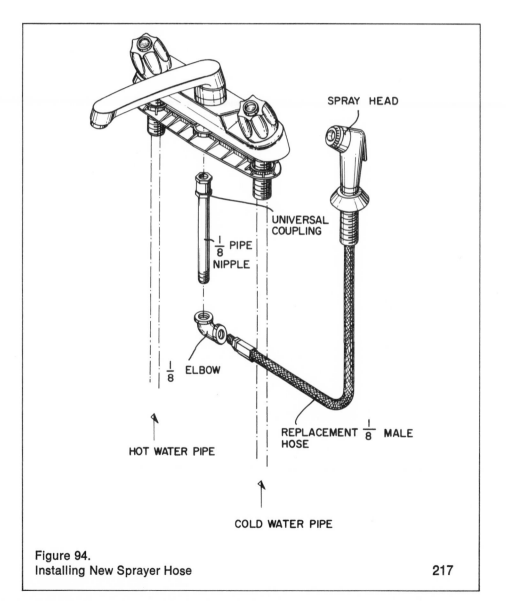

**Figure 94.**
Installing New Sprayer Hose

217

## 95. REPLACING SINK SPRAYER HEAD

Having a sink sprayer is a kick, we know. But it's absolutely no fun at all when it starts spraying you in the face. It's downright gloomy when it doesn't work at all. If your sprayer is malfunctioning in one fashion or another, you'll have to fix it. It looks like a tough job, but don't be fooled. It's as simple as installing a nozzle on a garden hose!

UTENSILS
*Pliers*
*Screwdriver*

INGREDIENTS
*New coupling and washer*
*New sprayer nozzle*

APPROXIMATE TIME: 15 MINUTES

□ *1.* Grasp nozzle in one hand (Fig. 95A).
□ *2.* With pliers in the other hand, grasp coupling firmly, but not too firmly.
□ *3.* Now unscrew the nozzle head in a counterclockwise direction and remove. The washer that is at the end of the hose must be snapped off. If it is still in good condition, keep it.
□ *4.* Slide coupling back slightly over hose. This will reveal the wire snap ring (Fig. 95B).
□ *5.* Pry snap ring off with screwdriver and retain.
□ *6.* Now slide old coupling off hose.
□ *7.* Now slide new coupling over hose so threads are facing outward.
□ *8.* Reinsert wire snap ring into place on rubber hose.
□ *9.* Place washer at the end of the hose, behind the coupling.
□ *10.* Screw new sprayer nozzle into coupling.
□ *11.* Grasp coupling with pliers and turn nozzle one-eighth of a turn. Do not overtighten!
□ *12.* Turn on water faucet and test new nozzle.

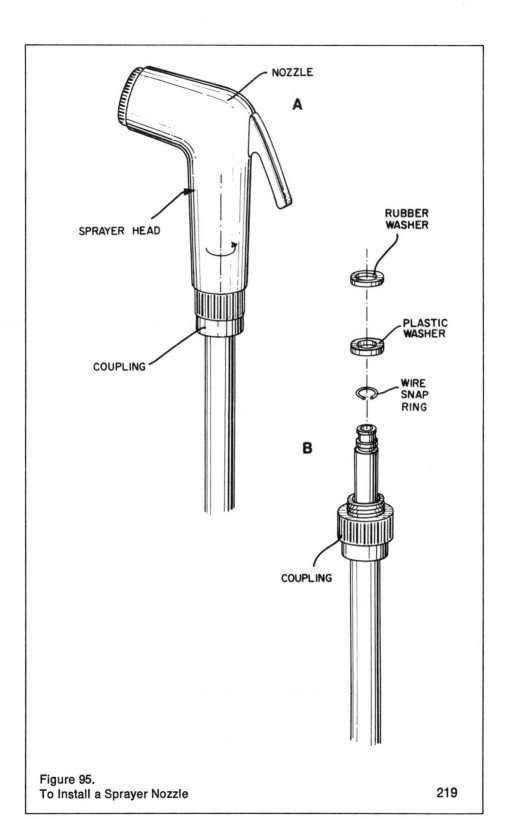

NOZZLE

A

SPRAYER HEAD

COUPLING

RUBBER
WASHER

PLASTIC
WASHER

WIRE
SNAP
RING

B

COUPLING

Figure 95.
To Install a Sprayer Nozzle

219

## 96. REPAIRING GARDEN HOSE

The next time you use your garden hose to wash your car or water the lawn and find that you are getting watered as much as the grass, it's time to check your hose for holes. Don't throw out the hose just because of a few sprinkle holes. Fix it. That's why you bought this book!

UTENSILS
*Pocketknife*
*Hammer*
*Shallow dish of hot water*
  *(for plastic hose)*

INGREDIENTS
*2 tubes epoxy glue, 1*
  *hardener, 1 adhesive*
*Proper size hose coupling*
*Hose coupling washers*

APPROXIMATE TIME: 15 TO 20 MINUTES PER COUPLING

- [ ] *1.* Cut away section of hose in need of repair (Fig. 96A).
- [ ] *2.* Take cutaway section to hardware store to match up couplings, whether male, female, or joint couplings.
- [ ] *3.* Mix small amount of epoxy glue as directed on package.
- [ ] *4.* Smear glue onto corrugated end of coupling (Fig. 96B).
- [ ] *5.* Insert corrugated end of coupling into hose. See Figure 96B.
- [ ] *6.* If hose is plastic, place ends of hose into hot water to soften, and then insert coupling (Fig. 96C).
- [ ] *7.* Hammer down fingers or clamps all the way around hose, tapping gently until secure (Fig. 96D and 96E), allow glue to harden.
- [ ] *8.* With female couplings, insert washer.
- [ ] *9.* Hose may then be connected to hose bib valve or other female hose.

220

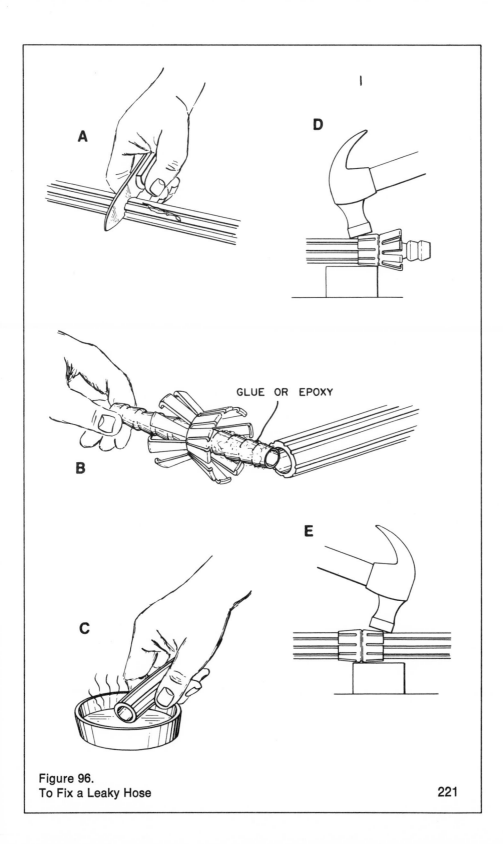

GLUE OR EPOXY

Figure 96.
To Fix a Leaky Hose

221

**PART V**

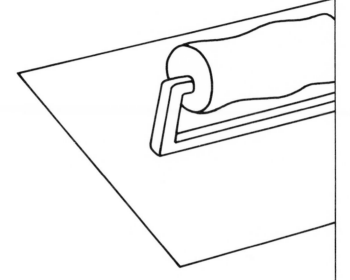

# Masonry

Sunlight, rain, wind, heat, and cold are all agents of erosion. And time, which waiteth for no man, will lay waste to your bricks and concrete in its course. It's a fact and a problem that must be dealt with by the homeowner. We cannot, unfortunately, prescribe the ingredients for a perfect brick wall. Even the wondrous Netherlands dikes have trouble. You all remember the Dutch boy and his famous finger of fate?

Fortunately, one or two or even a half dozen or so loose bricks on the facing of your home, or on your porch or stoop, will not bring down your house. Of that we can assure you. But, like the song says, ". . . if two and two and fifty make a million . . ." then things can be tough. Before that happens, look carefully at your walls and periodically check for loose or broken bricks and replace them immediately. And watch those concrete walls for unsightly and potentially dangerous cracks.

Masonry work is fun. There is no question about it. And what's more fun is all the money you'll be saving by doing it yourself. Have you any idea what a bricklayer charges these days?

The illustrations in this section will show you what beautiful masonry is all about. Check your brick walls against the ones shown and see if you can identify the bond style of your home. For that matter, look around at your neighbors' homes, and look at old buildings wherever you go. You'll be pleased at your ability to differentiate between the variety of bonds in existence.

The items below represent an adequate array of equipment and material to handle all but major jobs. If you have a really serious problem, do not hesitate to call in a person who can handle it quickly and expertly.

*Pointing tools, sizes as*
  *necessary*
*Cold chisel*
*Hammer*
*Wooden float trowel*
*Cement trowel*
*Smooth steel trowel, 12 inches*
  *long*
*Garden hose*

*Mixing pan*
*Steel water bucket*
*Mortar mix color and amount*
  *to meet your needs*
*Cement mixes of various types*
  *for different jobs*
*Burlap on canvas*
*Several pieces of 2 by 4 lumber,*
  *3 to 4 feet long*

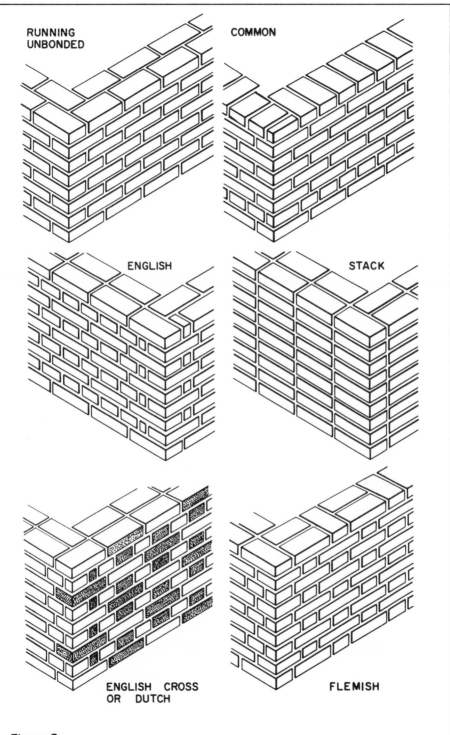

RUNNING UNBONDED

COMMON

ENGLISH

STACK

ENGLISH CROSS
OR DUTCH

FLEMISH

Figure G.
Brick Faces

# CEMENT COMPUTER

This handy chart contains valuable information for all large masonry repairs. Essentially, it is a purchasing guide, as it tells you precisely the quantity of materials you will need for a given job.

| KIND OF MIX | BAG WEIGHTS | COVERAGE AREA |
|---|---|---|
| **Mortar Mix**<br>For joints between brick, stone, cinder and concrete blocks | 20, 45, 80 pounds | 80-pound bag provides for laying approximately 40 to 50 bricks or 15 to 20 blocks |
| **Sand Mix**<br>For filling cracks in cement walks, steps, stucco walls, foundations | 11, 20, 40, 45, 80 pounds | 80-pound bag will cover 8 square feet with 1-inch topping |
| **Concrete Mix**<br>For post collars, building steps, and walks | 45, 90 pounds | 90-pound bag will make ⅔ cubic feet or enough to cover 12 inch by 12 inch by 9 inch area |
| **Waterproof Mix**<br>For topcoat surfaces around pools, on walks and steps | 45, 80 pounds | 80-pound bag will cover 16 square feet with ½-inch topping |
| **Blacktop** | 66, 80 pounds | 66-pound bag will patch 6-square-foot area, 1-inch thick |
| **Plaster Mix** | 2, 5, 10, 25 pounds | 1 pound covers 1 square foot 3/16 inch thick |

## 97. LOOSE BRICKWORK

Time was when a loose and removable brick was a sort of home vault behind which one's life possessions could be hidden. But today, we have bank and safe-deposit boxes, and a loose brick is nothing but a nuisance. The job takes a little time, but any person can reset single bricks or even an entire course of bricks with hardly any effort.

UTENSILS
*Cold chisel*
*Hammer*
*Garden hose*
*Water bucket or deep pan*
*Mixing pan*
*Small cement trowel or*
  *gardening trowel or*
  *2½-inch spackle knife*
*Spirit Level, 18 inches long*
*Burlap cloth or canvas*

INGREDIENTS
*Dry mortar mix, color to*
  *match*
*Water*

APPROXIMATE TIME: 60 MINUTES, SMALL JOB

☐  *1.* Remove all loose bricks (Fig. 97A).
☐  *2.* Remove old mortar that has adhered to bricks with hammer and chisel.
☐  *3.* Chisel brick beds clean of old mortar.
☐  *4.* Place bricks in water bucket and let stand for a few hours.
☐  *5.* Before mixing new mortar, wet down brick beds with garden hose.
☐  *6.* Mix mortar in pan, adding small quantities of water until the mortar becomes plastic but very thick. The drier the mix the better.
☐  *7.* Remove bricks from water and shake off excess water.
☐  *8.* With trowel, lay small amount of mortar into brick bed (Fig. 97B). Do not spread.
☐  *9.* "Butter" edges of brick with mortar.
☐ *10.* Place brick into position and tap down on it gently with trowel handle until mortar overflows under the pressure (Fig. 97C). Make sure that newly bedded brick is even with other bricks.
☐ *11.* Clean away excess mortar, making sure none falls on lower brickwork.

☐ *12.* Repeat procedure for all bricks, including top course, checking periodically for level.

☐ *13.* Place full water bucket on top course of bricks to prevent unwanted movement during hardening period.

☐ *14.* After several hours, the handle of the trowel or a pointing tool, or a pipe may be used to smooth out mortar. Mortar should be slightly recessed from brick face, not flush.

☐ *15.* Remove bucket from top course of bricks.

☐ *16.* After a full day of hardening, the brickwork may be cleaned with water. If any excess mortar has hardened on bricks, remove it carefully with hammer and chisel.

**A**

REMOVE ALL
LOOSE BRICKS

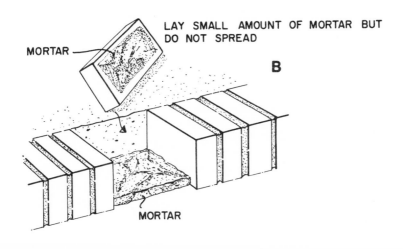

LAY SMALL AMOUNT OF MORTAR BUT DO NOT SPREAD

MORTAR

**B**

MORTAR

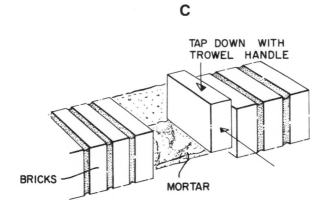

**C**

TAP DOWN WITH TROWEL HANDLE

BRICKS

MORTAR

Figure 97.
To Repair Loose Brickwork

229

## 98. POINTING IN BRICKWORK

If we cannot offer instant, magical brick repair, we can offer the next best thing—a *tool* that points brick mortar into place.

One word of caution: when working with bricks or other masonry, it is best to avoid direct sunlight. If this is not possible, keep a damp burlap cloth or canvas handy to cover brickwork, thus preventing premature hardening.

UTENSILS
*Hammer*
*Screwdriver or cold chisel*
*Garden hose*
*Mixing pan*
*Pointing tool*
*Steel bucket*
*Burlap cloth or canvas*

INGREDIENTS
*Dry mortar mix*

APPROXIMATE TIME: DEPENDS ON NUMBER OF BRICKS

☐ *1.* Chip away loose mortar between bricks with hammer and chisel (Fig. 98A).
☐ *2.* Water down brickwork with hose, washing away loose mortar.
☐ *3.* Mix concrete mortar in pan, adding water from the bucket a little at a time. The drier the mix the stronger and more workable it will be.
☐ *4.* With pointing tool, lay in a small quantity of mortar in desired place and smooth over (Fig. 98B).
☐ *5.* Continue as necessary until all joints have been repointed.
☐ *6.* Mortar must be recessed from brick face, not flush.
☐ *7.* Cover brickwork with damp burlap or canvas if in direct sunlight.
☐ *8.* Let dry overnight.

*Note:* Pointing tools come in all sizes, conforming to the variable spacing in different brickwork. Measure the joints in your brickwork before purchasing tool. Joints will vary from ¼ inch to 1½ inches. A ½-inch diameter plumber's pipe may be used in lieu of pointing tool.

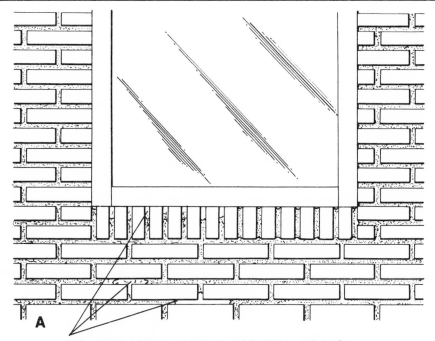

**A**

CHIP AWAY LOOSE MORTAR BETWEEN BRICKS
WITH HAMMER AND CHISEL

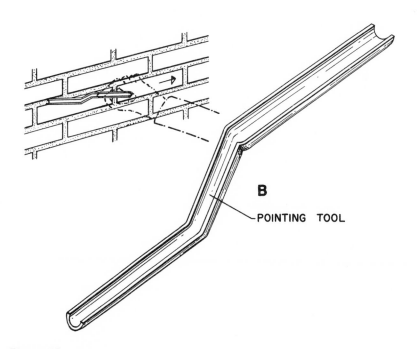

**B**

POINTING TOOL

Figure 98.
Use of Pointing Tool

## 99. PATCHING A FOUNDATION CRACK

Unfortunately, cracked concrete, like glass, can never be completely repaired. If you're worried about your foundation, don't play your Caruso records in the basement. If, however, a crack develops in the foundation wall, it is easily patched and will prevent leakage as effectively as when the wall was new. But remember: all foundation work can only be done on the inside of the structure as the exterior wall of the foundation is beneath the ground and very tough to get to.

UTENSILS
*Ball peen hammer*
*Cold chisel, 1-inch edge*
*Wire brush*
*Paintbrush*

INGREDIENTS
*Roll of fiberglass cloth*
*Quart can of polyester resin*
*Tube of polyester catalyst*

APPROXIMATE TIME: 90 MINUTES, DEPENDING ON SIZE AND LOCATION OF CRACK

☐ *1.* Chisel out a V-shaped groove where crack is located—approximately ½ inch deep into the foundation wall for the entire length of crack (Fig. 99A).
☐ *2.* Clean 12 inches both sides of groove with wire brush (Fig. 99B).
☐ *3.* Make chipping marks 6 inches on both sides of groove, 3 or 4 inches apart.
☐ *4.* Cut piece of fiberglass cloth to cover groove.
☐ *5.* Mix half of a can of resin, and catalyst, as directed on can. Observe precautions.
☐ *6.* Apply mixture liberally with paintbrush to groove and 12-inch adjacent area.
☐ *7.* Lay fiberglass cloth in groove (Fig. 99C).
☐ *8.* Apply heavy coat of resin mixture to fiberglass cloth, eliminating air bubbles as you go.
☐ *9.* Let dry 1 hour.
☐ *10.* Mix second half of polyester.
☐ *11.* Apply and reapply remainder of resin mixture over fiberglass cloth until mixture is gone.
☐ *12.* Let dry. This will do the trick.
☐ *13.* Discard can and brush in waste can.

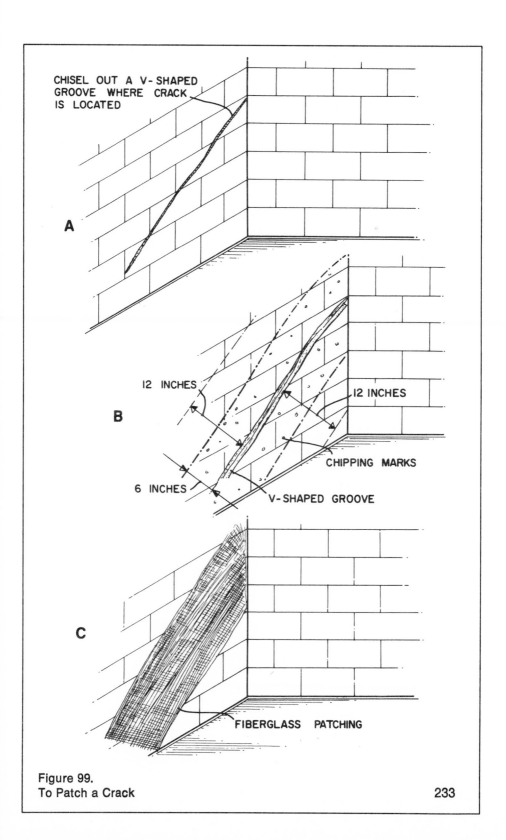

CHISEL OUT A V-SHAPED GROOVE WHERE CRACK IS LOCATED

A

B

12 INCHES

12 INCHES

6 INCHES

CHIPPING MARKS

V-SHAPED GROOVE

C

FIBERGLASS PATCHING

Figure 99.
To Patch a Crack

233

## 100. DRAWING A LEAK DOWN TO THE FLOOR: CRACKS IN FOUNDATION WALL

You've noticed by now that we are modest. But this recipe is simply spectacular! You can do it like a professional and save a fortune—to say nothing about restoring colossal strength to your foundation.

UTENSILS
*Ball peen hammer*
*Cold chisel*
*Wire brush*
*Sponge*
*Mixing pan*
*Smooth steel trowel, 12*
  *inches long*
*Water bucket*

INGREDIENTS
*Petroleum jelly*
*Dry mortar mix*
*Ball of heavy string*

APPROXIMATE TIME: 2 HOURS PER CRACK

☐ *1.* With hammer and chisel, form a V-shaped groove by chiseling 1 inch on either side of the foundation crack, using the crack itself as the center of the groove (Fig. 100A).

☐ *2.* Clean entire area with wire brush.

☐ *3.* Clean groove with wet sponge and allow to remain damp.

☐ *4.* Cut a length of string twice the length of the crack.

☐ *5.* Lubricate string liberally with petroleum jelly.

☐ *6.* Lay string gently into groove, allowing surplus string to lay on floor (Fig. 100B).

☐ *7.* Mix mortar. The drier the mix, the stronger it will be. Add water slowly, a bit at a time.

☐ *8.* Trowel mortar into groove, covering the string in the groove but allowing its tail to rest on the floor 90 degrees to the wall (Fig. 100C).

☐ *9.* Smooth out patched area with trowel.

☐ *10.* Let dry 1 hour.

☐ *11.* With chisel, press string gently into the wall-floor joint (Fig. 100C).

☐ *12.* With free hand, gently withdraw string. The petroleum jelly will allow for easy removal.

☐ *13.* Allow patch to dry overnight.

234

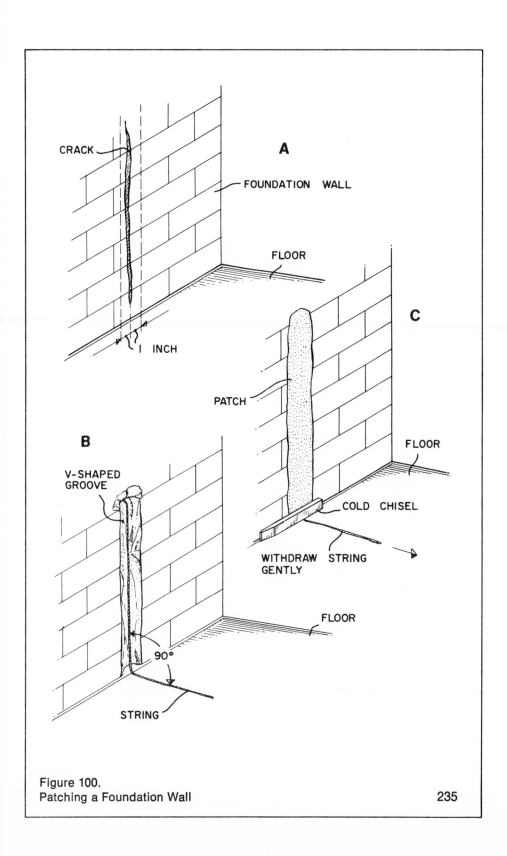

CRACK

FOUNDATION WALL

**A**

FLOOR

1 INCH

**C**

PATCH

FLOOR

COLD CHISEL

WITHDRAW STRING
GENTLY

**B**

V-SHAPED
GROOVE

FLOOR

90°

STRING

Figure 100.
Patching a Foundation Wall

235

## 101. PATCHING CRACKS IN CONCRETE

Now we come to the irksome subject of broken concrete. Don't turn the page, please. You already know the danger of falling into a hole in the ground. You already know about liability suits if someone takes a spill on your property, so we won't remind you of either. What we WILL pass on is this: we have it on good authority that Jack's legendary bean stalk actually grew out of a break in someone's concrete walk.

All kidding aside, it is wise to patch these unsightly and dangerous canals. We also advise that you check local municipal regulations concerning repairs on public street walks.

UTENSILS
*Hammer*
*Cold chisel*
*Garden hose*
*Mixing pan*
*1 piece of 2 by 4, 3 feet long*
*12-inch smooth steel trowel*
*Wooden float trowel*
*Water bucket*
*Burlap cloth or canvas*

INGREDIENTS
*Dry sand-mix concrete, in*
  *bag size necessary for*
  *the job*

APPROXIMATE TIME: YOU TELL US

☐ 1. Remove loose cement with hammer and chisel (Fig. 101A).
☐ 2. Wash crack thoroughly with garden hose.
☐ 3. Mix concrete in pan, adding water a little at a time. The drier the mix, the stronger and more workable it will be.
☐ 4. Pour concrete into area to be patched.
☐ 5. Level surface with 2 by 4 (Fig. 101B).
☐ 6. Remove excess concrete and smooth surface with steel trowel.
☐ 7. Allow to dry for 30 minutes.
☐ 8. Rub lightly over area in circular fashion with wooden float trowel. This will produce a granular surface extremely desirable for outdoor concrete. (For indoor concrete use steel trowel only.)
☐ 9. Lay damp burlap cloth or canvas over patched area until hardening is complete.

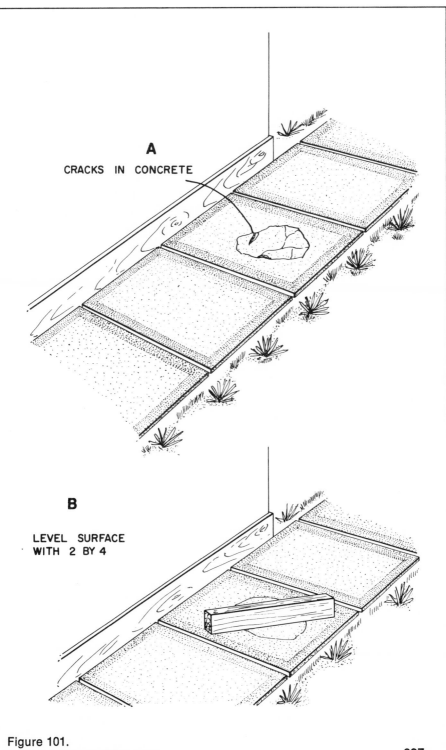

**A**

CRACKS IN CONCRETE

**B**

LEVEL SURFACE
WITH 2 BY 4

Figure 101.
To Patch Cracked Concrete

237

## 102. PATCHING ASPHALT DRIVEWAYS

Potholes in a driveway can be dangerous for many reasons. In cold weather they will collect moisture and form slippery ice pockets. Moreover, the pothole in the driveway is like the proverbial leak in the dike: the condition is progressive.

UTENSILS
*Shovel*
*Stiff broom*
*Tamping tool (rentable) or*
   *5-foot length of 2 by 4*
*6-inch by 6-inch by ¾-inch*
   *plywood, nailed to one end*
   *of 2 by 4*
*Paintbrush*

INGREDIENTS
*Gravel, if a large hole*
*Can of liquid tar*
*Asphalt cold patch, available*
   *at hardware stores*

APPROXIMATE TIME: DEPENDS ON SIZE OF HOLE

☐ *1.* Clean area to be patched with shovel and broom (Fig. 102A). Area must be dry.
☐ *2.* Fill in large holes with gravel to 1 inch below driveway surface (Fig. 102B).
☐ *3.* Tamp down gravel compactly with tamping tool (Fig. 102C).
☐ *4.* Paint area generously with liquid tar (Fig. 102D).
☐ *5.* Pour in asphalt cold patch (Fig. 102D).
☐ *6.* Tamp down with tamping tool or by running your automobile back and forth over patch.
☐ *7.* Add more asphalt and repeat tamping until surface is smooth and tight.
☐ *8.* Let surface dry for several days before driving or walking on it.

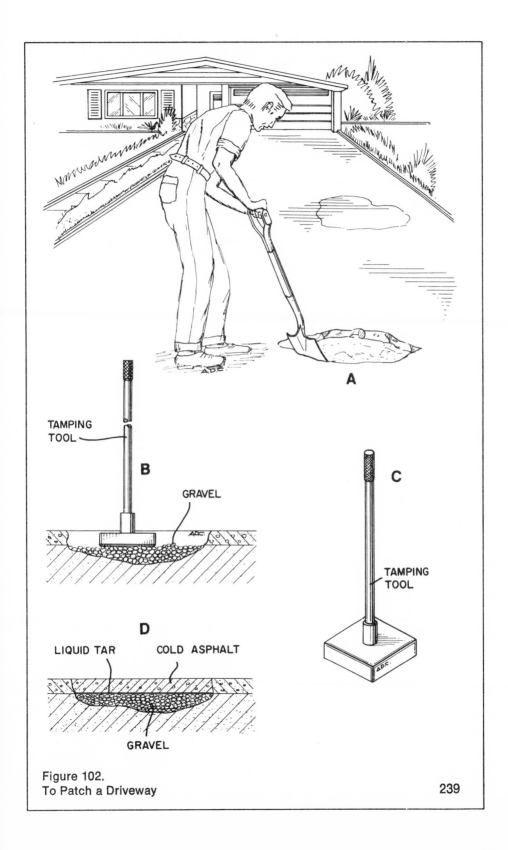

TAMPING TOOL

**B**

GRAVEL

**A**

**C**

TAMPING TOOL

**D**

LIQUID TAR   COLD ASPHALT

GRAVEL

Figure 102.
To Patch a Driveway

239

**PART VI**

# Charts
# and
# Tables

The following tables and charts are meant to be a miniature home-repair reference center for the reader. The information contained within them is valuable and timeless. Some of them, particularly the table of Ladder Safety Rules and the Fire Prevention Checklist, are meant to be studied carefully or even memorized. Others —charts on abrasives, lubricants, adhesives, etc.—can be used only when very specific information is required for a particular task.

## SCREWS AND NAILS

There is little we can tell you about screws and nails—except, of course, that they hold the world together and, like people, they come in all sizes, shapes, colors, with and without heads.

One's selection of screws and nails for home repair jobs is important: you simply cannot choose a 16 penny nail (see chart) to hammer together 2 quarter-inch pieces of plywood. Nor could you make use of a one-half-inch finishing nail to join a couple of two-by-fours. It simply won't work.

Screws must also be carefully selected for appropriate jobs. Screws fall into two general categories: wood screws and metal screws. But don't be confused—both types are actually *made* of metal. Wood screws have shanks tapered to a sharp point, and they are designed to be driven into wood. Metal screws have untapered shanks and are designed to be driven through *already existing holes in metal* and fastened at the other end with a nut.

Screws are calibrated in diameter size. Nails are measured in penny (d) weight. See the two charts that follow. We suggest that the reader stock up on screws and nails as a general household staple. Using the accompanying charts as a guide, go to your nearest hardware store and get a generous assortment of each.

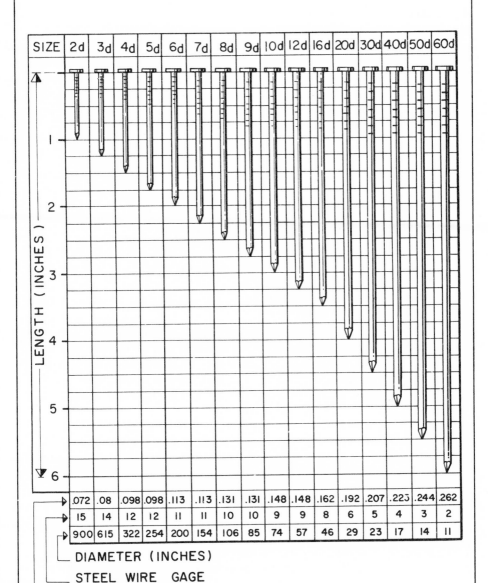

| SIZE | 2d | 3d | 4d | 5d | 6d | 7d | 8d | 9d | 10d | 12d | 16d | 20d | 30d | 40d | 50d | 60d |
|------|-----|-----|------|------|------|------|------|------|------|------|------|------|------|------|------|------|
| DIAMETER (INCHES) | .072 | .08 | .098 | .098 | .113 | .113 | .131 | .131 | .148 | .148 | .162 | .192 | .207 | .223 | .244 | .262 |
| STEEL WIRE GAGE | 15 | 14 | 12 | 12 | 11 | 11 | 10 | 10 | 9 | 9 | 8 | 6 | 5 | 4 | 3 | 2 |
| NUMBER PER POUND | 900 | 615 | 322 | 254 | 200 | 154 | 106 | 85 | 74 | 57 | 46 | 29 | 23 | 17 | 14 | 11 |

LENGTH (INCHES)

Figure H.
Common Nails Sizes

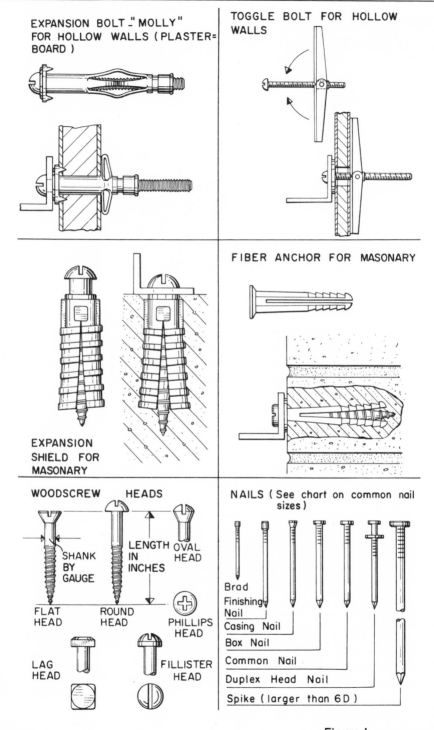

EXPANSION BOLT ."MOLLY" FOR HOLLOW WALLS (PLASTER=BOARD )

TOGGLE BOLT FOR HOLLOW WALLS

EXPANSION SHIELD FOR MASONARY

FIBER ANCHOR FOR MASONARY

WOODSCREW HEADS

SHANK BY GAUGE

LENGTH IN INCHES

OVAL HEAD

FLAT HEAD

ROUND HEAD

PHILLIPS HEAD

LAG HEAD

FILLISTER HEAD

NAILS ( See chart on common nail sizes )

Brad
Finishing Nail
Casing Nail
Box Nail
Common Nail
Duplex Head Nail
Spike ( larger than 6 D )

Figure I.
Common Fasteners

## LADDER SAFETY RULES

**Follow these instructions for your safety and that of others:**

Never use chairs or books. Never straddle a chair and a window sill. It's not worth a crippling fall. Use the proper ladder.

1. Inspect ladder carefully when you buy it and before each use. Test all movable parts for proper attachment and operation. Ladders that are damaged or defective after you've owned them a while should be marked Do Not Use.
2. Keep nuts, bolts, and other fastenings tight. Oil moving metal parts regularly. Obtain replacement parts from original manufacturer. Never use a ladder on which you have performed a makeshift repair. Never straighten a bent metal ladder.
3. Ladders must stand on a firm, level surface. Use the appropriate nonslip feet or nonslip bases. Take additional precautions if using ladder on a slippery floor.
4. Always FACE the ladder when ascending or descending.
5. Place ladder close enough to work to avoid hazardous overreaching. Keep your weight centered between the side rails.
6. Keep steps of rungs free of grease, oil, paint, and other slippery substances.
7. Ladder should be fully opened before ascending. Never stand on pail rest or on the top of the ladder.
8. Never ascend the rear steps of the ladder.
9. Never place ladders in front of doors unless precautions are taken.
10. Never stand on the top three rungs of an extension ladder.
11. Extension ladders, extending 30 feet or beyond, should be tied down with heavy lines. Shorter extension should be tied down on windy days.
12. Be sure all locks on extension ladders are securely hooked over rungs before ascending.
13. Make all height adjustments from the floor. Never extend a ladder when you are on it.
14. Never use wet or metal ladders when working with a live power source, as water and metal are excellent conductors of electricity.

15. Only one person at a time on any but very specialized ladders.
16. Never use ladders in horizontal position.
17. Store ladder in dry, cool, well-ventilated place, and where it is readily accessible.

## FIRST AID

**Call a doctor** when sudden serious injury or illness occurs. While waiting, what you do or do not do may mean the difference between life or death. First Aid is the help you can provide until professional medical aid arrives. Know the simple rules:

*Don't move an injured person*—especially after a fall, a crash or other violence, unless it is necessary to prevent further danger. Don't turn or lift him, or encourage him to sit up. Unnecessary movement may kill or cripple from internal injuries or a broken spine. Call a doctor.

**Shock**—Expect shock after any serious injury. Keep the patient lying down, with head lower than feet. Cover him and keep him warm, but not hot or sweaty. If he can swallow and is not semi-conscious, vomiting or with an abdominal wound, give him warm fluids or a shock solution: 1 tsp. salt and ½ tsp. baking soda dissolved in a quart of warm water. Call a doctor.

**Stop bleeding quickly**—Apply pressure directly over wound until bleeding stops, using towel, cloth, or the cleanest thing you can find, pressing hard with your whole hand. Use a tourniquet only if all other efforts have not stopped bleeding. Call a doctor.

**Burns and scalds**—For major burns, treat for shock. Cut clothing from burned area, but don't pull it away if it sticks. Cover with thick pad of sterile dressings, or a clean sheet or towel. Call a doctor.

**Drowning**—Lay victim on back and wipe foreign matter from mouth with fingers. Put your hand under neck and lift, tilting head back with other hand. Pull tongue forward if it has slipped back into throat. Place your mouth on victim's, pinch his nostrils and blow hard enough to make his chest rise. Remove your mouth and listen for exhaled air. Repeat until victim responds. Call a doctor.

**Broken bones**—Treat for shock. Apply ice bag to painful area. If bone protrudes through skin, stop bleeding. Do not try to push bone back in place or clean the wound. Wait for the doctor.

**Poisoning by mouth**—Call the doctor fast! Dilute poison by giving warm fluids to induce vomiting. Use antidote listed on container, or the universal emergency antidote: 2 Tbsp. crushed burnt toast, 1 Tbsp. strong tea, 1 Tbsp. Milk of Magnesia in ½ glass water. Do not induce vomiting if the poison is corrosive—acid, alkali, kerosene or gasoline.

## FIRE SAFETY CHECKLIST

| HAZARD | YES | NO | CORRECTION |
|---|---|---|---|
| Combustible or flammable ashtrays in all rooms? | ☐ | ☐ | Use only noncombustible ashtrays. |
| Careless disposal of glowing matches and cigarettes? | ☐ | ☐ | Douse all matches and cigarettes till dead. |
| Matches in combustible container? | ☐ | ☐ | Keep in metal container. |
| Matches within reach of children? | ☐ | ☐ | Keep in high place, out of children's reach. |
| Family members smoke in bed? | ☐ | ☐ | Strict rules against smoking in bed. |
| Do you run electric cords under rugs and over nails and hooks? | ☐ | ☐ | Run cord along baseboard and over doorways. |
| Keep lamp and appliance cords in bad condition? | ☐ | ☐ | Repair frayed lamp and appliance cords. |
| Overload outlets in your home? | ☐ | ☐ | Don't overload. |
| Use 30-ampere-fuses on lighting circuits? | ☐ | ☐ | Use 15-ampere-fuses for lighting circuits. |
| Do you use flammable cleaning fluids? | ☐ | ☐ | Use only when necessary. |
| Do you store flammable liquids improperly? | ☐ | ☐ | Store in closed containers. |
| Attic or basement filled with rubbish, papers, oily rags? | ☐ | ☐ | Keep free of trash and combustible materials. |

247

| HAZARD | YES | NO | CORRECTION |
|---|---|---|---|
| Gas range leaking gas? | ☐ | ☐ | Call gas company. |
| Gas range greasy? | ☐ | ☐ | Clean top of range. |
| Is cooking closely supervised? | ☐ | ☐ | Be present during cooking. |
| Is chimney free of cracks? | ☐ | ☐ | Repair cracks. |
| Are chimney flue and furnace cleaned before heating season? | ☐ | ☐ | Clean thoroughly before heating season. |
| Fire escapes in bad condition? | ☐ | ☐ | Have landlord repair them. |
| Fire escapes cluttered? | ☐ | ☐ | Remove all items from fire escape. |
| Do you store paint, varnish, lacquer and enamel improperly? | ☐ | ☐ | Store in closed metal containers. |

## USEFUL DATA

To find circumference of a circle, multiply diameter by 3.1416.

To find diameter of circle, multiply circumference by .31831.

To find area of a circle, multiply square of diameter by .7854.

To find surface of a ball multiply square of diameter by 3.1416.

Area of a rectangle = length multiplied by breadth. Doubling the diameter of a circle increases its area four times.

To find area of a triangle, multiply base by ½ perpendicular height.

Area of ellipse = product of both diameters × .7854.

Area of parallelogram = base × altitude.

To find side of an inscribed square, multiply diameter by 0.7071 or multiply circumference by 0.2251 or divide circumference by 4.4428.

Side of inscribed cube = radius of sphere × 1.1547.

To find side of an equal square, multiply diameter by .8862.

Square. A side multiplied by 1.4142 equals diameter of its circumscribing circle.

A side multiplied by 4.443 equals circumference of its circumscribing circle.

A side multiplied by 1.128 equals diameter of an equal circle.

A side multiplied by 3.547 equals circumference of an equal circle.

To find cubic inches in a ball, multiply cube of diameter by .5236.

To find cubic contents of a cone, multiply area of base by ⅓ the altitude.

Surface of frustrum of cone or pyramid = sum of circumference of both ends × ½ slant height plus area of both ends.

Contents of frustrum of cone or pyramid = multiply area of two ends and get square root. Add the 2 areas and × ⅓ altitude.

Doubling the diameter of a pipe increases its capacity four times.

A gallon of water (U.S. standard) weighs 8⅓ lbs. and contains 231 cubic inches.

A cubic foot of water contains 7½ gallons, 1728 cubic inches, and weight 62½ lbs.

To find the pressure in pounds per square inch of a column of water, multiply the height of the column in feet by .434.

Steam rising from water at its boiling point (212 degrees F) has a pressure equal to the atmosphere (14.7 pounds to the square inch).

A horse power is equivalent to raising 33,000 lbs. one foot per minute or 550 lbs. one foot per second.

A standard horse power: the evaporation of 30 pounds of water per hour from a feed water temperature of 100 degree F into steam at 70 pounds gauge pressure.

To find capacity of tanks any size, given dimensions of a cylinder in inches, to find its capacity in U.S. gallons: square the diameter, multiply by the length and by .0034.

To ascertain heating surface in tubular boilers, multiply ⅔ the circumference of boiler by length of boiler in inches and add to it the area of all the tubes.

# U.S. WEIGHTS AND MEASURES

## SQUARE MEASURE (Measures of Surface)

| Sq. Ins. | | Sq. Ft. | | Sq. Yards | | Sq. Rods | | Roods | | Acre |
|---|---|---|---|---|---|---|---|---|---|---|
| 144 | = | 1 | | | | | | | | |
| 1296 | = | 9 | = | 1 | | | | | | |
| 39204 | = | 272¼ | = | 30¼ | = | 1 | | | | |
| 1568160 | = | 10890 | = | 1210 | = | 40 | = | 1 | | |
| 6272640 | = | 43560 | = | 4840 | = | 160 | = | 4 | = | 1 |

640 Acres = 1 square mile.
An Acre = a square whose side is 69.57 yards or 208.71 feet.

## LIQUID OR WINE MEASURE

The U.S. standard gallon measures 231 cubic inches, or 8.33888 pounds avoirdupois of pure water, at about 39.85 degrees F., the barometer at 30 inches.

| Gills | | Pints | | Quarts | | Gallons | | Tierces | | Hogs-heads | | Punch-eons | | Pipes | | Tun | | Cubic Inches |
|---|---|---|---|---|---|---|---|---|---|---|---|---|---|---|---|---|---|---|
| 4 | = | 1 | = | | | | | | | | | | | | | | | 28.875 |
| 8 | = | 2 | = | 1 | = | | | | | | | | | | | | | 57.75 |
| 32 | = | 8 | = | 4 | = | 1 | = | | | | | | | | | | | 231. |
| 1344 | = | 336 | = | 168 | = | 42 | = | 1 | | | | | | | | | | |
| 2016 | = | 504 | = | 252 | = | 63 | = | 1½ | = | 1 | | | | | | | | |
| 2488 | = | 672 | = | 336 | = | 84 | = | 2 | = | 1½ | = | 1 | | | | | | |
| 4032 | = | 1008 | = | 504 | = | 126 | = | 3 | = | 2 | = | 1½ | = | 1 | | | | |
| 8064 | = | 2016 | = | 1008 | = | 252 | = | 6 | = | 4 | = | 3 | = | 2 | = | 1 | | |

A cubic foot contains 7½ gallons.
The British imperial gallon contains 277.27 cubic inches and = 1.2 U.S. gallons.

## LONG MEASURE (Measures of Length)

| Ins. | | Feet | | Yards | | Fathoms | | Rods | | Fur-longs | | Mile |
|---|---|---|---|---|---|---|---|---|---|---|---|---|
| 12 | = | 1 | | | | | | | | | | |
| 36 | = | 3 | = | 1 | | | | | | | | |
| 72 | = | 6 | = | 2 | = | 1 | | | | | | |
| 198 | = | 16½ | = | 5½ | = | 2¾ | = | 1 | | | | |
| 7920 | = | 660 | = | 220 | = | 110 | = | 40 | = | 1 | | |
| 63360 | = | 5280 | = | 1760 | = | 880 | = | 320 | = | 8 | = | 1 |

6080.26 Feet = 1.15 statute miles = 1 nautical mile or knot.

## CUBIC MEASURE (Measures of Volume)

| Cu. Ins. | | Cu. Ft. | | Cu. Yards |
|---|---|---|---|---|
| 1728 | = | 1 | | |
| 46656 | = | 27 | = | 1 |

A cord of wood = 128 cubic feet, being 4 feet × 4 feet × 8 feet.
42 Cubic Feet = a ton of shipping.
1 perch of masonry = 24¾ cubic feet, being 16½ feet × 1½ feet × 1 foot.

## AVOIRDUPOIS OR COMMERCIAL WEIGHT

The grain is the same in troy, apothecaries and avoirdupois weights.
The standard avoirdupois pound is the weight of 27.7015 cubic inches of distilled water weighed in the air at 35.85 degrees F., barometer at 30 inches. 27.343 grains = 1 Drachm.

| Drachms | | Ounces | | Lbs. | | Long Qrs. | | Long Cwt. | | Long Ton |
|---|---|---|---|---|---|---|---|---|---|---|
| 16 | = | 1 | | | | | | | | |
| 256 | = | 16 | = | 1 | | | | | | |
| 7168 | = | 448 | = | 28 | = | 1 | | | | |
| 28672 | = | 1792 | = | 112 | = | 4 | = | 1 | | |
| 573440 | = | 35840 | = | 2240 | = | 80 | = | 20 | = | 1 |

The above table gives what is known as the long ton. The short ton weighs 2000 pounds.

## DRY MEASURE

The standard bushel contains 2150.42 cubic inches, or 77.627013 pounds avoirdupois of pure water at maximum density. Its legal dimensions are 18½ inches diameter inside, 19½ inches outside, and 8 inches deep; and when heaped, the cone must be 6 inches high, making a heaped bushel equal to 1¼ struck ones.

| Pints | | Quarts | | Gallons | | Pecks | | Bushels | | Cubic Inches |
|---|---|---|---|---|---|---|---|---|---|---|
| 2 | = | 1 | = | | | | | | | 67.2 |
| 8 | = | 4 | = | 1 | = | | | | | 268.8 |
| 16 | = | 8 | = | 2 | = | 1 | = | | | 537.6 |
| 64 | = | 32 | = | 8 | = | 4 | = | 1 | = | 2150.42 |

The British imperial bushel contains 2218.2 cubic inches and = 103. U.S. bushels.

## TEMPERATURE CONVERSION

1.8 × Centigrade + 32 degrees = Fahrenheit.
Fahrenheit − 32 degrees × .5566 = Centigrade.

## FLOORING AND SIDING

In estimating matched flooring, a square foot of ⅞-inch stuff is considered to be 1-foot board measure.
If the flooring is 3 inches or more in width, add ¼ to assumed board measure to allow for the forming of tongue and groove; for less than 3 inches in width, add ⅓.
A square foot of 1⅛-inch finished flooring is considered to be 1¼ feet board measure.
To calculate the board measure of same, figure as if 1 inch thick and add 60 percent to cover extra thickness and waste in tonguing, grooving, etc.
Siding is measured by superficial foot.
6-inch siding nominal width actually measures 5⅝ inches.

## BRICKWORK

Brickwork is estimated by the thousand, and of various thicknesses of wall, runs as follows:

8¼-inch wall, or 1     brick in thickness, 14 bricks per superficial foot
12¾-inch wall or 1½ brick in thickness, 21 bricks per superficial foot
17  -inch wall, or 2     brick in thickness, 28 bricks per superficial foot
• 21½-inch wall, or 2½ brick in thickness, 35 bricks per superficial foot

An ordinary brick measures about 8¼ × 4 × 2 inches. 27.343 grains = 1 drachm. The average weight is 4½ pounds.


# THE METRIC SYSTEM

## WEIGHTS

### Metric Denominations and Values

| Names | | No. Grams | |
|---|---|---|---|
| Millier or tonneau | = | 1,000,000 | = |
| Quintal | = | 100,000 | = |
| Myriagram | = | 10,000 | = |
| Kilogram or kilo | = | 1,000 | = |
| Hectogram | = | 100 | = |
| Dekagram | = | 10 | = |
| Gram | = | 1 | = |
| Decigram | = | .1 | = |
| Centigram | = | .01 | = |
| Milligram | = | .001 | = |

### Equivalents in Denominations in use

| Quantity of water at maximum density | | Avoirdupois weight | |
|---|---|---|---|
| 1 cubic meter | = | 2204.6 | pounds |
| 1 hectoliter | = | 220.46 | pounds |
| 10 liters | = | 22.046 | pounds |
| 1 liter | = | 2.2046 | pounds |
| 1 deciliter | = | 3.5274 | ounces |
| 10 c. centimeters | = | 0.3527 | ounce |
| 1 c. centimeter | = | 15.432 | grains |
| .1 c. centimeter | = | 1.5432 | grains |
| 10 c. millimeters | = | 0.1543 | grain |
| 1 c. millimeter | = | 0.0154 | grain |

## MEASURES OF LENGTH

### Metric Denominations and Values    Equivalents of Denominations in use

| Myriameter | = | 10,000 meters | = | 6.2137 miles |
|---|---|---|---|---|
| Kilometer | = | 1,000 meters | = | 0.62137 mile, or 3,280 feet 10 inches |
| Hectometer | = | 100 meters | = | 328 feet and 1 inch |
| Dekameter | = | 10 meters | = | 393.7 inches |
| Meter | = | 1 meter | = | 39.37 inches |
| Decimeter | = | .1 meter | = | 3.937 inches |
| Centimeter | = | .01 meter | = | 0.3937 inch |
| Millimeter | = | .001 meter | = | 0.0394 inch |

## MEASURES OF SURFACE

### Metric Denominations and Values   Equivalents in Denominations in use

| Hectare | = | 10,000 square meters | = | 2.471 | acres |
|---|---|---|---|---|---|
| Are | = | 100 square meters | = | 119.6 | square yards |
| Centare | = | 1 square meter | = | 1550 | square inches |

## MEASURES OF CAPACITY

| Metric Denominations and Values | | | Equivalents of Denominations in use | | |
|---|---|---|---|---|---|
| *Names* | *No. Liters* | *Cubic Measure* | *Dry Measure* | *Wine Measure* | |
| Kiloliter | = 1,000 = | 1 cubic meter | = 1.308 cubic yards | = 264.17 | gallons |
| Hectoliter = | 100 = | .1 cubic meter | = 2 bush. 3.35 pecks | = 26.417 | gallons |
| Decaliter = | 10 = 10 | c. decimeters | = 9.08 quarts | = 2.6417 | gallons |
| Liter = | 1 = 1 | c. decimeter | = 0.908 quart | = 1.0567 | quarts |
| Deciliter = | .1 = | .1 c. decimeter | = 6.1022 cubic inches | = 0.845 | gill |
| Centiliter = | .01 = 10 | c. centimeters | = 0.6102 cubic inch | = 0.338 | fluid oz. |
| Milliliter = | .001 = 1 | c. centimeter | = 0.061 cubic inch | = 0.27 | fluid oz. |

## UNITED STATES AND METRIC CONSTANTS

*Note:* To convert measures from United States to metric constants, reverse multiplication process to division, and division to multiplication, as necessary.

### Long Measure

| Millimeters | × | .03937 | = inches |
|---|---|---|---|
| Millimeters | ÷ | 25.4 | = inches |
| Centimeters | × | .3937 | = inches |
| Centimeters | ÷ | 2.54 | = inches |
| Meters | = | 39.37 | = inches (Act of Congress) |
| Meters | × | 3.281 | = feet |
| Meters | × | 1.094 | = yards |
| Kilometers | × | .6214 | = miles |
| Kilometers | × 3280.8 | | = feet |
| Kilometers | ÷ | 1.6093 | = miles |

### Square Measure

| Square millimeters | × | .00155 | = square inches |
|---|---|---|---|
| Square millimeters | ÷ 645.2 | | = square inches |
| Square centimeters | × | .155 | = square inches |
| Square centimeters | ÷ | 6.452 | = square inches |
| Square meters | × | .1550 | = square inches |
| Square meters | × | 10.764 | = square feet |
| Square meters | × | 1.196 | = square yards |
| Square kilometers | × 247.1 | | = acres |
| Hectares | × | 2.471 | = acres |

### Cubic Measure

| Cubic centimeters | × | 0.06102 | = cubic inches |
|---|---|---|---|
| Cubic centimeters | ÷ | 3.69 | = fluid drachms (U.S.P.) |
| Cubic centimeters | ÷ | 29.57 | = fluid ounce (U.S.P.) |
| Cubic meters | × | 35.315 | = cubic feet |
| Cubic meters | × | 1.308 | = cubic yards |
| Cubic meters | × 264.2 | | = gallons (231 cubic inches) |

### Liquid Measure

| Liters | × 61.022 | = cubic inches (Act of Congress) |
|---|---|---|
| Liters | × 33.84 | = fluid ounces (U.S. Phar.) |
| Liters | × .2642 | = gallons (231 cubic inches) |
| Liters | ÷ 3.78 | = gallons (231 cubic inches) |
| Liters | ÷ 28.316 | = cubic feet |

Hectoliters   ×   3.531   = cubic feet
Hectoliters   ×   2.84    = bushels (2150.42 cubic inches)
Hectoliters   ×    .131   = cubic yards
Hectoliters   ÷ 26.42   = gallons (231 cubic inches)

### Weights

Grammes                ×     15.432   = grains (Act of Congress)
Grammes                ×   981.       = dynes
Grammes (water)    ÷    29.57   = fluid ounces
Grammes                ÷    28.35    = ounces avoirdupois
Grammes                ×      .0353 = ounces
Grammes per cubic
   centimeter       ÷    27.7     = pounds per cubic inch
Joule                    ×      .7373 = foot pounds
Kilograms            ×    2.2046 = pounds
Kilograms            ×   35.3      = ounces avoirdupois
Kilograms            ÷   907.2     = tons (2,000 pounds)
Kilograms            × per square centimeter 14.223 =
                                   pounds per square inch

# BASIC ADHESIVES CHART

| JOB DESCRIPTION | DESIRABLE ADHESIVE(S) |
|---|---|
| All-purpose woodworking, hard and softwoods | Casein glue<br>Animal glue<br>Plastic resin glue<br>Polyvinyl glue |
| Gluing metal to wood | Epoxy glue<br>Rubber cement |
| Repairing broken ceramics or masonry | Epoxy glue |
| Doweling work | Polyvinyl glue<br>Plastic resin glue |
| Veneering | Plastic resin glue<br>Polyvinyl glue |
| Cabinetwork | Plastic resin glue<br>Polyvinyl glue |
| Repairing leather, canvas, or cloth fabric | Clear cement<br>Fabric mending adhesive |

254

| JOB DESCRIPTION | DESIRABLE ADHESIVE(S) |
|---|---|
| Gluing plastic to metal, wood, or plastic | Epoxy glue |
| Gluing glass to glass | Epoxy glue |
| Repairing cracks in wood beams and joists | Casein glue |
| Gluing rubber to metal, wood, or glass | Contact cement Rubber cement |
| Gluing metal to metal | Epoxy glue |
| Gluing linoleum to wood | Plastic resin glue Casein glue Contact cement |
| Gluing chipboards to wood | Plastic resin glue Casein glue Contact cement Polyvinyl glue |
| Tile setting and waterproofing | Silicone adhesive |

# TYPES OF SANDPAPER AND THEIR USES

| JOB DESCRIPTION | TYPE WORK | GARNET, ALUMINUM OXIDE, OR SILICONE CARBIDE | | EMERY CLOTH | FLINT |
|---|---|---|---|---|---|
| | | Grit | "O" Series | | |
| Wet sanding, for high-satin finish. Also for wet sanding lacquer and varnish topcoats. | Ultra-light | 600 500 400 360 320 | (10/0) ( 9/0) | | |
| Wet and dry sanding finishing undercoats. No sanding marks visible. | Very Light | 280 240 220 | ( 8/0) ( 7/0) ( 6/0) | (Dry only) Extrafine | |

| JOB DESCRIPTION | TYPE WORK | GARNET, ALUMINUM OXIDE, OR SILICONE CARBIDE | | EMERY CLOTH | FLINT |
|---|---|---|---|---|---|
| | | Grit | "O" Series | | |
| Wet and dry final sanding of wood and smoothing old paint. | Light | 180 | ( 5/0) | 3/0 | (Dry only) |
| | | 150 | ( 4/0) | 2/0 | |
| | | 120 | ( 3/0) | | Fine |
| General wood sanding, initial smoothing of paint and plaster. | Medium | 100 | ( 2/0) | 0 | (Dry only) |
| | | | | ½ | |
| | | 80 | ( 0 ) | 1 | |
| | | | | 1½ | Medium |
| | | 60 | ( ½ ) | | |
| General rough wood sanding. | Heavy | 50 | ( 1 ) | 2 | |
| | | 40 | ( 1½ ) | 2½ | Coarse |
| | | 36 | ( 2 ) | | |
| Sanding with high-speed, heavy machinery only. | Ultra-heavy | 30 | ( 2½ ) | 3 | Extra coarse |
| | | 24 | ( 3 ) | | |
| | | 20 | ( 3½ ) | | |
| | | 16 | ( 4 ) | | |
| | | 12 | ( 4½ ) | | |

## BASIC LUBRICATION CHART

| UNIT | LUBRICANT | WHERE TO LUBRICATE | QUANTITY | WHEN |
|---|---|---|---|---|
| Doors, sliding closet | Silicone | Channels and wheels | 1 to 2 drops and spread evenly | Twice yearly |
| Doors, sliding and overhead garage | Graphite oil | At locks, pulleys, along tracks | 1 to 3 drops and work movable parts | Twice yearly |
| Doors, sliding shower and medicine cabinet | All-purpose white lubricant | Channels | 1 to 2 drops and spread evenly | Twice yearly |

256

| UNIT | LUBRICANT | WHERE TO LUBRICATE | QUANTITY | WHEN |
|---|---|---|---|---|
| Doors: storm door check | All-purpose white lubricant and lightweight household oil | On check's sliding surface, and/or rod | 2 drops in check and 1 drop white grease on sliding surface | Twice yearly |
| Drawers, furniture doors | Silicone, soap, or paraffin | Sliding surface | Light coat and spread | Twice yearly |
| Furnace blower motors | Heavy household oil | In cups (some have none and don't need lube job) | 2 to 3 drops | Twice per heating season |
| Hinges | Lightweight household oil | Hinge pin | 1 to 2 drops: remove pin, lubricate, and replace | Twice yearly |
| Locks | Graphite oil | Apply through keyhole | 2 drops: insert key and work back and forth | Twice yearly |
| Mowers, power | Heavy household oil | As suggested by manufacturer | 1 to 3 drops | Twice yearly |
| Machinery, heavy | Heavy household oil | As suggested by manufacturer | As suggested by manufacturer | Twice yearly |
| Machinery, light | Lightweight household oil | As suggested by manufacturer | 1 to 3 drops | Twice yearly |
| Plumbing fixtures | Graphite oil | Moving surface | 1 to 2 drops | Twice yearly |
| Tools, hand | Lightweight household oil or all-purpose white lubricant | Where metal hits metal | 1 to 2 drops and work in | Twice yearly |
| Tools, outdoor | Graphite oil | Exposed metal | Thin coat | After use |

| UNIT | LUBRICANT | WHERE TO LUBRICATE | QUANTITY | WHEN |
|---|---|---|---|---|
| Tools, power | Lightweight household oil | As suggested by manufacturer | 1 to 3 drops | Twice yearly |
| Window, casement and jalousie channels | All-purpose white lubricant | Channels | Thin coat, work in by moving window | Twice yearly |
| Window, casement and jalousie cranking mechanism | Lightweight household oil | Hand crank | 1 to 2 drops | Twice yearly |
| Windows, double-hung | Silicone, soap, or paraffin | Channels | Thin coat, work in by moving window | Twice yearly |
| Window, latches | Lightweight household oil or all-purpose white lubricant | At joint | 1 to 2 drops | Twice yearly |

## EXTERIOR PAINT SELECTION CHART

| SURFACE TO BE PAINTED | PAINT(S) |
|---|---|
| Wood siding, clapboard, vertical and horizontal | Oil-base paint<br>Latex paint |
| Wood shingles and shakes | Latex paint |
| Asbestos shingles | Latex paint |
| Aluminum siding | Oil-base paint |
| Plastic siding | Oil-base paint |
| Masonry | Latex paint |
| Wooden windows and doors | Oil-base paint<br>Alkyd enamel |

| SURFACE TO BE PAINTED | PAINT(S) |
|---|---|
| Trim and cornice | Alkyd enamel |
| Metal windows and doors | Oil-base paint<br>Alkyd enamel |
| Wooden gutters | Oil-base paint<br>Latex paint<br>Alkyd enamel |
| Metal gutters | Oil-base paint<br>Alkyd enamel |
| Downspouts | Oil-base paint<br>Alkyd enamel |

# INTERIOR PAINT SELECTION CHART

| SURFACE TO BE PAINTED | PAINT(S) |
|---|---|
| Plasterboard walls and ceilings in bathroom and kitchen | Gloss alkyd enamel<br>Gloss latex |
| Plasterboard walls and ceilings (other rooms) | Flat latex<br>Flat alkyd |
| Plaster walls and ceilings in bathroom and kitchen | Gloss alkyd enamel<br>Gloss latex |
| Plaster walls and ceilings (other rooms) | Flat latex<br>Flat alkyd |
| Masonry walls (basement) | Flat latex |
| Wood doors and windows | Flat latex<br>Flat alkyd<br>Gloss alkyd enamel<br>Gloss latex<br>Varnish |
| Metal doors and windows | Flat alkyd<br>Gloss alkyd enamel |
| Baseboards and woodwork | Flat latex<br>Flat alkyd<br>Gloss alkyd enamel<br>Gloss latex<br>Varnish |

| SURFACE TO BE PAINTED | PAINT(S) |
|---|---|
| Wood paneling | Flat latex<br>Flat alkyd |
| Radiators and pipes | Flat alkyd |
| Tile floors | Latex floor paint |
| Furniture, cabinets | Gloss alkyd enamel<br>Gloss latex<br>Varnish |

# HOW TO COMPUTE QUANTITY OF PAINT NEEDED

**PERIMETER OF STRUCTURE** (2 × width plus 2 × length in feet)

HEIGHT OF STRUCTURE IN FEET

| | 100 | 125 | 150 | 175 | 200 | 225 | 250 | 275 | 300 | 325 | 350 |
|---|---|---|---|---|---|---|---|---|---|---|---|
| **10** | 1000<br>2½ | 1250<br>3 | 1500<br>3½ | 1750<br>4½ | 2000<br>5 | 2250<br>5½ | 2500<br>6 | 2750<br>7 | 3000<br>7½ | 3250<br>8 | 3500<br>8½ |
| **12** | 1200<br>3 | 1500<br>3½ | 1800<br>4½ | 2100<br>5 | 2400<br>6 | 2700<br>6½ | 3000<br>7½ | 3300<br>8 | 3600<br>9 | 3900<br>9½ | 4200<br>10½ |
| **14** | 1400<br>3½ | 1750<br>4½ | 2100<br>5 | 2450<br>6 | 2800<br>7 | 3150<br>8 | 3500<br>8½ | 3850<br>9½ | 4200<br>10½ | 4550<br>11½ | 4900<br>12 |
| **16** | 1600<br>4 | 2000<br>5 | 2400<br>6 | 2800<br>7 | 3200<br>8 | 3600<br>9 | 4000<br>10 | 4400<br>11 | 4800<br>12 | 5200<br>13 | 5600<br>14 |
| **18** | 1800<br>4½ | 2250<br>5½ | 2700<br>6½ | 3150<br>8 | 3600<br>9 | 4050<br>10 | 4500<br>11 | 4950<br>12 | 5400<br>13 | 5850<br>14 | 6300<br>15 |
| **20** | 2000<br>5 | 2500<br>6 | 3000<br>7½ | 3500<br>8½ | 4000<br>10 | 4500<br>11 | 5000<br>12 | 5500<br>13 | 6000<br>15 | 6500<br>16 | 7000<br>17 |
| **22** | 2200<br>5½ | 2750<br>7 | 3300<br>8 | 3850<br>9½ | 4400<br>11 | 4950<br>12 | 5500<br>13 | 6050<br>15 | 6600<br>16 | 7150<br>17 | 7700<br>19 |
| **24** | 2400<br>6 | 3000<br>7½ | 3600<br>9 | 4200<br>10½ | 4800<br>12 | 5400<br>13 | 6000<br>15 | 6600<br>16 | 7200<br>18 | 7800<br>19 | 8400<br>21 |
| **26** | 2600<br>6½ | 3250<br>8 | 3900<br>9½ | 4500<br>11 | 5200<br>13 | 5850<br>14 | 6500<br>16 | 7150<br>18 | 7800<br>19 | 8450<br>21 | 9100<br>22 |
| **28** | 2800<br>7 | 3500<br>8½ | 4200<br>10½ | 4900<br>12 | 5600<br>14 | 6300<br>15 | 7000<br>17 | 7700<br>19 | 8400<br>21 | 9100<br>22 | 9800<br>24 |
| **30** | 3000<br>7½ | 3750<br>9½ | 4500<br>11 | 5250<br>13 | 6000<br>15 | 6750<br>17 | 7500<br>18 | 8250<br>20 | 9000<br>22 | 9750<br>24 | 10500<br>26 |

Top number in each column represents area in square feet to be painted;
lower number indicates number of gallons needed for the job.

## TROUBLESHOOTING FURNACES

Waking up on a February morning with icicles on your eyelashes is no fun. But every homeowner runs into this problem at least once. The following checklists for your furnace, whether gas, oil, or electric, will usually help to keep things humming. We suggest you make your check in August. We also advise that the system be cleaned, oiled, and its safety devices checked at least once yearly by a competent service company.

### Checklist for Oil Furnaces

1. Check oil burner emergency switch. It should be in the "on" position. This is also called a remote control switch.
2. Check for blown or loose fuses at main burner switch box or central fuse box. Replace fuses if necessary with fuses of identical amperage.
3. Check water level in gauge glass on your furnace and fill to more than half full at all times (for steam systems only).
4. Raise thermostat to 5 degrees above room temperature and wait 15 minutes. It is not unusual for clock-type thermostats to be out of cycle. You must check to see if the day and night settings have been confused. If so, correct.
5. Check your oil tank gauge to see if you have fuel.
6. Press or turn recycling button at the burner control box. Do this only once or twice. If the furnace runs for a minute or two only, DO NOT PUSH THE RECYCLING BUTTON AGAIN! Shut off your emergency switch (step 1) and call a serviceman.

### Checklist for Gas Furnaces

1. Check furnace switch (electrical), if you have one. It must be in the "on" position.
2. Check for blown or loose fuses at main burner switch box or central fuse box. Replace fuses if necessary with fuses of identical amperage.
3. Check water level in gauge glass on your furnace and fill to more than half full at all times (for steam systems only).
4. Raise thermostat to 5 degrees above room temperature and wait 15 minutes. It is not unusual for clock-type thermostats to be out of cycle. You must check to see if the day and night settings have been confused. If so, correct.

5. Check main gas valve, which must be in the "on" position.
6. In warm air systems, clean and/or replace filter(s).
7. If pilot light is not burning, relight as per instructions attached to the furnace.
8. If none of the above restores furnace to operational order, call utility company or competent serviceman.

**Checklist for Electric Heating**

1. Check with neighbors to see if there is a local blackout. If so, you'll just have to wait until power is restored.
2. Check main circuit-breaker panel box or fuse box for disconnected switches or burnt fuses. Reset and/or replace as necessary with fuses of identical amperage.
3. Raise thermostat to 5 degrees above room temperature. It is not unusual for clock-type thermostats to be out of cycle. Check to see if day and night settings have been confused. If so, correct.
4. If none of the above restores heating system to operational order, call utility company or competent electrician.

# INDEX